Cat America

Self-Renewal Centers and Retreats

Patricia Christian-Meyer

John Muir
Publications
Santa Fe,
New Mexico

This book is dedicated to my parents, William and Dorothea Christian, who fostered within me a thirst for the spiritual side of life. Although we now drink from different wells, our thirsts are quenched by the same groundwater.

John Muir Publications, P.O. Box 613, Santa Fe, NM 87504

© 1989 by Patricia Christian-Meyer
Cover © 1989 by John Muir Publications
All rights reserved. Published 1989
Printed in the United States of America

First edition. First printing

Library of Congress Cataloging-in-Publication Data

Christian-Meyer, Patricia, 1946–
    Catholic America.
        1. Retreats. 2. Retreats—United States—Directories.
I. Title.
BX2375.A3C57   1989   269'.6'02573   88-43538
ISBN 0-945465-20-3

Typeface: Eras and Garamond
Typesetter: Publications Development Co.
Designer: Marcy Heller
Printer: McNaughton-Gunn

Distributed to the book trade by:

W. W. Norton & Company, Inc.
New York, New York

Contents

Foreword   vii

Acknowledgments   xi

Miscellaneous Notes   xv

Introduction   1

The Value of Making a Retreat: Comments from Leading Retreat Directors   10

What Kinds of Retreats Are Available?   16

Practical Advice for Making Retreats   28

The Desert Experience: Solitary Retreats   43

The Retreat Experience without the Retreat: A Modest Suggestion from Father Thomas Keating   52

Personal Retreat Experiences   57
    Desert Experience No. 1   57
    A Jesuit-Directed Retreat   61
    Desert Experience No. 2   63
    Time in a Trappist Monastery   67

Directory of Retreat and Renewal Centers   75

Appendix   255
    Roman Catholic Beliefs in Brief   257
    Resources   263

Foreword

If you told, say, 100,000 American Catholics that *Catholic America* was a new book's title and asked them to guess the subtitle, it is very unlikely they would suggest *Self-Renewal Centers and Retreats*. Patricia Christian-Meyer has matched two halves that few people—Catholics or others—would have readily recognized as an integral whole. In *Catholic America: Self-Renewal Centers and Retreats,* the colon is like a road sign. "Where is Catholic America?" you wonder; "Self-Renewal Centers and Retreats," the sign says. "That is where it is."

But isn't that a bit simplistic? It would be, if we claimed that this was all. It is not. That there is a great deal more to Catholic America than renewal centers and retreats is only too obvious, sometimes painfully so. It would not even be correct to look in those places for the heart of America's Catholic Christianity. Its heart is in the Eucharist, it is in the grateful life of service that flows from human and divine communion and sows seeds of God's Kingdom. The heart of Catholic America beats among the poor and exploited, most of whom will never get a chance to visit a self-renewal center or go on retreat. What is it, then, that makes those places so important? The answer: their vitality.

In many parts of the world today, religious institutions lack vitality; Catholic America (if that means the Church in the United

States) is no exception. Proof: the increasing emphasis on law and order under pressure from the Vatican; the fearfulness of religious officialdom; the nervous efforts to impose conformity. As long as a shared vision has vitality enough to inspire commitment, unity will be enhanced by the variety of forms in which this commitment finds expression. But when the vision gets blurred, inspiration flags, commitment fails, power will try to fake unity through enforced uniformity. Vitality cannot be brought about by command and decree.

This raises a crucial question: where should religious institutions look for the source of their vitality? To God? We cannot go wrong with that answer; but it does not get us very far. God is everywhere. To the Holy Spirit, "the Giver of Life"? Yes, indeed. But where does God, where does God's Holy Spirit, touch the life of an institution? The answer: where human hearts were touched before there was an institution; where the Church came into being in the first place, in a personal encounter with God. The vitality of a religious institution springs from the living faith of its members. Faith comes alive as we experience God. That is where religious vitality has its source.

God is apt to burst in on us unannounced, when we least expect it, in most unlikely places. But that is God's business. Our responsibility is to prepare ourselves, expose ourselves, open ourselves for that encounter. For those of us who have the necessary health, time, and—let us be blunt—money to do so, this means a responsibility to avail ourselves of self-renewal centers and retreats. Our handicapped and materially impoverished sisters and brothers will not be the losers; God, who cares for the oppressed and exploited, will see to that. But what excuses shall we, to whom those opportunities are offered, find if we waste them.

How, then, do I get started? That is where Patricia Christian-Meyer offers assistance. What kind of retreat will suit my personal needs? She presents a wide range of options. What should I expect from a retreat? What should I not expect, so as to avoid disappointment? Ask almost any question of this kind and you

Foreword

may expect to find a practical answer in this book. The author has gathered here veterans in retreat work to offer advice. You are likely to find among them just the right person to consult. There is also a descriptive listing of retreat and renewal centers and—thanks to Father Thomas Keating—even a hint or two on getting the benefits of a retreat without going to any of those places.

This book is a first, a pioneering venture. Patricia Christian-Meyer is staking out a trail. She deserves our thanks and our admiration, even where she is roughing it, as pioneers are wont to do. I admire her gallantry, even when she is trying to do the impossible, like summing up "Basic Roman Catholic Doctrine" in a baker's dozen of paragraphs. I am grateful to her for giving hope to "wounded Catholics" (as Mother Tessa calls them) almost despairing of finding genuine religious experience within the institutional Church. But most of all, I admire her sure instinct for where the source of vitality lies—her placing that colon in the book's title precisely at the spot where it speaks the truth.

For decades, a mere handful of Benedictine monasteries in France and Germany were the cold frames in which seedlings awaited the springtime that Pope John XXIII brought to the Church. Some of the retreat and renewal centers listed in this book may well be the cold frames that nurture the Church's vitality through the nasty weather of our own time. From a renewed Church in the twenty-first century, someone may look back and say, "I've forgotten the title of that book and the name of its author, but I am very happy it fell into my hands. It led me to a personal encounter with God, which I had never thought possible in Catholic America."

Brother David Steindl-Rast
April 1989

Acknowledgments

In his book *Gratefulness, The Heart of Prayer,* Brother David Steindl-Rast wrote, "The greatest gift one can give is thanksgiving." It is difficult for me to believe that as I try to thank everyone who has made this book possible—I am overwhelmed by the enormous generosity and selfless assistance received from so very many people on this project. Gratitude seems the very least I can give back to them.

This book never would have come into existence had it not been for the vision of a friend, Don Morreale. We had often talked about doing a survey of Buddhist centers in the United States, but Don is a man of action; he found a publisher and put such a book in motion, asking me to write an essay for it based on my ten years of Zen training. His request coincided with a growing need to reconcile my training with my Christian upbringing—to become a *whole* person—and my research on the subject led to this book. At the same time, Don made it possible for me to meet and work with my publisher, John Muir Publications, in Santa Fe. Everyone on the staff has been unbelievably helpful, tolerant, and literally patient as saints with this novice author. Deepest gratitude to all of them.

For this person to finally hear and perceive the original truth of Christ, a journey deep into silence and solitude was first necessary. This is not an easy journey to make, as readers of this book will discover. For the careful and caring guidance that made that journey possible for this person, I owe unending thanks to Roshi Philip Kapleau, my Zen teacher.

For her early encouragement and for introducing me to Brother David, I am deeply grateful to my dear friend Marion Rigney. She carried a rough draft of the book proposal to a retreat with Brother David, a longtime friend of hers, and asked him to write the foreword—action truly above and beyond the call of friendship! Were it not for Marion, I might not have met this beautiful, kind, and gentle monk, and my life would be that much poorer. To Brother David himself, who not only has written the foreword but graciously gave me his time and valuable advice last summer, I say only, "Thank you! A thousand times times a thousand times, thank you!"

To all the wonderful, extraordinary people who allowed themselves to be interviewed by this rank novice, I give my heartfelt thanks. Mother Tessa Bielecki, Father William McNamara, and Father Dave Denny of the Spiritual Life Institute in Crestone, Colorado, and Nova Scotia were founts not only of information but, more important, of bubbling encouragement and excitement; and the entire community in Crestone was wonderfully supportive during my visit there. Father Robert Arida was very generous with his time and comfortingly emphatic in urging me to continue my quest. Dr. James Finley's kindness and enthusiasm for the book are deeply appreciated. Father Thomas Keating's gentle response to my importunate letters and his generous invitation to visit and interview him were a great surprise and joy. And Abbot David Geraets, Brother Daniel Stramara, Sister Ann, and all the members of the Pecos Community were also very kind and helpful.

I am very blessed to live in a city with so many fine retreat centers, and many of the directors were very kind and extremely generous with their time, encouragement, and advice in the preparation of the questionnaire. Great gratitude goes to Sister Jean Reardon of the Cenacle, Sister Doris Mattingly of the Center

Acknowledgments

for Spirituality, Father Wilfrid Tunink of Christina House, Father John Schork of Our Lady's Retreat House, Sister Carol Hoelscher of Seton Center, the Reverend Martin Seeley of Thompson Center, and Father Denis Daly of the White House Retreats.

To the people who generously contributed essays to this book, my endless thanks: the anonymous author of the essay about a Jesuit retreat, Cynthia Stebbins and Michelle Reineck for their desert retreat experiences, and Mary Alice Strom for her account of an intensive centering prayer retreat. It is very difficult to write one small part of a book without being able to see the surrounding parts, but all these people did so beautifully. And to Father Tom Gedeon, executive director of Retreats International, my gratitude for his continuing advice and support on this project. His busy schedule made his planned essay contribution to the book impossible, but his interest and encouragement were very welcome.

In the course of developing the manuscript, many people were shown bits and pieces and contributed helpful advice. Of these, I wish to single out for special thanks Father Donald Reck, SJ, for his assistance on the section about Roman Catholic doctrine. Three people have been especially generous in their willingness to plow through the entire manuscript, and to them I owe a debt of gratitude: my parish priest, Father Dimitrie Vincent of St. Thomas the Apostle Orthodox Church, and my good friends Marlene Beavans and Gil Marsh.

Many thanks to everyone who took time to complete the questionnaire. I received numerous calls from retreat center directors across the country telling me that the questionnaire was being answered by consensus, with everyone in the community participating in the preparation of the answers. This was so wonderful to hear! And all of the callers were unfailingly excited and enthusiastic in their encouragement to me, for which I am very grateful.

I also owe thanks to two special colleagues, neither of them Roman Catholic but both of them shining examples of loving and open human beings, who gave me access to a computer on which to compose the manuscript: to Clyde Crittenden and Sol Guber, thank you for helping me keep sight of the distinction between "book-learned religion" and true charity!

To all the above-mentioned saints in progress, my undying gratitude.

Finally, I must thank the one person who set all this in motion. She loved me when I was a small child devoted to her; she waited patiently through all my teen and adult years when I turned my back on her; she heard my agonized cry for help last year and has answered all my pestering prayers since; and she has guided and is still guiding my every step on this journey: dear Mary, Mother of God, thank you.

Miscellaneous Notes

About the Bible: Unless otherwise noted, all quotes from the Bible used in this book have been taken from *The Revised Standard Version Bible,* with the Apocrypha/Deuterocanonical Books, Ecumenical Edition. This version has been approved by the Roman Catholic, Orthodox, and Protestant churches.

About the word "Catholic": St. Ignatius of Antioch, a second-century bishop, was the first to use the word "catholic" to describe the Church. At that time it was a word which meant "full, perfect, complete, lacking nothing." This is the sense in which the word is still used by Eastern Orthodox Christians today to describe their Church. Later the word "catholic" took on its secondary meaning of "universal," signifying that Christ came to save *all* human beings. Over time and after divisions in what was once a single, unified Christian Church, "catholic" gradually came to be identified primarily with the Roman Christian Church and was capitalized, as in "Roman Catholic Church." Unfortunately, the appropriation of the word "catholic" solely to the Roman Church is inaccurate and a source of irritation to others who also consider themselves "catholic," notably, both Orthodox Catholics, who are *not* part of the Roman Church, and Church of England Catholics.

Complicating matters is that the idea of lay people making retreats and the development of retreat centers flow out of a monastic tradition that has its original roots in the Mediterranean area of early Christendom—often called "the East." Just using the terms "East" and "West" is confusing, because one must distinguish between Christian and non-Christian traditions or between Eastern Christian and Western Christian traditions!

Several ecumenical centers listed in the directory are not members of the Roman Church. However, the Roman Church's Cardinal Ratzinger has written:

> The Church universal is not a secondary fusion of local Churches; the Church universal, catholic, gives birth to the particular Churches, which can remain Churches only in communion with catholicity. On the other hand: catholicity requires the multiplicity of tongues, the reconciliation and reunion of the wealth of humankind in the love of the Crucified. Catholicity is not therefore only an external thing, but also an internal characteristic of personal faith: . . . Catholicity demands an open heart, as St. Paul says to the Corinthians: "You are not restricted by us, but you are restricted in your own affections. In return—I speak as to children—widen your hearts also" (2 Cor. 6: 12–13). This "widen your hearts" is the enduring imperative of catholicity.

Thus, although this book focuses on the Roman Catholic Church, every effort has been made to use terminology clear to all. Perhaps we can take one small step toward mutual understanding and respect here, if not reunification in Christ.

Introduction

Deus, deus meus es. Solicite te quaero, te sitit anima mea. Desiderat te caro mea, ut terra arida et sitiens, sine aqua.
—Psalm 62 (Vulgate)

(God, you are the God of my own True Self. I restlessly search for you. The life-force within me is dying of thirst for you, my physical self yearns for you, like land which is barren and parched from lack of water.)
—Author's Translation

This is a book about the direct experience of God: where to look for it, how to prepare for it. The experiential side of Roman Catholicism had been virtually lost from the sixteenth century until perhaps thirty years ago. (Although Father Thomas Keating, in his book *Open Mind, Open Heart,* traces the revival of mystical theology in the Roman Catholic Church back to the publication of a book about the teaching of John of the Cross in 1896, I suspect the average layperson was not aware of it.)

Accompanying the rise of intellectual movements such as humanism and the Renaissance, as well as the Reformation movements, was a deliberate effort by the Roman Catholic hierarchy to suppress the mystical writings in its tradition, for fear they would be misunderstood and misused by a largely uneducated laity. These writings then had to be rediscovered in our own century by the now-educated laity.

In his early years at Gethsemani Abbey, Thomas Merton wrote that his impression of the Cistercian way to contemplation was to throw oneself into one's labor with gritted teeth while muttering, "All for Jesus." This set him off on a search through the ancient and mystical writings of the early Christian church, a search he eventually shared with his readers.

Partly as a result of this opening into the mystical side of

Roman Catholicism, many books have appeared on the subject of Christian contemplation. Writers such as Father Thomas Keating, Father William McNamara, and Father M. Basil Pennington have emphasized that contemplation—the experiential encounter with God—is the natural birthright of every human being, rather than the esoteric practice of a few saints. The teaching of the Roman Catholic Church until the sixteenth century, according to Father Keating, "held that contemplation is the normal evolution of a genuine spiritual life and hence is open to all Christians."

Meditation techniques and methods of interior prayer, means to prepare for and enter a state of readiness for the contemplative experience, are now accessible in books and are routinely taught in some retreats and workshops.

There thus seemed to be compelling reasons to write a resource directory for Catholic contemplative training. Our entire social fabric seems to be unraveling and chaos is now the "order" of the day. Karlfried Graf Von Durckheim wrote in his classic book, *Hara: The Vital Centre of Man:* "Western ways of life have come to the end of their fruitfulness, rationalism has made its final contribution and modern man will succumb increasingly to physical and spiritual decay unless he finds some new way of coming back to his essential self and the true sense of life." Now that we flower children of the sixties have matured, perhaps it's time for us to stop looking *outside* ourselves for answers and start looking *inside,* to discover our essential Christ-nature. We already attend workshops, seminars, continuing education classes, training camps, and spas in unprecedented numbers, for all sorts of reasons: to lose weight, to hone our business skills, to improve our tennis serve or golf swing. One of the finest management trainers I have met counsels people in his workshops to spend a minimum of twenty days each year improving their management skills. How much more vital is it to improve the spiritual skills in our lives?

Most of the material in this book has been gathered in interviews with leading retreat directors in the Catholic Church today:

Introduction

- Brother David Steindl-Rast has been a Benedictine monk since 1953. The author of *Gratefulness, The Heart of Prayer* and *A Listening Heart,* Brother David is one of the leaders in ecumenical dialogue with non-Christian religions. In 1968 he helped found the Center of Spiritual Studies, and now spends part of each year secluded in a hermitage in Big Sur, California.
- Mother Tessa Bielecki is cofounder with Father William McNamara, O.C.D., and Mother Abbess of the Spiritual Life Institute in Crestone, Colorado, a Carmelite hermitage for men and women. A Carmelite for more than twenty years, Mother Tessa has lived the semieremitical life and now lectures and leads retreats in Christian contemplation. I first met Mother Tessa at a conference on Christian and Buddhist meditation practices, and her warmth and openness captivated me. She explained the solitary hermitage-style retreats offered at her Nada Hermitage and insisted that I visit there. Mother Tessa divides her time between the Crestone foundation and its sister, Nova Nada, outside of Kemptville, Nova Scotia.
- Father Dave Denny is the Prior at the Nada Hermitage in Crestone and graciously agreed to be interviewed early one morning during a rare trip to Denver for a Catholic conference. Thus it was that some of Denver's power-breakfast eaters were treated to the rare sight of a Carmelite hermit being interviewed and tape-recorded at 7:00 A.M. in the lobby of the staid Brown Palace Hotel. Thanks to Father Dave's generous spirit, I was able to hear both the male and the female voices of Nada Hermitage, and I can only pray that I transmit them accurately here.
- Dr. James Finley is a Catholic layman who studied for six years under Thomas Merton at Gethsemani Abbey in Kentucky and holds his doctorate in clinical psychology from Fuller Theological Seminary. The author of *Merton's Palace of Nowhere,* he leads weekend retreats in the United States and Canada. His voice as a lay person, husband, and father in the Roman Catholic Church who is actively engaged in leading retreats is very important. Dr. Finley also attended the previously mentioned conference on meditation practices. Although he was much in demand,

we managed to squeeze an interview into his schedule by huddling together late one hot afternoon on the corner of a noisy parking lot, with just a tape recorder and a mutual dedication to retreats between us.

- Father Thomas Keating is a Cistercian (Trappist) priest who lives at St. Benedict's Monastery in Snowmass, Colorado. He is the author of a number of books, including the wonderful *Open Mind, Open Heart,* which explains the system of centering prayer meditation he has helped to develop and teaches around the country. Father Keating allowed me to visit him at his monastery on the western slope of the Rocky Mountains. After a truly breathtaking drive over a 12,000-foot mountain pass, I was treated to a rollicking discussion of centering prayer. Father Keating invited me to stay for his "contemplative sit-down" Mass that evening, where I experienced for perhaps the first time a true Eucharistic celebration.

- Father William McNamara has been a Discalced Carmelite since 1944 and was ordained a priest in 1951. In 1960 he founded the Spiritual Life Institute, with double (male/female) hermitages in Crestone, Colorado, and Nova Scotia, with a mandate from Pope John XXIII. He has written extensively about the essential spiritual journey and has coined the term "earthy mysticism" to describe a natural life filled with God. His books, especially *Christian Mysticism* and *The Human Adventure,* elaborate his spiritual teachings. Since Father William now spends most of his time in his hermitage in Nova Scotia, I was unable to meet with him. However, Mother Tessa was kind enough to carry a list of questions and some blank tapes to him for a "long-distance" interview. He sat up late one night and taped his answers—admitting it was the first time he had used one of "these mechanical devices" for such a purpose!—and then had some departing retreatants mail the tape when they returned to the United States. The tape I received from Father William, filled as it is with not only his wisdom but also his extraordinary spirit, has become one of my most treasured possessions. The excited

Introduction

encouragement I have received from Father William and Mother Tessa has been a great joy.

In addition to these Roman Catholic leaders, a wonderful grace was given me when I met and interviewed Father Robert Arida, an Eastern Orthodox priest and Dean of Holy Trinity Cathedral in Boston. In addition to his parish in Boston, Father Arida has what he calls the "little parish" of his wife and four young children. He has led retreats and appeared at the same conference where I met Mother Tessa. Because he is Orthodox, Father Arida gave me an essential understanding and appreciation of the mystical traditions in Christianity, practices that have remained very fresh and alive in the Orthodox (Eastern Christian) Church, while they had disappeared from the Roman (Western Christian) Church. As Father McNamara had told me, "The thing to aim at is to rediscover the mystical tradition of Christianity, and it is lost in the West. You don't hear it preached in the typical (Roman) Catholic parish. Orthodoxy plays an important role in the understanding of mysticism because they are even more steeped in this tradition than we in the West are."

Without an understanding of the roots of Christian contemplation, and that this tradition has remained alive and unbroken somewhere in Christianity from the earliest times, one risks falling into the arrogant error of thinking that one has discovered something new. Unfortunately, the Western Christian tradition has never had a strong element of lineage or personal transmission. The result has been a series of renewals in which individuals had to rediscover—and in some cases, literally reinvent—the mystical side of Roman Catholicism.

But each rediscovery or reinvention misses something in the process, so that the message becomes weaker at each step. One has only to read the classic Orthodox text on spirituality, *The Ladder of Divine Ascent* by St. John Climacus, to see how pale our modern mysticism is by comparison. The only valid "new age" for a Christian is one founded on Christ and the Apostles, that is, a contemplative tradition that leads to a personal encounter with the personal God, "Abba," "Our Father."

All of these leaders discuss the value of making retreats and give practical advice on how to do so in this book. Because it is relatively new and unknown, the desert experience of the hermitage-style retreats in Crestone and Nova Scotia, among other places, is discussed in detail by Mother Tessa. Also treated at length is Father Keating's system of centering prayer. There's a chapter explaining the rich selection of types and styles of retreats available in Catholicism today. There are personal essays by individuals who describe their own retreat experiences.

The information in the Directory was gathered in an extensive questionnaire sent to every retreat center I could find. Every center director, every layperson I contacted said the same thing: we need a catalog to tell us everything available; right now the only way we learn about retreat centers is by word of mouth! Mother Tessa said, "I get asked this question all the time: where can I go? With whom can I connect? And although I certainly have no time for such a project, I've had it in my mind to put together some sort of a listing of places myself. So this book is a wonderful, a fabulous contribution!"

In the back of the book is a brief overview of Roman Catholic doctrine and an Appendix listing books, tapes, and other resources for those who wish to explore the subject in greater depth.

This book has grown out of my own journey back to the Christian path I abandoned nearly twenty-five years ago. In all my interviews, one theme constantly recurred: everyone warned me not to try to write this book in a detached way; they urged me to explain my personal interest, saying my story is so typical of the baby-boom generation that it might help others. Reluctantly, then, let me briefly tell you why this particular person is writing this particular book.

I was sitting in a silent retreat, meditating, when I heard a bell carillon in the distance pealing out a medley of lovely hymns to

Mary—hymns that had been engraved on my heart when I was a small child in a Roman Catholic school. Suddenly the room seemed bathed in blindingly bright light and I felt an overwhelming sense of love and joy far beyond the mere human emotions I had experienced all too briefly in my life. Although I had had glimpses of this vast enveloping warmth before, they had always been detached, a-personal. Somehow, this time, I knew that this boundless love and joy was demanding that I call it by name.

I suddenly found myself praying fervently to God, something I had not done in many years. I still don't understand what really happened. I felt so very much at peace, and yet I was acutely uncomfortable. This was, after all, the third day of a very intensive Zen Buddhist retreat!

A year later, in answer to one of my questions in our "long-distance" interview, Father William McNamara explained that there are two basic experiences in a contemplative retreat: "First, one is found by God. Since everyone feels a terrible sense of exile and loneliness in this world, there is great delight when one is found by God. At the same time it is dreadful, because one has been found by the all-consuming God who makes devastating demands of love."

And so my quest began. In the process, I have rediscovered a rich spiritual heritage I had lost. After Roman Catholic grade school I attended a Roman Catholic high school and a Jesuit college, with its obligatory courses in Scholastic theology. Thus, when I finally decided I did not believe in Christianity, I was certain I knew everything about it. What I have discovered has shown me that I really knew nothing. Mother Tessa Bielecki refers to people like me as "wounded Catholics," and explains that she often meets people who "compare a Sunday-school-level grasp of Christianity to sophisticated Eastern (i.e., non-Christian) contemplative practices, and it's a totally unfair comparison. They know nothing about Christian mysticism, and so they think there's nothing to it." Until the sixties, Christian mysticism was a taboo topic, never taught or discussed in Roman Catholicism. So naturally we know nothing about it!

As a fairly typical member of the baby-boom generation, I proceeded after college to pursue material success. I truly believe that those of us who grew up in a strong Roman Catholic environment and then left the Church walk around with a large hole in our hearts. We are always seeking to replace that center of gravity we lost, and we're quite creative in our choices of replacements: careers, BMWs and Mercedes Benzes, palatial homes, status symbols ad nauseum, exotic vacations, adventurous hobbies, and—most important—relationships with other human beings just as empty as ourselves. And so I had what my friends considered the ideal marriage (it was hell), the ideally-decorated home (it was drudgery), and a brilliant career that made me a vice president in an international corporate headquarters (it was a morass of petty politics) at the advanced age of 35. What I didn't have was lasting happiness, a sense of self-satisfaction, and a center to my life. Cardinal Joseph Ratzinger of the Vatican said,

Because the desire of liberty belongs to the essence of a human being, such a person necessarily seeks from the start the path to 'being like God': all other things in fact are not sufficient for human beings, insatiable where finite things are concerned. Our time in particular demonstrates this, with its passionate cry for total freedom and anarchy in face of the insufficiency of all bourgeois freedom, however broad it may be, and for all libertinism.

When material things and love affairs failed to satisfy me, I took the next step typical of my generation and became deeply involved in an Eastern meditation tradition (Zen Buddhism), even spending a year as attendant to my teacher. And that was very satisfying, indeed; it healed a lot of my wounds, and led me to a point where I was open enough to face the question: why was I baptized a Catholic? All my Buddhist training told me there had to be a good reason, that it was not chance.

In his book *Christian Mysticism,* Father McNamara wrote that a Westerner needs first to be firmly rooted in the Christian tradition. When I asked him why, he explained,

Introduction

Because you were born and raised in a Christian culture and have experienced, at least to some degree, the wisdom of the Christian tradition. Although there are rare exceptions, Westerners who claim to be Eastern mystics usually come across as not quite totally genuine and authentic. What is much more likely to happen is that, by dipping into the wisdom of non-Christian Eastern traditions, one reconfirms and strengthens and broadens and deepens one's own grasp of Christian wisdom, one's own attraction to Christ as the "mystic par excellence." This is what happens to the best practitioners—they become better Christ-men and Christ-women.

The Christian tradition involves an intensely personal relationship with God. Cardinal Ratzinger wrote, "On the presence of the personal God depends the indestructible value of the human person." Non-Christian traditions have a well-developed sense of the transcendent aspect of the Absolute. But those of us who grew up with Jesus Christ need more, because there is so much more in Christianity—a whole other side to the divine coin. Transcendence is balanced with immanence, with God-become-man. (This is not true for some Protestant denominations that do not share this Christological outlook.)

The detachment of a non-Christian tradition is very comforting and very comfortable, because one can pick and choose one's responses. It is only in Christianity, in personal involvement in the love life of the Trinity, that one encounters those "devastating demands of love" that are not necessarily the choices of one's small ego-self. Paradoxically, it is only by losing oneself in those devastating demands that one finds one's True Self—one's Christ-self.

In the Divine Liturgy of the Orthodox Christian Church, the priest intones, "Wisdom! Let us be attentive!" before readings from Holy Scripture. The words on the following pages are not the author's; they come from some of the finest retreat directors in the country, people who have dedicated their lives to helping others on the spiritual path. Their words contain much wisdom. Let us be attentive to them.

The Value of Making a Retreat: Comments from Leading Retreat Directors

> *To make a retreat is to go into training to be Christian. In the same way that walking and running are a means of exercising the body, a retreat is a spiritual exercise which prepares the soul to make an ever better response to the call we have received.*
> —Cardinal Joseph Ratzinger

What is a retreat? What does it mean to make a retreat? Those of us who attended Roman Catholic high schools in the fifties and sixties probably remember being herded off to large retreat houses once a year where a priest preached to us about "life," we said a lot of prayers, and we had to keep quiet. The girls always went to a cloistered convent or a center run by nuns; the boys always went to a monastery or a center run by priests or monks. And most of us had absolutely no idea of what we were doing, aside from getting out of classes for a few days.

Now that we're busy, working adults, it's a good bet that a retreat, whatever form it may take, will bear no resemblance to our high school memories. For one thing, the very nature of retreats has changed. But so have we. Dr. James Finley said, "I sometimes tell people that a retreat is a retreat from our retreat! We're always retreating in our normal, daily lives. So to make a spiritual retreat is to be willing to risk abandoning our daily 'retreat.' The idea that one is running away from life is completely wrong. Life starts in your heart, in the silence of yourself. And you can only hear that on a retreat."

So a retreat is an opportunity to stop and reorient ourselves

The Value of Making a Retreat

to God as the center of our lives. It's the time we take to turn down the volume of the "buzz" of daily life and tune in to the voice of God. Cardinal Ratzinger wrote, "In the multiplicity of our daily tasks it can easily happen that God becomes secondary. God is patient and silent, those other things are urgent and demanding; it is much easier to put off listening to the word of God than to so many other things."

If a retreat is listening to God, the question then becomes, how do we do that? How do we hear something we normally cannot hear?

The Value of Silence

Everyone interviewed for this book agreed that silence is a critical ingredient of the retreat experience: not silence that is repression or suppression but rather a silence that grows naturally out of our desire to improve our lives. Because the "hesychast" tradition, or the way of silence ("hesychia" is a Greek word meaning silence) is so integral a part of the Orthodox path, Father Robert Arida explained the value of cultivating an interior silence. In a public talk entitled "The Language of Silence," Father Robert explained how important silence is as the foundation of all forms of communication:

> I am sure that no one here would disagree that the pollution of our atmosphere is in part made up of meaningless and empty babbling. The language of silence, therefore, requires us to become reacquainted with the nature of language, as dialogue. . . . Silence puts to death the false meaning of words and teaches us how to speak anew.

But silence is much more than this. Father Robert traced the development of the hesychast tradition from its earliest times, when it referred to one who lived in solitude and thus denoted an environment conducive to interior peace. From there the understanding of the hesychast way expanded, so that the idea developed that the monastics (from "monos," meaning one) were not the only people called to be one; *everyone* is called to have total integration with God, himself or herself, and the world. Thus, a return to silence is really a return to wholeness.

A New Point of View

All the wisdom of the East and West, Christian and non-Christian, has taught that we don't really see and hear accurately in our normal daily lives. One can go back to Plato's *Republic,* in which Socrates presents a vivid metaphor of the human condition as that of people who are chained inside a cave with their backs to the entrance; behind them a huge bonfire is built and all the world parades between them and the fire, so that all they can see are silhouettes cast upon the cave wall. Socrates then asks what it would be like to be released from those chains and the dark cave—that is, what would the retreat experience be like, encountering God directly instead of as a shadow? The assembled company all agree that one who learns to see the true nature of reality will have difficulty adjusting at first, but will grow accustomed to "living in the direct light of the sun" and will rejoice in it. So it is with making retreats. Brother David Steindl-Rast calls this type of experience a "radically experiential approach" to God. That is, one bypasses the usual intellectual and mental exercises and strives to come face-to-face with the Absolute on a visceral level.

One critical point is that the retreat experience is not a turning away from daily life but rather an opportunity to learn a more natural way to live daily. Father Dave Denny said,

A retreat is an end in itself. We've lost our natural taste for a more contemplative life and so it can be hard at first; some people may have difficulty starting in retreat work. But it's an acquired taste. Once it is reawakened, people then realize they have this great hunger and thirst for more silence in their lives, more prayer, more solitude. At Crestone, we try to get rid of the distractions and superficial stimuli, the bombardment by advertising, for example, so that we can hear what is going on underneath it all, which is the love of God, and rediscover that. Our whole thrust comes from the book of Hosea: 'Come into the desert to pray and there I will speak to your heart.' [Editor's Note: This is an old Vulgate translation, no longer found in the RSV Bible, of

Hosea 2:14.] Very few things in our life today really speak to our hearts—television certainly doesn't! We are living in a kind of heartless society now, one which is highly secularized. People sometimes make the accusation that 'monastics couldn't handle the real world.' We consider the love life of the Trinity to be the *real* world, and sometimes it helps to go into the desert to rediscover that, the presence of God in the world.

Father Dave's superior, Father William McNamara added, "Retreats are one of the most important means of human growth, human wholeness, of bringing to a screaming halt the tendency to become indolent, lazy, to go through a day mindlessly. Thoreau was a layman who was also a solitary, and he once said he would give first prize to the person who managed to live one day *deliberately*. This cannot be done unless one breaks out of one's ordinary way of daily life."

Relation to Daily Life

One theme that recurred in these interviews was that a retreat must be seen in light of one's whole life. Although a radical change is needed from daily life today, for one to benefit, the retreat attitude and atmosphere must be translated into the language of daily life and carried home.

Father Thomas Keating is firm in his belief that "the purpose of retreats for lay people is to reinforce a practice they should already be doing. A retreat is not a substitute for daily life. It should be a booster and an accelerator of the spiritual journey—like taking a plane instead of a train or a horse to a certain destination—you go a long way in a short time. But if it is not continued then by some daily process, its primary benefit and effect will be missed."

Father William discussed the theme this way:

> We try to set the stage and create the environment in which people will develop habits that will continue and endure when they return home. When we speak to retreatants, we always speak in terms of how will this affect you, in your home and on your streets and at your work?

This is not meant to be an isolated religious experience in your life but is meant to touch the core of your being so that you will never be the same again, but will act thoughtfully and mindfully in the everyday circumstances of your life. We are constantly making that connection between the desert and the city.

People end up belonging to a religion rather than to God, so that religion stops being the supreme *means.* That is the great hunger of young people, they want a kind of direct and immediate experience of the living God—at least as much as is humanly possible. They don't want to go through so much religious rigamarole that it gets put off, it gets postponed, and in the meantime they suffer a terrible deadening boredom—to such an extent that most of them give up religion entirely.

It is only the *mystical* dimension of religion which attracts and draws people, because it is the longest and deepest tradition of the Christian church, but the church has forgotten it, so it does not *convey* its mystical tradition effectively. Thus so many go to Eastern [non-Christian] traditions.

There is a danger of coming home from a retreat and thinking of it as a sort of isolated high experience. The point is to make a significant move toward the end of becoming one's best self. This is *sanctity,* a movement much deeper into holiness. One shares more intimately in the Christ-life, and thus redeems the ordinary world.

An Experiential Approach to God

Contemplation, then, or this radically experiential approach to God, is really the natural state of human life. But contemplation is one of three stages in the development of an experiential Christian. It might help to look at these three stages—prayer, meditation, and contemplation—more closely to understand them better. It needs to be emphasized, however, that these are not neat, discrete events; rather, one who practices rightly may move—or, more correctly, be moved by the Spirit of God—back and forth among the three stages of activity in any given prayer session.

Prayer: Although in the Orthodox Church the word "prayer" has remained all-inclusive and refers to all three stages, Western Christianity had come to use the term only in reference to the recitation of formulaic prayers. (This is changing somewhat with the teaching of centering

The Value of Making a Retreat

prayer.) Brother David makes a distinction in his writing and talks between "prayer" and "prayers," using the first to refer to an attitude which may or may not be found in combination with the second, which refers to standard verbal patterns.

Meditation: This term has gained in use in the last few decades as a result of the popularity of non-Christian Eastern traditions, many of which teach specific techniques for calming the mind and stilling the body that are called "meditation."

Contemplation: With the exception of American Tibetan Buddhists, who use these terms differently, the word "contemplation" in both Christian and non-Christian traditions refers first to the altered state of consciousness that sometimes results from advanced meditation practice. A Christian would call this "union with God." The hallmark of a true contemplative state is that the person is totally unaware of being in it until he or she emerges from it—if you think you're "contemplating," you're not.

Prayer and meditation, steps in which the individual consciously and deliberately makes an effort to encounter God on a personal level, are necessary to set the stage for contemplation. Prayer and meditation, when performed on a regular basis, help one reach a level of involvement in life where one is in a constant state of readiness for God. Thus prayer and meditation are habits over which we have complete control, whereas contemplation is in God's control. We cannot deliberately force God to meet us face-to-face, we can only be ready for when he chooses to do so. In the New Testament (James 4:8) it is written, "Draw near to God, and he will draw near to you." Commenting on this verse, Tito Colliander, a well-known Orthodox writer, said, "It is for us to begin. If we take one step towards the Lord, he takes ten towards us—he who saw the prodigal son while he was yet at a distance, and had compassion and ran and embraced him."

Summing up these three steps of prayer activity under the term "prayer," St. John Climacus wrote, "The beginning of prayer is the expulsion of distractions from the very start by a single thought; the middle stage is the concentration on what is being said or thought; its conclusion is rapture in the Lord."

Since we must take the first step in this love affair with God, we need to know what steps may be taken, what steps people before have taken. We need to know what kinds of retreats are being offered today.

What Kinds of Retreats Are Available?

> *He who does not meditate acts as one who never looks into a mirror and so does not bother to put himself in order, since he can be dirty without knowing it. The person who meditates and turns his thoughts to God Who is the mirror of his soul, seeks to know his defects and tries to correct them, moderates himself in his impulses and puts his conscience in order.*
> —Padre Pio

When I described this book project to Father Tom Gedeon of Retreats International and mentioned the need for this chapter, his initial reaction was, "Impossible! It can't be done!" But how else can anyone know the wide range of Catholic retreats today?

And the range is indeed wide! Father Gedeon is correct in that the same words are used by different centers to describe different types of retreats and, conversely, the same type of retreat is described in several different ways by different centers! But this is valuable information for the would-be retreatant, because it helps one avoid the error of assuming "all retreats are the same so it makes no difference where I go." Dr. James Finley advised: "A person needs to seek out that kind of retreat which best addresses where he or she is on the spiritual path at any given time. For example, people who feel a need for a contemplative type of retreat should look for retreat houses which offer those kinds of retreats, as opposed to more conference-style ones. The important thing is that the individual must be in touch with his or her own needs, believe in them, and then seek out places and people who can fill those needs."

As recently as twenty-five years ago, there was one standard retreat offered for lay people in the Roman Catholic Church. It

What Kinds of Retreats Are Available?

was based very loosely on the Ignatian Exercises (which will be explained later), and usually lasted three or four days.

This type of retreat was always led by a priest. Men would go to a monastery or a retreat house run by monks or priests, while women would congregate at centers staffed by nuns. Such retreats included the Mass every morning, periods of silence and private prayer, formal talks by the director, question-and-answer periods, and such devotional practices as the rosary and the Stations of the Cross.

The general outline followed was, first, to arouse sorrow for one's sins, and second, to meditate on the life of Christ as exemplar; then to explore the retreatants' vocation (for lay people, what it meant to be a Christian husband and father or wife and mother). The retreats concluded with practical resolutions by participants on ways to follow Christ more closely in their daily lives. These traditional types of retreats can still be found, and are considered beneficial by people who make them. They have their place in a Christian life, and may be a good place to start for someone with no experience in meditation or retreats.

However, since Vatican II there has been a renewed emphasis on the more contemplative, or mystical, paths of spiritual development, and new retreat forms have sprung up to meet this need.

In two of his books, *Finding Grace at the Center,* written with Pennington and Clarke, and *Open Mind, Open Heart,* Father Keating has discussed the loss of this particular tradition in Roman Catholicism. He points out that St. Ignatius originally had three levels of prayer in his *Exercises,* but the two more advanced methods were suppressed until well into our own century, leaving only the lowest form of discursive meditation to be taught.

A variety of other historical, social, cultural, and ecclesiastical events and trends contributed to the further decline of what had been a vibrant tradition of contemplation up until the sixteenth century.

Father Keating wrote, "The genuine Christian tradition, taught uninterruptedly for the first fifteen centuries, is that contemplation [which he defines earlier as 'the knowledge of God based on the intimate and loving experience of His presence'] is the normal evolution of a genuine spiritual life and hence open to all Christians. All these historical and cultural factors help to explain why the traditional spirituality of the Western church has gradually been lost in recent centuries, and why Vatican II had to address itself to the acute problem of spiritual renewal."

When I asked Dr. Finley about the changes in lay retreats that he has observed in the last twenty to twenty-five years, he said, "I have a strong sense that the real renewal which has taken place in the [Roman Catholic] Church has been a renewal of spiritual awakening among the laity. You can now find Bible study groups and prayer groups in most parishes in the U.S., and if you sit and listen to those groups you will find a very alive and exciting commitment to the spiritual path. And I have the impression that retreat houses have become rather like 'centering places' where such people can gather together and meet each other and explore what they are doing."

Brother David added, "Not only can lay people now make contemplative and meditative types of retreats, which they could never do before, but there are today some excellent women retreat directors around who are adding a wonderful depth and richness to the choice of retreats!"

An indication of the changes that have taken place can be seen most easily by looking at the problems encountered in developing a questionnaire to send to centers for this book. When I interviewed directors of retreat centers with my draft questionnaire, I discovered that the categories of retreats were a problem for all of them. I had developed those categories based on books and periodical articles I had read, some quite recent, but they did not represent what was going on in the centers.

For example, a major problem arose with the word "directed." For some, it meant a "preached" retreat, which is similar to the traditional retreat just described; but for others,

What Kinds of Retreats Are Available? 19

"directed" meant just the opposite—they used it to mean a private, one-on-one retreat.

The same thing happened with the word "private"—some used it to mean a one-on-one retreat with a director, others defined it as a solitary, undirected retreat. And then there were all the new categories, many of which do not qualify as true retreats —prayer days, encounters, seminars, workshops, retreats for problems such as chemical dependence, which are heavily weighted toward therapy, and so on.

Many of the innovative retreats that sprang up in the 1970s (one thinks immediately of clowns) have mercifully disappeared from the retreat landscape of the late 1980s, rendering much of the existing literature on the subject outdated.

The result of the questionnaire interviews was to make that section on types of retreats and programs much looser and open to essay. We narrowed the "standard" retreat categories to four:

- *Directed/Group:* What most people think of as the traditional Roman Catholic retreat. One attends as a member of a group and is guided by one or more directors. This is also most commonly known as a "preached" retreat.
- *Directed/Private:* The most common example of this type of retreat would be the Ignatian Exercises. One resides in a retreat center, but as an individual rather than a member of a group. However, one is guided by a spiritual director rather than following one's own schedule. Many retreat centers can accommodate this sort of retreat, but it is almost never listed in their brochures—one must request it. Under normal circumstances, a person making this sort of retreat already will have made group retreats and will be seeking one-on-one assistance of a specific spiritual nature.
- *Conference:* This is a group retreat in which the person guiding it acts as a "facilitator." These retreats are generally not as silent as the preceding types, and are often weighted in a psychological direction. Group members share their thoughts and feelings as the retreat progresses. Journal retreats are an example of this type.
- *Hermitage/Solitary:* This is a fairly recent development in lay retreats. Although a lay person could always go off in the woods alone, it is now possible to find retreat centers that provide individual hermitages or rooms, but offer no regular spiritual direction. The

individual is on his or her own, making an unguided retreat but in a monastic atmosphere and with access to the Liturgy and Sacraments. An entire chapter is devoted to this type of retreat, because it is so new and is becoming so popular.

A glance through the listings of the Directory of this book will reveal a wide range of variations on the basic types being offered today.

The questionnaire next presented a list of other types of retreats that have become more common in the last two decades and asked the centers if they are offered. Most of these are not, strictly speaking, true retreats, but rather programs that deal with a specific theme or problem area:

- *Ecumenical:* A loose description for any workshop or program that emphasizes an effort to explore the common ground of various Christian denominations.
- *Charismatic:* The charismatic movement has grown within the Roman Catholic Church since Vatican II, and many parishes now include charismatic prayer groups and/or healing prayer groups. The charismatic movement will be covered later in this chapter with a description of the Pecos Community in New Mexico.
- *Prayer Days:* Also called Days of Recollection, these are one-day gatherings at a retreat center, often scheduled in conjunction with some liturgical highlight of the year, such as Lent or Advent. The center directors I interviewed felt very strongly that these should not be called retreats.
- *Parent-Teen:* Often a weekend, these programs usually emphasize family communications.
- *Marriage and Engaged Encounters:* These are not true retreats, but programs with a specific psychological purpose. Marriage Encounter brings married couples together for a weekend, under the direction of a team of other couples and a priest, for the purpose of improving communications. Engaged Encounter does the same thing with engaged couples.
- *Cursillos:* The cursillo movement started in Spain in 1949 and in the United States in 1957. The basic program is a three-day weekend in which lay people explore their potential for Christian community living and apostolic action. Follow-up programs and weekly local group meetings are an integral part of the movement.

The third category on the questionnaire concerned special retreats. These are "theme" retreats, and most often revolve around chemical dependence or alcoholism. Another major area is dealing with grief and the separation of divorce; dealing with AIDS is becoming a more common theme. Retreat centers that offer their facilities as hosts for other groups often have an extensive schedule of such retreats.

The final question asked centers to list any programs that do not fit into the three previous categories. There was a wide variety of answers, and one needs to request program brochures from the centers that interest one. In the Directory I have listed only those programs that were unusual; if the programs fell into the common categories, I said that the center offers "miscellaneous programs."

The most common category is psychological—such programs as Enneagram, Meyers-Briggs, Jungian analysis, and Intensive Journaling are ubiquitous. One area more frequently offered is the development of lay ministry and lay spiritual directors.

One interesting program is the "19th Annotation." Based on the 19th annotation, or paragraph, of the Spiritual Exercises of St. Ignatius of Loyola, these programs are designed for people who cannot make a strict retreat.

Generally, the person meets once a week with a spiritual director and prays and meditates the rest of the week within the context of his or her daily life. This program, which is becoming a frequent offering at retreat centers, is opening the realm of a deeper prayer life to far more lay people than previously were touched by the traditional approach to retreats.

In addition to the four standard types of retreats listed above and the various workshops and programs, it is helpful to know about some of the more prominent threads, or approaches running through all retreat offerings. For example, the Ignatian Exercises have set the standard for Roman Catholic retreats for centuries, but today—thanks to new translations of St. Ignatius—a lay person is much more likely to find an authentic Ignatian approach. So a look at the basic Ignatian Exercise pattern might be a good idea.

Second, there is a contemplative approach called centering prayer, based primarily on the teaching in the fourteenth-century *Cloud of Unknowing,* which has become very popular. Taught by people like Father Basil Pennington and Father Thomas Keating, centering prayer is a method of Christian meditation that will be readily familiar to anyone who has ever investigated a non-Christian Eastern tradition.

Third, there is a movement among Roman Catholic retreat directors to teach some form of the Jesus Prayer, the traditional mystical or contemplative path of Orthodox Christianity. The Jesus Prayer is part of the common heritage that predates separations in Christianity, and so it is not unusual that Roman Catholics might investigate it as part of their renewal. However, one needs to understand that a Roman Catholic approach to the Jesus Prayer and a Roman Catholic way of teaching it will be radically different from the Orthodox approach, as will be seen later in this chapter when we look at the Jesus Prayer in depth.

Fourth, there is the charismatic movement which, although far from being mainstream in Roman Catholicism, is having a definite impact. And last, an in-depth look at the solitary or hermitage retreat movement is long overdue.

The Exercises of St. Ignatius of Loyola are generally presented in a four-week period. The time frame may be compressed or expanded, but the outline is always the same. The first period (week) is the "way of purgation," with an emphasis on examination of conscience and development of a spirit of compunction (repentance, sorrow for one's sins, desire to improve). By meditating on the question of a human's final end, one is brought to a state of mind where one is ready to learn how to improve.

The second week, therefore, concentrates on the life of Jesus as our role model, the perfect human being. As one's understanding and appreciation of the life of Christ develops, one moves into the third week and concentrates on his Passion and Death. The purpose of meditating on Christ's sacrifice is to develop a spirit of humble gratitude and to strengthen the resolve to improve that was set in the first week.

The fourth week considers Christ's Resurrection and engenders a spirit of faith, trust, and consolation in the retreatant. It culminates in a meditation to develop selfless love and a life wholly dedicated to service to God. The Ignatian Exercises are, first and foremost, a visualization form of meditation. Ideally, the director will be very experienced at leading a retreatant through the vivid visualization of the meditation subjects and the resultant examinations of conscience and application to one's own life.

Centering prayer, our second approach, is a way of meditation, but not of visualization. My intention is not to reproduce what Father Keating and Father Pennington have so well explained in their own books (refer to Appendix for suggested further reading). However, since one of the personal retreat essays in this book concerns an intensive centering prayer retreat, and since centering prayer groups are springing up all over the country, a brief overview of the method is called for.

In his book *Open Mind, Open Heart,* Father Keating wrote, "Spiritual disciplines, both East and West, are based on the hypothesis that there is something that we can do to enter upon the journey to divine union once we have been touched by the realization that such a state exists." He calls centering prayer "a discipline designed to reduce the obstacles to contemplative prayer."

Ideally, one practices centering prayer twice a day, preferably morning and evening. One takes a comfortable position in an environment as empty of noise and distraction as possible and chooses a sacred word that will act as a reminder of what one is trying to do, that is, move toward God. The sacred word is not spoken, and it is not concentrated on with the intellect or the imagination. Rather, one tries to achieve a sort of "bare attention" in which one is not thinking but is fully aware, using the sacred word only as a lasso to pull one back from runaway thoughts.

Prayer periods are usually twenty to thirty minutes long. One does not consciously try to stop thinking, because then one is thinking about stopping thinking. One lets go and relaxes into a different level of awareness from normal life, a level that is a state of readiness for God (but not *conscious* readiness!).

And now we come to the Jesus Prayer. Some of the incidents in the New Testament in which people cry out to Jesus as he passes by, "Son of David, have mercy on me!" have been cited as forerunners of the Jesus Prayer. In its current form it is usually recited, "Lord Jesus Christ, Son of God, have mercy on me, a sinner." One finds very early references to a type of Jesus Prayer, albeit unstructured and unspecified, in *The Ladder of Divine Ascent* by John Climacus, a mystical writer of the late sixth and early seventh centuries in the Eastern Christian (Orthodox) tradition. However, the Jesus Prayer, sometimes called the "Prayer of the Heart," was rather unfortunately popularized by a short story of J. D. Salinger's ("Franny and Zooey") and a slim volume called *The Way of the Pilgrim*. Most members of the baby-boom generation first read Salinger's story, in which a college-age woman reads the story of the pilgrim, starts saying the prayer on her own, and has a nervous breakdown. The point of the story seems to have been lost on us, since sales of the pilgrim's story went up after Salinger's story appeared.

This trivialization aside, many Roman Catholic monastics in the fresh air of Vatican II turned to the Orthodox tradition to relearn their mystical heritage, and there are now prominent retreat directors who include the Jesus Prayer among the methods of contemplation that they teach.

The pilgrim, a nineteenth-century peasant, hears St. Paul's admonition to the Thessalonians to "pray unceasingly" (1 Thess. 5:17) and sets off on foot across Russia to find a spiritual teacher who can instruct him in how to do this. His journey is a very telescoped and idealized version of the development that might occur with the practice of the Jesus Prayer. The reality, at least today, is something quite different.

In their introduction to Volume I of the *Philokalia,* the translators and editors (G. E. H. Palmer, Philip Sherrard, and Kallistos

Ware) have this to say about hesychasm, the spiritual path in which one finds the Jesus Prayer practiced:

> It must be stressed, however, that this spiritual path known as hesychasm cannot be followed in a vacuum. Although most of the texts in the *Philokalia* are not specifically doctrinal, they all presuppose doctrine even when they do not state it. Moreover, this doctrine entails an ecclesiology. It entails a particular understanding of the Church and a view of salvation inextricably bound up with its sacramental and liturgical life. This is to say that hesychasm is not something that has developed independently of or alongside the sacramental and liturgical life of the Church. It is part and parcel of it. It too is an ecclesial tradition. To attempt to practice it, therefore, apart from active participation in this sacramental and liturgical life is to cut it off from its living roots. It is also to abuse the intention of its exponents and teachers and so to act with a presumption that may well have consequences of a disastrous kind, mental and physical.

It is important to keep this in mind when reading the words of Father Robert Arida, an Orthodox priest, on the Jesus Prayer. I asked Father Robert about the Jesus Prayer in our interview and heard far more than I bargained for! He made me realize that the Jesus Prayer is a very powerful and advanced practice, never to be undertaken lightly. One must keep in mind that, although Father Robert uses the same words one hears in Roman Catholicism —words like "Church," "community" and "parish"—he means them in a very different context, the context explained above by the translators of the *Philokalia*.

It is here that one begins to see the fundamental difference between Orthodox and other Christians, and what they mean when they use the word "catholic" to mean "full and complete": Orthodoxy is a whole made up of interlocking parts, all of which are necessary to have the fullness and completeness of Christ's Church on earth. This point of view is diametrically opposite the "cafeteria" approach, in which one picks and chooses one's beliefs and practices according to one's personal inclinations. Father Robert said,

> I myself do not teach the Jesus Prayer, and there is great reluctance among Orthodox teachers to do so. First of all, because it is a very

powerful practice which, if misused, can lead to insanity. But second, you must understand that for an Orthodox teacher to instruct someone in the Jesus Prayer would make him responsible for that person; there would have to be a very deep spiritual bond of the sort found in monasteries.

Still more important, however, is the fact that the Jesus Prayer has a specific context in which it is practiced, and that context is the Christian community—the Church, the parish. Someone doesn't just walk in off the street, like the pilgrim, and say, "Father, I want to learn the Jesus Prayer." First the person must be deeply involved in the life of the community, actually living the life that underlies the Jesus Prayer. In a certain sense, the Jesus Prayer is never really practiced alone, even if one is locked in one's room while doing it. One must understand the concept of the church as the mystical body of Christ on earth in order to understand the communal context of the Jesus Prayer and practice it rightly.

There are a number of stages or levels of development in the practice of the Jesus Prayer, and one needs very careful guidance through all of them. One of the first pitfalls is the temptation to use it as a replacement for other standard Orthodox forms of worship, and that is not its purpose. The Jesus Prayer is a practice to unite mind and heart, which means that I am not only praying intellectually, but that these words are real words, they are not just sounds. And they are really *my* words, I am *being* them, they are not someone else's words. That is why there are various stages to the Jesus Prayer—there is the audible stage, the mental stage, and finally there is the stage of the heart, which is *total integration.*

The fourth major approach in retreat centers is the charismatic movement, which tends to call itself a "renewal" in the Roman Catholic Church. When I visited the Pecos Community in New Mexico, Brother Daniel Stramara pointed out that their monastery considers itself in the avant-garde of Roman Catholicism, because of its double nature (both men and women are members) and its leadership in the charismatic movement. The movement is growing, and a number of the centers listed in the Directory bill themselves as specifically charismatic.

In early 1967, a small group of faculty and students at a Catholic college in the United States gathered on a weekend retreat and prayed for the presence of the Holy Spirit. The group experienced what they called the gifts of praying in tongues and prophecy, and the movement started to spread—first to other colleges, then to groups of lay people within parishes.

Today, much of the emphasis of charismatic retreat centers and programs is on healing, although praying in tongues and prophecy are still important parts of their regular prayer meetings. Abbot David Geraets of the Pecos Community, for example, is studying to become a Jungian analyst to enhance his ability to help people heal in a holistic way. Abbot David said, "The greatest attraction of the Pecos Community is the deep prayer experience, which leads people to experience a healing in spirit, in psyche, and also sometimes in the body."

Pecos is in a beautiful and peaceful river valley not far from Santa Fe, the buildings are adobe, and the two dormitories have roofs of solar panels. The monastery has become a very popular center for charismatic retreats, and is noteworthy for its intensive School for Charismatic Spiritual Directors. When I asked Abbot David why people are drawn to his community, he replied, "The best way to communicate a religious experience is in a loving community. Human love is probably the best medium to communicate the Holy Spirit. So people come into our community and they sort of "catch" the Spirit, they "catch" prayer, they "catch" Christianity more than having it taught to them."

Finally, we come to the desert experience. Because this is such a new and exciting direction in retreats, and also because it is only for experienced retreatants and needs a clear understanding and a detailed explanation, another chapter will treat the subject in depth.

Practical Advice for Making Retreats

> *There are many who live in the mountains and behave as if they were in the town, and they are wasting their time. It is possible to be a solitary in one's mind while living in a crowd, and it is possible for one who is a solitary to live in the crowd of his own thoughts.*
> —Amma Syncletia,
> *Sayings of the Desert Fathers*

One of the biggest obstacles to making a successful retreat is lack of knowledge of what to expect and what to do. Most people learn the hard way, by going on retreat, making mistakes, and knowing better the next time. But experience is a costly teacher—in terms of money and time. Everyone interviewed for this book was asked practical questions that beginners are usually too shy to ask. In addition, every retreat center director was asked on the questionnaire for advice on making a retreat. Highlights from the interviews follow in question-and-answer format.

General Advice

The first question concerned general advice given to people considering making a retreat. I asked each person, "If someone were to approach you with a desire to make a retreat and ask for your advice, what would you say?"

Father William McNamara: When people come on our retreat—the eremitical, the desert or wilderness experience—the first thing I urge them to do is to *not* try to get anything out of the retreat. I am convinced that our society is built on the principle of "only that which is useful is good." They should spend as much time as possible on a retreat, because it takes a few days to settle in, since it is such a contrast. And then I urge them to waste the time, which they find rather shocking! But the only way that I can prove that I love God and take him seriously, that he absorbs me and fascinates me, is that I simply *be there*. I must have no designs on God; I must not go on retreat to get something out of it; rather, I must go because God is there, to enjoy the presence and company of God. What St. Thomas called "holy leisure" is contemplation. My favorite definition of contemplation is "taking a long, loving look at the Real"—with no designs on the Real. In this society we keep coming up with very clever ways of avoiding the essential human act of just *being*.

Father Robert Arida: First, I would say all people need a kind of break sometimes. But the great danger is that breaks can become escapes. Retreats should be periods of spiritual, mental, and physical refreshment. If they become something other than that, I don't think that's healthy.

Father Dave Denny: Sometimes people complain that Christian spirituality is so distinctively monastic. And yet when you compare it, for example, with the Buddhist tradition, Christian spirituality is far less monastic and much more of a kind of organic, natural way of developing a life of prayer whatever situation you're in. The key is to develop that "leisurely spirit." People often come on retreat with an agenda and work too hard to accomplish some particular thing. I think it's very important to realize that the desert experience is full of surprises. You might think you're going for one reason and it turns out that something else entirely develops. We need to be very open-ended and open-minded about where a retreat leads us. One needs to be open to being led by God in a direction not anticipated and having one's plans shattered by God.

Brother David Steindl-Rast: Before starting on any method of meditation, there are some general guidelines which must be understood as basics, or givens: discipline, regularity (you do it whether you feel like it or not), and the cultivation of mindfulness. You are really training for a lifestyle that goes on twenty-four hours a day, not just at certain times. So the main point regarding any retreat work is that as far as possible it should be personalized. This means, first of all, that the basics—the discipline, the regularity, the mindfulness—must come from inside oneself, must become natural as opposed to forced. But it also means that whoever helps you should first know what kind of psychological background you have, what kind of a psychological type you are. I believe very much in the usefulness of psychological types.

Mother Tessa Bielecki: The most valuable piece of advice I can give anyone is: be silent. Our culture is so noisy, we are so inundated with words, that at least on retreat, be silent. And come to feel at home in silence, so there will be a growing hunger for it and a conviction that one should enter into it on a more regular basis.

I really feel that people should make a retreat at least once a year, absolutely. A lengthy retreat once a year, and in as much as one's vocational demands allow, shorter periods throughout the year. But most important of all is that every day has to have some kind of contemplative time built into it. When lay people really become convinced that this is of value to them, then they will do it. But they must be convinced, or it won't happen.

Also, I think it's very important that one go on retreat alone, not with a friend. If you don't go alone, you go with habitual mind, and you will use the other person as a crutch. Whatever is unfamiliar or somewhat frightening to you, you will try to keep at bay by running to the other person. But it's very important to allow yourself to encounter the uncomfortable, the unfamiliar, whatever is different, and to break through it in some way.

Practical Advice for Making Retreats 31

Getting Started

I next asked how one might go about getting started in making retreats. "Where does one look for a center, what does one do to find the retreat that is just right?"

Dr. James Finley: Speaking from my own experience, I would advise people who feel a need for a contemplative type of retreat to go to their local retreat houses first and see if they offer meditation-style retreats. Look for those retreats which address where you are on the spiritual path right now. This, of course, presupposes that one is aware of one's spiritual needs. And if you can go only once a year, then this might involve some travel, you may not find what you need locally. But if you are in touch with what your real need is, then look for someone who gives that specific kind of retreat.

Father Robert Arida: The retreat experience must begin in the home. For example, within the daily life of the Orthodox Christian there are set times for prayer. A good way to start is to keep those times. There has to be a rhythm, a rule of prayer before anything else. I always advise people to start with the short version, to handle what they can handle. And then they can build up and expand on that in various ways. It might include other hours of the day, or it might be expanded in how one begins to see things, how one begins to react to things, how one begins to approach things. So that in fact, then, the life becomes prayer; our life becomes God's life. But the "system," if you will, already exists and it is simply a matter of availing oneself of it. One thing that must be made clear, though, is that daily prayer is not a divorce from daily life. Once it becomes that it becomes an escape.

Father William: Don't mull over it, don't think about it, just stop everything and go! It has to be a pretty abrupt thing, otherwise you'll never do it. When you look for the most appropriate and convenient time and place, it never happens. You put it off and put it off. Stop what you're doing and come into the desert to pray!

Advice for the Experienced Retreatant

I asked everyone what advice they might give to a person who is somewhat experienced in making retreats but feels a need to "move up" his spiritual mountain, perhaps to try something different. It was on this subject that I received the most divergent opinions.

Father William: There are all kinds of different retreats, and one can become in a sense sated with one kind of retreat. The traditional style of retreat, for example, goes through the same steps over and over again, and if you have made that kind of retreat for years, perhaps you need to try something new. But the desert experience is indispensable. The central biblical experience is the desert experience, and yet so few people have it. So I would say to anyone who is experienced in making retreats but has not spent any time in a hermitage, "You're missing something vital!"

Father Thomas Keating: Pay no attention to dry spots. It seems to me that every new direction leads to a contemplative practice. It may be that one would feel a need for a change in one's teacher or one's method of practice of contemplative prayer, sure, that could happen. But I think most of the time people who persevere in their practice are going to go through that kind of interior desert. So, I think that if a person is comfortable with his or her teacher and practice, just continue. But if they feel it is limiting them in some way, then they might look for a more receptive method.

Mother Tessa: An experienced retreatant who feels the need to do more must go deeper, whatever that means. That might mean a longer retreat, that might mean more frequent retreats, it would certainly mean more silence and more solitude, it would probably mean less intellectual input, more time spent in prayer, or just something different. It depends on whether the person is moving or the person is stuck—they're two different situations. The person who is stuck may need to make some radical changes in the kind of retreat he or she is attending.

Brother David: There are two possibilities for the person with retreat experience: Either one really deepens one's experience and continues to go where one feels enabled to do this—when you have found water, keep digging! Or, if one is not a particularly venturesome person, then one should look around and try to find some other type of retreat that one has never tried before. But if one is the venturesome type—always looking around and trying the latest things—then I would say, bend backwards and stay in the same place! It is always a matter of counteracting our too-extravagant tendencies. Frequently, what we want to do is exactly wrong for us, and we need to do what we *don't* want to do.

Dr. Finley: For the seasoned person, the old warhorse, I try to help put them in touch with what they already know from their own experience, which is that it really is a matter of always starting over. As soon as you start accumulating spiritual fodder, it's heavy to carry around; this is the time to maybe just let go of a lot of stuff and start all over. Relisten, renew, recommit.

Advice for the Beginner

Some people had specific advice for people who are just beginning on the path of making retreats. They dealt more with the idea of what it means to be a beginner.

Mother Tessa: I really don't deal with beginners very much at all, since a beginner would never make a hermitage retreat. But in general I would advise such people to start with a short retreat.

Dr. Finley: For beginners I usually talk about silence on the opening night of a retreat. The mere fact that we're not talking doesn't mean that we're in silence. Silence is an *attentiveness* and a sincerity without expectations. Sometimes people come in with expectations, and I work with them to just be very sincere, very childlike, very open. Beginners need to learn how to trust in the unforeseen that arises out of that openness. The whole idea of being a beginner is very profound, really, and so beginners are in a very good space. That's often the trouble with us—we don't know how to be beginners, or we forget.

Brother David: For the person making a retreat for the first time, I would say, ask someone who knows you very well which type of retreat to make and which place to visit. Don't just go someplace because someone else went there, because you may be someone very different from the person who enjoyed it so much. So get good advice from someone who knows you well.

Father Thomas: Centering prayer would probably be better for someone who already has some retreat experience, because not everyone will take to it the first time. But any kind of retreat would be helpful, I think, as a starting point. But start with a short one. A retreat in a monastic atmosphere has a lot going for it because one is with a community that is praying, and that can be very exciting for people the first time they experience it.

Father Dave: I think balance is essential. In the course of the retreat day, try to lead as balanced a life as possible. This would mean doing some reading, spending some time in the chapel, exercising, getting outside. Monasteries are almost always in beautiful locations and there's a reason for that: one doesn't just shut oneself up in a room, one gets out and back in touch with nature. And then, cultivate a leisurely spirit: leisure is the basis of prayer. One needs to be relaxed and peaceful, and even in a somewhat playful frame of mind, for God to break through.

Integration with Daily Life

A very important consideration is the need to avoid making any sort of split between one's retreat work and one's normal daily life. On this subject there was a lot to be said:

Father Robert: I think the retreat director must simply state, in the course of the retreat, that the idea is to come to an oasis and then go back. First one needs to drink from the water and taste its sweetness; then one goes back and strives to transform wherever one is into an oasis. This is why everyone needs retreats, because it's so easy to forget that such an oasis can exist. There are some people who really have, somehow, by God's grace cultivated an oasis in the midst of their lives. I've seen them, and they are unaware of it, it's just there. One sees it in their faces, one sees it in how they live and in how they interact with other people and especially in how they pray. It's manifested in every aspect of their lives. In order to become such people ourselves, we as parents must understand that the home has to be a church—in the Orthodox way, the nuclear family is the little church. And a retreat nurtures this idea and helps us cultivate it into a reality.

Brother David: This is very much the responsibility of the person who leads or organizes the retreat, the one who facilitates it. On the very first day of a retreat, in the very first talk, I already emphasize, "Let's prepare for the reentry panic." What can one take home from a retreat? I tell people to enjoy all the elements in a retreat that one doesn't have anywhere else, but don't cling to them, don't focus on them. That is not the important point. The important thing is what one can take along and integrate into daily life outside of retreat.

Dr. Finley: Usually my last talk on a retreat is, "What does it mean to go back?" What happens in a retreat is so beautiful, until one gets out to the parking lot and comes to the first traffic light.

People can just go into a nosedive after a contemplative retreat. And when one gets back home, not only is there the usual stuff, but there's a backlog of the usual stuff as a result of being away. The whole idea of a contemplative prayer retreat is to invite people to discover a certain level of reality that exists all the time. What makes it so powerful is the fact that it is not a devotional superstructure which is built up on top of the ordinary; rather, it is *the holiness of the ordinary* that is realized! Once one has a taste of this truth a kind of quiet trust develops so that, when the phone rings, it's not necessarily a distraction. The more one is awakened to the spirituality of ordinary experience, the more one is able to see that life is practice.

Mother Tessa: There are problems which make integration into daily life difficult: lack of community support—having no one else who shares the same values—is probably the biggest problem. There can also be very painful conflict between spouses who share different spiritual value systems, and there are certainly problems for newly married couples who have young children. The burdens of early child-rearing are tremendous. A sort of schizophrenia could develop, a split between retreat time and daily life: one remembers it seemed so pleasant in solitude without a bunch of screaming children around, and then there one is again with a bunch of screaming children around. But that's the vocation. That is what is asked, what is demanded, what needs to be surrendered to, and that is the place where the contemplative life has to be lived.

Some signs that one is making retreats incorrectly, or is making the wrong kind of retreats, might be isolationism, withdrawal from reality, a refusal to meet the demands of life, a reneging on life commitments for selfish reasons—because solitude was so pleasant that you want to prolong that, and so you neglect your family, you neglect your spouse. Irresponsibility, other-worldliness, a lack of groundedness are all danger signals.

A good retreat would result in such things as greater conviction, greater commitment, living more deliberately, being faithful to a discipline of prayer, not being swept along with the current and succumbing to peer pressure. One comes to know God better and oneself better. An awareness of global needs and an increase in love are also signs of a beneficial retreat. The result of any kind of authentic prayer, any kind of authentic solitude, any kind of authentic practice from a Christian standpoint is an increase in love: am I becoming a better lover? If you are, whatever you're doing is right. If you're not, you're doing something very wrong. Something may be happening when you're meditating or praying, but it is not authentic prayer, or you'd be ending up a better lover, of God and of his whole creation.

Going In/Coming Out

A lot of the problems people encounter in making retreats stem from either going into them incorrectly or coming out of them incorrectly. We all know—common sense tells us—not to make abrupt transitions, but sometimes we all need to be reminded of it. In addition, experienced retreat directors have seen people enter and exit retreats in every imaginable way. Their insights on this subject may save some of us a lot of trouble.

Dr. Finley: Going on retreat is like going to a session of psychotherapy. Sometimes people walk in and they say, "Boy, it's been a hell of a week and I dashed over here in this rush hour traffic and I don't really know what to say." It takes twenty minutes just to get into it and then it's half over. It's difficult to prepare for a retreat and sometimes it's really counterproductive. People have to get ready to leave their daily lives, so there's even more detail to cover and they go dashing around. Then the first half of the retreat is often devoted to just resting up enough to be there. However, if people are already doing some sort of spiritual practice, such as a daily quiet time, they should let the object of that quiet time be an anticipatory awareness of the retreat. Get in touch with the felt need for the retreat—just listen to that need. If it's logistically possible and if they would find it helpful, they might expand that quiet time a bit during the week before the retreat. Afterward, the challenge is how to carry interiority out into the world. Leaving the retreat house is carrying this compassion and this depth out into the midst of life.

Brother David: Be as rested as possible, because otherwise when you get to the retreat, any reasonable retreat master will say, "Sleep, rest." Even if one goes on retreat and just sleeps and then goes home, that would be better than continuing in a rat race. If one is planning a retreat as part of a vacation, don't plan it for the beginning but for the end of that vacation. And don't stay up late the last few days before going on a retreat. Get there rested. For coming out, focus on the elements that can be taken back home into daily life.

Father Thomas: If one could just slow down a little a few days before, that would be very helpful. In this culture of ours it will take a full day or two for most people to unwind. Just as centering prayer is the keystone of the whole lifestyle or commitment to the contemplative dimension, so retreat is a kind of renewal or refurbishing. It's like having your rug cleaned. You might not only have to clean the rug, but you might have to do a little dusting, maybe even throw out a few things. We suggest a series of practices to bring interior silence into daily life. [Editor's Note: see chapter 12 in Father Keating's *Open Mind, Open Heart.*] People need to understand that the spiritual journey is a total commitment, a response to Jesus' invitation to "follow me." It involves progressively more and more of daily life and our attitudes there. So when one returns from a retreat one should think of it as just the beginning, not the end, and the challenge is to bring the new insights into one's relationships.

Mother Tessa: The way to enter and the way to exit a retreat are one and the same: Slowly! Don't slip into a retreat from a rushed, frantic situation, but ease into it gradually and sort of depressurize or debrief gradually on the other end of it. For example, we encourage people when they leave us to just take a day at home first alone. Don't just go home on Sunday evening and have to report to work on Monday morning, but ease into it, even if you have to cut your retreat short a day to have a day on the other end, it's very helpful to do that. Easing into a retreat may often mean sleeping at the beginning of it.

The way we structure a retreat in our centers is specifically geared to a gradual immersion. If a person is coming for a week, we encourage him or her to arrive on a Thursday. In this way, they will have periods of prayer, a community meal, and community work on Friday. On Saturday they will help us with chores to get ready for the Sabbath, and Sunday is celebration and play, which means they again have some community time. Only then, on Monday and Tuesday, do they move into really radical solitude. And then on Wednesday when they come out they have a community meal, which is usually an opportunity to share what has happened and to celebrate what has happened on the retreat.

One important thing we do with every person before they leave us is to discuss with them what they can expect when they go home. What is going to be an obstacle for them, and how they can minimize those obstacles and maximize the positive dimensions. Everything in our society works against this. The lack of community support is one of the biggest obstacles to integrating the retreat lessons into daily life.

Father Dave: The whole thrust is to emphasize that divinization or sanctification is simply a process of humanization. So that, if one really makes a good retreat, it should mean that he or she will become a better mother, a better father, a better son or daughter. A well-made retreat doesn't in any way conflict with what our basic vocation is, it amplifies it, it recharges us with more life, more vigor. Gandhi, when he was running India, would spend one day a week meditating. If Gandhi could do that with how busy he was, surely I can stop one day a week with my little responsibilities. And I think that's true for everyone. It's a matter of priorities, and you always find that whatever your highest priorities are you can accomplish. God doesn't distract you from your vocation.

Advice from Retreat Center Directors

On the questionnaire sent to retreat centers, I asked, "What is the most important advice you would give someone who wishes to make a retreat?" A few of the answers were practical, such as a reminders to pack comfortable clothes or to bring walking shoes. But the majority of the answers provided spiritual advice, most of them similar to the following sampling:

- Be open to the inspiration (surprises) of God.
- Be open to new ideas and choose a retreat that will spiritually guide you to be a whole and holy person.
- Be open to God's loving presence.
- Come with an open mind and a loving heart.
- Be open to the movement of the spirit at work in you and in those around you. Listen and meditate upon what you hear and see. God is speaking all the time.
- Be open to whatever God sends you on retreat, and de-escalate your own expectations and agenda.
- Be open—don't set too many expectations.
- Come with an openness that will allow the Lord to speak in all that happens.
- Be open to meet the Lord however he chooses to come.
- Put aside expectations. Let happen what happens.
- Be willing to listen to the Lord. Let Him tell you how to solve your problems.
- Ask for the grace to be open to the promptings of the Spirit!

When the Desert Fathers were flourishing in the early centuries of Christianity, they were visited by a steady stream of pilgrims, all seeking advice. The most common way of asking for advice seems to have been, "Father, please say a word," or

"Father, please give me a word." The responses were filled with the wisdom of the Spirit and the discernment developed in the desert. The wise pilgrim or would-be disciple listened carefully and accepted the proffered advice into his or her heart.

Every individual hears the same words differently and applies those words to his or her own life at the moment of hearing. For this reason, it is a good practice to expose ourselves to as much wisdom as possible, for we never know when mere words will strike us with the force of *The Word* and change our lives. Herewith is a sampling of the best advice offered to would-be retreatants by directors of retreat centers across the country:

- Plan the time away well in advance and let nothing interfere.
- Go often.
- Be good to yourself as God is good to you.
- Let go of control and *be* in the quiet mystery of God.
- Take time to become whom you profess to be.
- Take time to reflect on your life experience if you want to deepen your relationship with God.
- Come and see what good can come from Nazareth!
- Be aware of what you desire as you prepare to come.
- The most important religious experience is that God loves you.
- Seek God.
- Pray. In your prayer, try not to grab but rather to receive what is given.
- Be still and know that He is God! Learn to listen!
- Learn how to pray and reflect in quiet.
- Leave your worldly baggage at home and travel light to the Lord.
- Come to become more fully yourself.
- Trust your prayer!
- Give yourself time to just be. Don't overplan or overschedule.
- Come and take some time to be with your God.

- Come, let God love you during this time for peace and quiet. Become aware of God's presence and call.
- Come, see, make peace with God and self.
- Come apart so you can get back together and be present to others again.
- Be still and taste the goodness of the Lord.
- Don't worry about what should be done on retreat, you've already done it by being here. The Lord does the work, you simply dispose your heart.
- Learn to see all of life as a journey from the self to the Self.
- Expect God to do wonders for you when you are open and attentive.
- Be still and listen, then respond to the Lord.
- Love yourself enough to come away for some alone time.
- Take time to be with the Lord, and you will come to know the peace, healing, compassion, and freedom that only He can give.
- Be gentle with yourself.
- Pray for openness and generosity.
- Allow God time in your life.
- Accept yourself where you are today and know that God loves you.
- Retreat is a time to seek God. Let that be your only motive.
- Come because you want to come.
- "Seek God and you will find Him."
- Make it a vacation with the Lord.
- Be still and listen to your heart.
- Come with an empty heart and let God fill it.

The Desert Experience: Solitary Retreats

Be still and know that I am God.
—Psalm 46:10

Certain images have always served as metaphors for the spiritual journey—most notably, a voyage at sea, a climb up a mountain, or the solitude of the desert. This latter image, however, has been much more than a metaphor in Christianity.

Christianity considers itself the fulfillment of the Old Testament and thus traces its origins to the covenant between God and Israel. Father McNamara said that the central biblical experience is the desert experience. The prophets encountered God most often in the desert or on a mountain. Anyone familiar with the landscape of the Middle East knows that there the two are essentially the same.

In the early centuries of Christianity, holy men and women moved to the desert areas, especially in Egypt, to withdraw from the pagan society around them and nurture their Christ natures in silence and solitude. These were those whom we now revere as our Desert Fathers and Mothers. Out of that movement eventually grew all of Western monasticism. When the desert experience was carried into Western Europe, allowances had to be made for the radically different landscape, and monasteries took root in deep wooded valleys or on forested mountains. But silence and solitude remained essential elements.

It was the bane of monasteries in the West, due to their

function as repositories of knowledge during the Dark Age not experienced in the East, that wherever they were established they were followed by people who built towns around them. Hence the high walls and cloistered atmosphere and attitude of European monasteries.

Thus, the desert experience retreat would be one that is not only silent, but also solitary. Today this is often called a hermitage-style retreat. These are just beginning to become popular, and for good reason: they are an advanced contemplative experience that should never be attempted by a beginner to meditation. Meditative or contemplative-style retreats have been developed and offered to lay people only in the past two decades, and it can easily take a person ten years (if ever!) to reach a point where he or she is ready for the desert experience. Mother Tessa said that in the early years in Crestone there was very little solitude available, even for the monastics themselves, because "in the history of the church one traditionally grows into solitude, having first proven oneself in community virtue. As a community, we have now grown into solitude. Initially, the week-long periods of solitude that we have were open to the monastics only, not to lay people. But now we are beginning to see a hunger for solitude among society at large."

Hermitage-style retreats are currently available in only a few places, and those centers are usually booked well in advance. The Nada Community in Crestone, for example, has space for only three or four outside retreatants at a time, and people routinely book space six or eight months beforehand.

On the other hand, there is a small hermitage outside my hometown of St. Louis, Missouri, called Christina House. Its director, Brother Wilfrid, told me there are certain times of the year—notably winter—when it might be possible to book a hermitage a week or two in advance. He added that a phone call is always a good idea, since people sometimes cancel at the last minute and a hermitage becomes available.

Still, the norm is that a solitary retreat needs to be—and should be, from the point of spiritual development—planned

The Desert Experience

and booked well in advance. This is not the sort of thing one does on a whim.

Because the desert experience is primarily contemplative in nature, i.e., mystical, I asked Father McNamara why he feels so strongly that the contemplative or mystical experience is the basic spiritual path for everyone. He makes a strong case in his books for what he calls "earthy mysticism," and both words are important. He explained, "Without that 'earthy,' mysticism can become very dangerous. There is a tendency to move from 'mist' into 'schism'! Earthy mysticism is not a flight from the world. It is coming face-to-face with Reality itself."

Father McNamara described the importance of the mystical experience:

> In the mystical or contemplative experience, God touches one at the core of one's being, so that one can never be the same again. That's the difference. You are not rearranging things on the surface of your life. You are exposing yourself with utter abandon and vulnerability to the living God.
>
> A mystic is one who no longer knows God by inference or hearsay, but by experience—the way the lover knows the beloved. Actually, there is no other way to know God! God is love, and the mystic is wooed into his love, into his mystery. This is exactly what Jesus does in the New Testament; he lures people into deeper levels of life, knowing that if they really live, they will pray. This is the kind of prayer that is going on full tilt all the time at the heart of the world, the prayer of Christ. All we have to do is climb aboard. We don't have to come up with a red-hot prayer of our own, we just have to climb aboard the prayer that is going on full tilt and full-time, the prayer of Christ himself from beginning to end and from one end of the universe to the other. Jesus is sheer prayer.

Probably one of the best-known centers for making a solitary retreat is Christ in the Desert Monastery, a Subiaco Benedictine foundation in Abiquiu, New Mexico. Thomas Merton had high praise for it in his *Asian Journal*. It is almost always booked to capacity, making early reservations essential.

At present the community consists of ten members, one of whom is a priest and the others, monks. The monastery is in a remote desert canyon, reached via a twelve-mile dirt road. The monks follow the traditional Benedictine way of life consisting of prayer, reading (Lectio Divina), and manual labor.

Individual lay men and women are welcome to go there for "private" retreats—meaning you are on your own. Regular spiritual direction is not provided. Rather, retreatants are encouraged simply to blend into the regular monastic rhythms, which include coming together eight times a day for the Divine Office and a daily Mass, and to take advantage of the privacy and silence for personal reflection and prayer.

Conditions are rugged and primitive: the monastery is at an elevation of 6,500 feet and there are no electricity and no telephone; retreatants have rooms in a guest house, not individual hermitages. Thus, one would be well advised to develop self-discipline in prayer and meditation before making the trek to this monastery. To do otherwise would be to waste a glorious opportunity.

Another center becoming known is the Hermitage at Big Sur, California. This is where Brother David Steindl-Rast resides, and it is a true hermitage-style center with a small number of hermitage rooms. They are self-contained, each having a small enclosed garden, a view of the ocean, and a small rudimentary kitchen. The main meal is provided by the community and is received through a hatch in the wall, so that one may spend one's retreat in total solitude if desired. However, one is certainly encouraged to participate in the liturgy that is celebrated. The brothers are working to construct some paths on their grounds for solitary walks on the cliffs above the ocean. Again, they only admit people who have retreat experience, and a first visit is limited to three days. After that, if one handles the radical solitude without difficulty, one may return for longer periods.

I asked Mother Tessa to explain how they work with lay retreatants at Nada Hermitage in Crestone. Much of what she said applies to all solitary retreat experiences. But, more important, her comments on how to integrate the desert experience into daily life apply to everyone seeking to uncover his or her Christ nature.

The Desert Experience

Mother Tessa first described those qualities that make the Crestone center so different from others:

What makes us unique is primarily the solitude, and that is why people come to us. We don't do preached retreats, we don't do directed retreats. People come to us because they want to be alone with God. Although we check people out very carefully beforehand and keep an eye on them, we don't see them on a regular basis during their stay with us. The whole idea is for them to discover what they can learn directly and immediately—from God, from themselves—through their solitude. Everyone has a separate hermitage, and that makes a huge difference in the freedom of spirit with which you make your retreat. Whether your prayer leads to weeping or screaming or dancing or singing or whatever, there are no inhibitions and you have total freedom to really be able to be who you are and be expressive. That's very special.

We're also unique in the sense that we are what I like to call an "open" monastery. Most times when you go to a monastery for a retreat you are in a guest house, separate from the monks, maybe even separated from them in the chapel. We like to say there's this wonderful dance going on between us and our retreatants: we pray together, we eat the three communal meals each week together, we work together, we play together. So there's a wonderful spirit. We really are enriched by our retreatants because they keep us engaged in a certain realistic way. And at the same time, because our retreatants can see us and relate to us in a normal, intimate, family way, they are greatly enriched. You don't often get to sit down at table or work with a monk!

Another dimension that is different is the fact that we are a mixed community of men and women monks, and obviously that has a certain spirit that affects the quality of a person's retreat. That marvelous man-woman complementarity, which is such an integral part of how we live, gives great vibrancy to a solitary retreat experience.

By the way, everything I say about our center in Crestone applies equally to Nova Nada, our place up in Nova Scotia. The only difference, really, is the lack of electricity in Nova Scotia. And of course the climate and landscape vary. But in terms of retreat style and how we live, both places are much the same.

I asked Mother Tessa what it's like to make a retreat at Crestone, and this is her reply.

Solitude does not mean that you are locked up in your hermitage; solitude simply means that you are alone. We emphasize a spirit of silence so that there isn't that very uncomfortable tension people sometimes experience when they feel they're being forced into something unnatural. We have, for example, several hours of solitude every day. Then two days of every week, Monday and Tuesday, are in complete solitude. And then one week out of every month is solitude. So if in those periods you pass someone on the path somewhere, there's not any kind of weird, inhuman refusal to acknowledge the presence of another person; you nod, you may say hello, you may even say good morning; but you don't engage one another in any kind of conversation.

We encourage retreatants to do some work, because the life is so solitary. It is not a requirement, and there's also great flexibility depending on the individual. Let's say you come in and you work on a computer all day long in the city; well, we would definitely encourage you to be outside a lot and doing some kind of manual labor. That would be a very important part of breaking open parts of your being that normally remain closed. Or let's say you're a farmer with a cow and a berry business, and you're working outside all the time. In that case you would be encouraged to do an awful lot of reading, and to spend time cultivating the more intellectual dimension of the contemplative life, to develop a balance between the two life-styles.

The play aspect is extremely important. We really celebrate the Sabbath in very special ways—the Sabbath is the day when we engage in playing and praying, the two highest human acts. So people who haven't played in years will play volleyball or charades, or it might be a costume party.

We have two periods of communal meditation for prayer, daily on days that are not solitary. Those are primarily the Divine Office, with a half hour of silent meditation in each. I'm very frustrated when I go to other monasteries where they pray the Office and you whip through the Psalms and then you're gone and done. No, no, no! We begin with the introductory prayers, three psalms, a reading from an ecumenical reading book that we put together, and then in silence we have a half hour of meditation. Then the bell rings and we conclude with prayers.

We deliberately do not teach a specific form of meditation to groups of people. We will help people one-on-one. But our understanding of meditation and prayer is that they are so personal, so unique to each individual, that we will present only universal principles and then a person needs to find his own way. We make many broad suggestions, and a person finds his or her own way through experimentation and listening. Most people who come to us are already doing some kind of spiritual practice and they just need some help to refine it.

Nada Hermitage, Spiritual Life Institute, Crestone, Colorado

The most unusual aspect of Crestone retreats is the development of "Foundations." This is the community's term for the basic elements necessary in any human life. Without them, a retreat will not have any lasting benefit. Those who join the Crestone community, for example, go through training in Natural Foundations, Intellectual Foundations, Spiritual Foundations, and Monastic Foundations. Mother Tessa said this training is not readily available to lay people and she is trying to adapt it for a larger audience. "What we have learned over the years is that there's a great hunger for this information and that this process needs to be made more broadly available beyond our monastery. There is a real dearth of practical, concrete, step-by-step, stage-by-stage teaching in Christianity," she said.

Mother Tessa summarized what these Foundations entail:

When we talk about Natural Foundations, we look at how natural a person's life is—do they exercise? Do they gaze at the stars? Do they know the names of the animals and plants around them? Do they go for walks? Do they listen to music (good, edifying music)? How and what do they eat? How much have they managed to detach themselves from the overriding artificiality of our society? In other words, are they in harmony with the natural environment around them?

The Intellectual Foundations concentrate on the mental and rational side of our human natures: How alive is your mind? How clearly do you think? How and what do you read? What do you think about? Is your reading balanced, to keep you balanced? Do you challenge your mind, to keep it alive and clear?

When we get to the Spiritual Foundations, then we start looking at practices: Do you have a regular and disciplined practice of prayer and meditation? Do you participate in the Liturgy and the Sacraments? Do you practice Lectio Divina—this is a very important part of our training. Lectio is a sort of slow, selective, disciplined, meditative reading, usually of scriptures. Other reading material may be used, but the idea is to provide a sort of ground in which meditation is enabled to flower. You read only a very little, and then meditate on it.

The whole area of Monastic Foundations, of course, would not be relevant to lay people. But instead of looking at what it means to be a monastic, and specifically a Carmelite, lay people need to look at their own vocations in the same way: What does it mean to be, first of all, a lay person? And then, what does it mean to be a husband, wife, son, daughter, single person, married person, and so on? And what sort of career is being pursued, and how is it being pursued?

Mother Tessa explained that it is only after they have put down these foundations that they start teaching prayer and meditation, and still later that they get into contemplation and mysticism. Without this natural progression, they find that people tend to pick up spiritual practices and try to stick them into lives that do not provide a context for them—they make no connection between the practice and the life.

She concluded:

> We firmly believe that contemplation is our birthright as human beings. People are naturally contemplative, but they have become out of touch with the ability. So this natural capacity needs to be reawakened. Part of the way we do that is by setting these foundations, creating an environment which will make contemplation happen rather naturally. When people leave us, they try to incorporate as many elements of this natural environment we teach them into their daily lives as possible: a measure of solitude, a discipline of daily meditational prayer, play, celebration of the Sabbath, meaningful community and family times, and so

on. We strive for a natural environment, an ordered environment, and a balanced environment.

This chapter has covered a few of the retreat centers that offer hermitage and solitary retreats. The Directory lists others. Each is different, because the essence of a solitary retreat is its uniqueness.

The Retreat Experience without the Retreat

A Modest Suggestion from Father Thomas Keating

> *But the Lord answered her, "Martha, Martha, you are anxious and troubled about many things; one thing is needful. Mary has chosen the good portion, which shall not be taken away from her."*
> —Luke 10:41–42

"One thing is needful," Jesus told Martha. And that one thing is time attending to the Word of God without distraction, in order to do the will of God.

When I interviewed Father Thomas Keating in Snowmass, I asked him if he could think of anything I had overlooked on the subject of making retreats. He immediately responded with a most emphatic "yes!" As he explained, "I think we need to develop some creative ways of making retreats available to people where they are. This is especially important for people who are elderly or for shut-ins. But there are also a great many people who simply cannot afford the cost of making a retreat." He suggested several ways to experience a mini-retreat without leaving home, and his suggestions are explored here.

The Need for Mini-Retreats

Aside from cost and the physical inability for some to make a retreat, there are other reasons to consider mini-retreats. Padre Pio said, "If we wish to reap it is necessary not so much to sow abundantly as to spread the seed in fertile soil, and when this seed becomes a plant, our chief anxiety should be to watch that the weeds do not suffocate the tender plants."

Mini-retreats are an ideal way to prepare to hear the word of God more clearly and to nurture that word within. Leading retreat directors emphasize the need to improve daily lifestyle to benefit from a retreat.

Another reason to incorporate mini-retreats can be found in Exodus, in the Third Commandment: "Remember the sabbath day, to keep it holy. Six days you shall labor, and do all your work; but the seventh day is a sabbath to the Lord your God; in it you shall not do any work . . . therefore the Lord blessed the sabbath day and hallowed it." (Exodus 20:8–11) Father William McNamara feels very strongly that we have lost sight of the importance of observing Sunday as a special day. He told me, "In our society today, we keep coming up with very clever, very inventive ways of avoiding the essential human act of just being. And we do this by performing too many 'good' deeds, you see, we don't do necessarily 'bad' things. We simply try to fill our lives up with doing too many good things and therefore the best thing escapes us: we never get around to doing the best thing. We never really celebrate the Lord's Day, we never really keep the Sabbath, because we are so busy doing all the little things in our lives that we never do the one big thing. And so we end up feeling very frustrated in our lives without ever really knowing why."

One way to build mini-retreats into one's life is to schedule them around the celebration of the Eucharist on Sunday. Even a half hour of silent meditation or Lectio Divina before and after Sunday services will make a big difference, and not only on Sunday. The effect is likely to last the whole week at a subtle level. And that really is the point: to effect a slow transformation in the daily fabric of life, a change that will provide fertile soil for the growth of a contemplative life.

Finally, parents must consider the need to educate children in Christian values. This is becoming increasingly difficult as parochial schools slowly disappear and the traditional Sunday school is viewed as more and more of an intrusion in our lives.

Those of us who grew up within the framework of a traditional value system at least have some dim memory that standards of conduct do exist in this world. But what of our children? In our zeal for a completely nonpartisan, nonsectarian, nondenominational, nonjudgmental society, are we depriving our children of an essential ingredient? Will they grow up with the thirst for God so deadened in them that it may never awaken? Are our good intentions creating, finally, a truly godless society? The implications for our future are staggering.

Five years ago a survey of executive ethics conducted by a major university found that, although the top executives of large corporations gave lip service to such values as honesty and fairness, when participating in case-study situations they invariably chose the course of action that was most pragmatic and profitable. Father Keating's suggestion of mini-retreats may be an ideal way to teach our children how to live Christian lives. And given the busy round of work and school activities during the week, Sunday seems the ideal day to do this.

The late Father Alexander Schmemann, a seminal theologian in modern Orthodoxy, wrote:

> Church attendance should be complemented from the earliest days of childhood by the home atmosphere which precedes and prolongs the mood of the church. Let us take Sunday morning. How can a child sense the holiness of that morning and of that which he will see in church, if the home is filled with the noise of radio and TV, if the parents are smoking and reading the papers, and if there reigns a truly profane atmosphere? Church attendance should be preceded by a sense of being "gathered in," a certain quiet solemnity . . . the home must reflect the church, must be illuminated by the light which we bring back from worship.

How to Make a Mini-Retreat

I have a friend who suffers from multiple sclerosis and is often confined to a wheelchair in her apartment. But she has a large library of spiritual talks on cassette tapes that she uses frequently. Father Keating is interested in a cable TV program that would guide people through a day of meditation. He already offers audio and video cassettes (see the Appendix). Tapes are beneficial if you can afford them, because they bring you closer to the retreat director. For example, it is one thing to read one of Father Keating's or Father McNamara's books; it is quite another to hear their wise and insistent voices, leading one deeper into the spiritual life.

An even easier way to get started is through the method of Lectio Divina. If you don't have any good spiritual reading on your own bookshelves, a quick trip to the library will solve that problem. One simply has to make a commitment and then choose the time and place for a mini-retreat.

Still another method is to use a meditation technique, such as Father Keating's centering prayer. Ideally, any mini-retreat will be a blending of all of these ingredients: perhaps a recording of a Gregorian Chant to set the tone, followed by a brief taped talk by a retreat director, then some slow spiritual reading and meditation.

The ingredients of a mini-retreat can be blended in any configuration, and may be repeated to fill up an entire day. One might consider starting with a few hours on a Sunday, structured around reception of the Eucharist or a Sunday service. Then, if desired, the mini-retreat can be expanded into a half day and later a full day. One should not strain or make it difficult or unnatural; rather, it should over time become the most natural part of the week. There is a tradition in the Orthodox Catholic Church that might be worth emulating: Vespers are held each Saturday evening to prepare for the Lord's Day. This is not to say that every Orthodox Church is packed on Saturday nights, but the opportunity exists for those who wish to take advantage of it. This is very different, of course, from attending a Mass on Saturday evening "to avoid being bothered on Sunday."

The sites for mini-retreats are as open to innovation and experimentation as the time and materials to be used. Certainly alone at home is a good place to start. But what about inviting a friend or friends to share the experience? Or perhaps a group might meditate before and after Mass, using the church basement or hall and issuing an open invitation to the parish at large. This would be a giant step toward developing communities that are supportive of a more contemplative lifestyle.

In short, Father Keating's idea of mini-retreats opens a realm of exciting possibilities. He also suggested that such mini-retreats would be a wonderful way to prepare for and return from formal retreats, so that the two types would bless each other.

Ultimately, the goal of all retreat effort is to learn to live in union with God on a day-to-day, moment-to-moment basis. This is why so many retreat directors emphasize the need for retreats to be integrated into one's entire life. If one sanctifies one's time and activities, if every act of every moment is imbued with a consciousness of Christ, then where is the need for a retreat? But at the same time, the way to develop such a Christ consciousness is by means of a retreat—a drawing back from unsanctified time and unsanctified activities.

Personal Retreat Experiences

> *We should before all things else seek to dwell in a retired place. In so doing, we should be able to overcome our former habits whereby we lived as strangers to the precepts of Christ . . . and we could wipe away the stains of sin by assiduous prayer and persevering meditation on the will of God. It is impossible to gain proficiency in this meditation and prayer, however, while a multitude of distractions is dragging the soul about and introducing into it anxieties about the affairs of this life.*
> —St. Basil, *The Long Rules*

Desert Experience No. 1
Cynthia Stebbins

For the past several years I have made my annual retreat at Nada Carmelite Monastery. The monastery lies between the towering Sangre de Cristo range and the desert expanse of the San Luis Valley, as if caught between the call to mysticism and earthly involvement.

The spirit of Nada is reflected in its physical layout. Surrounding the chapel and Agape, the main community house, are multiple hermitages for the monks and retreatants. The wondrous thing is that the architecture does no violence to the landscape. The simple lines reflect both a rootedness in the earth and a stretching toward the heavens. So even in its buildings Nada pictures its special mission—a call to earthy mysticism.

The monks themselves best reflect the spirit of Nada. There is so much falsity in today's world; so much passes for love that is not love; so much of our laughter is mere tittering; even our religion is marred by a "what's in it for me" attitude. The monks of Nada live with a love that is real, laugh with a from-the-gut freedom, and center all on Christ who teaches us how to be human. Often to be "only human" is an excuse for frailty. At

Nada human frailty is an avenue to the humanity of Christ and an invitation to celebrate so high a calling.

Ordinarily I use the day-and-a-half drive to Nada as preparation and transition. The monastery is not visible until the last bend is navigated, and then, suddenly, I am there. As I step from the car I never fail to be struck by the immensity of the silence. It is more than the absence of sound. It is a thundering stillness, pregnant with presence, promise, and possibility.

At Nada I experience an at-easeness that comes from being home. From the first moment of greeting at Agape, to settling in at the hermitage, I am made to feel like an honored guest. Usually one of the aspirants takes charge of the orientation, telling the ins and the outs. In each hermitage is a folder with literature describing the spirit of Nada as well as a schedule. Each hermitage is furnished simply, with a bed, chair, desk, and wood-burning stove. There is a small kitchen. All meals are taken alone except for dinner in common Wednesdays and Fridays after Mass. Sunday brunch and dinner are also in common. All common meals are suspended during weeks of solitude.

Nada does not offer retreats, it offers an atmosphere where each retreatant is free to pursue his or her own path. If the need for guidance arises, as it invariably does, each guest is assigned a monk as a soul-friend. Over the years, whether I am stumbling in the depths or dancing on the heights, my own soul-friend has been an immeasurable and unfailing help.

My retreats take form by entering into the rhythm of the community. At Nada the monastic rhythm flows in a four-week cycle: one week of solitude, one week of work, and two regular weeks with a balance of solitude and work. Over the years my retreats have evolved into a two-week stay, ordinarily beginning with a week of solitude followed by a regular week.

There is nothing easy about a week of solitude. It can be intimidating, but over the years I have come to welcome it as a holy time for special listening, at the same time knowing that the first two or three days will sometimes be marked by agitation and maybe a touch of craziness. I've come to accept that as a necessary unsettling, a purgation of the noisiness I carry within and without. My weeks of solitude have taught me the efficacy of waiting, the wisdom of silence. Silence is only a seeming emptiness, and solitude is only seeming aloneness. To perceive the fullness and presence in each, each must be entered into and likewise allowed to penetrate to the marrow. A taste for solitude must be acquired. It does not come easily or naturally, but must be actively pursued. Initially I found it difficult with so much time to fill. This only highlighted an attitude problem—that time is meant to be filled. Whether with the profound or trivial is of little importance, as long as it is filled. At Nada there are no artificial fillers, and the lesson I am coming to learn is that time is a gift—to be lived, cherished, and celebrated but never filled only to avoid emptiness.

I stumble around the first few days as if in unfamiliar territory, but slowly a rhythm and balance begin to emerge. On waking, sans alarm clock, I begin the day with a simple breakfast followed by prayer. I might take my coffee on the porch, watching the sun rise over the nearby mountains.

During the day I try to strike a balance between physical, mental, and spiritual activities. Ordinarily I reserve an hour morning and evening for meditation in the chapel. I find it good to break the day with some work and there is something for everyone—digging ditches or baking bread, chopping wood or helping in the library. Using the hands as well as the head and heart allows every part of myself to participate in the retreat. Manual labor is a wonderful contemplative activity, and it provides a diversion from myself without being a distraction from my purpose.

With so much of nature's beauty about, theophanies abound waiting only to be discovered, so walking is a favorite pastime.

I usually allow one day for adventure. With backpack full I set off, with or without a goal in mind. Last time I decided to camp overnight at a nearby creek. It was wonderful. What a gentle way to waken—to the sounds of song—the simple praises of creation: birds soaring on voice and wing, waters rushing, the sigh of breeze-kissed branches. To such praises I added my own lauds and experienced uniquely the liturgical intent of blessing, celebrating, and offering a new day.

Late afternoon I prepare dinner. That in itself is an adventure, since my culinary skills have been dampened by years of fast food. The menu is determined by what is in the cabinet, what's growing in the garden, and what the refrigerator holds. The results are often scrumptious serendipities.

After dinner and evening prayer comes one of my favorite times. The hour or so before sunset is reserved for a leisurely walking rosary. At dusk the deer come out to feed, and sometimes, carried on the wind, a coyote chorus can be heard. That primordial song stirs in me a like desire to erupt in one long heartful howl of sheer delight.

After returning to my hermitage I usually spend an hour or two reading and writing. And then to bed. The day which at rising loomed so long and empty has been filled—but not by me. All I have done is wait and watch and listen.

The week culminates with the Sabbath. At Nada, Sabbath begins the evening before with compline followed by exposition and an all-night vigil. Each monk and retreatant signs for an hour of solitary adoration. I usually pick an hour midway through the night. Walking through the darkness with trusty flashlight, under stars and moon, is a unique experience.

The chapel is lit only by vigil lights placed either side of the monstrance. Sometimes the hour is long and marked by a struggle against sleep, other times it is a time for love-making and all too brief. However it is spent, it is a time of prayer. It never fails to surprise me when I rise the next day refreshed, none the worse for interrupted sleep.

Sunday begins with the celebration of Mass followed by a communal brunch. One flows into the other as silence and solitude erupt into conversation and conviviality. It is the Lord's Day, a day set aside for play, laughter, and revelry. Work and worry can wait. Weather permitting, volleyball is a favorite pastime. All are invited, from rank amateur (myself) to benign fanatic (most of the monks).

The day ends with another communal meal. There is nothing self-consciously spiritual about the table conversation. It can run the gamut from climbing in the Himalayas to local projects to help the poor, from pottery to poetry, from the World Series to the latest encyclical. All of life is embraced.

Each year I return not knowing what God has in store. I arrive without agenda, with only a desire to remain open, trusting that God will give what I need, knowing that He knows better than I. Never have I been disappointed.

Each retreat is different—so different. One year is like a volcano, a making love—tender touches, soft whispers, and fire. The next refreshes gently as cool water for a thirsty pilgrim. Always it is gift. And always I am ready to leave at retreat's end, full to overflowing and eager to live what I have received.

A Jesuit-Directed Retreat

This anonymous account of a retreat experience is reprinted from Echoes, *newsletter of the White House Retreat in St. Louis, Missouri. Its director, Father Denis Daly, SJ, granted permission to reprint because it is such an exceptional report of a first-time retreatant. The author is a man in his twenties.*

My friends in God, I would like to take this opportunity to summarize my attitude as a first-time retreatant.

First the invitation: "Well, that's awful nice of you to ask; but I . . . Well, I . . . I know all that stuff and anyway I have faith in God. I go to church on a weekly basis and say my prayers occasionally!" Quite a skeptical attitude, eh? Well, thanks be to God, through the ones I love, for his persistence. I am here today.

The first evening: Silence? Not really, that control and faith I thought was in my life was tumbling around inside of me. Silence, though, enabled me to hear and understand this turmoil. My faith was like the house built on sandy ground. Well, I was quick to realize that tools were made quite accessible here to build a more sound faith. Such as the buildings here at the White House Retreat with their white solid stone walls and invincible foundation, which have survived all the elements. The most important tool made available was silence. Don't get me wrong, Father Maginnis, the conference master, you were so very helpful. I would like to know half of everything you have ever forgotten.

The first full day: On this day I felt like a champagne bottle all iced up and seal unbroken. One problem: the bottle was located on the back of a bouncy bus. Sure, I looked good from the outside, patiently waiting for the right person to pop my cork. While I waited, the longer I waited, the more pressure mounted on the inside. Thanks to Father O'Brien, my cork was popped and not a drop of champagne was lost. I spent some time waiting for the bubbles to calm down, so I could see how clear my relationship with Jesus really was. Total silence at last! Thanks be to God! Silence, yes, but I was not yet at peace with myself.

The second full day: The preparation we received for the sacrament of reconciliation was simply remarkable. After receiving the sacrament I had reached a peaceful plateau. Like a marathon runner puts his body through great pain and weariness to accomplish his goal, so did I put my soul through great turmoil and weariness to accomplish my goal. It was time to go away into a quiet place by myself and rest a little.

At last, the gift of sound, in the golden silence all around us. Peacefulness through my entire body and soul. Presently able to hear yet understand, to see and also recognize that God has been reaching out to me since I was able to reason. I have learned so much that I can't begin to express to you in words.

One outstanding observation though: it has long since been known to me that the richest, most powerful people in the world are seldom recognized for their happiness and joy. It has been noted by many a millionaire that the richest person is the person in good health. Even your good health can be whisked away in a second and ultimately will be. Therefore, we have learned on this retreat that the preservation of everlasting happiness is through a Spirit filled by Our Lord Jesus Christ!!

Desert Experience No. 2
Michelle Reineck

Finding out what we really want, and having the courage to be, do and have what we desire, requires facing the enemy within. To face the enemy within means facing the obstacles and rejections of the outer world as we move toward what is real, toward what our real self wants. It means going against the wishes of those we love and admire. It means leaving secure, comfortable ways of doing things to pursue something strange and frightening.
—*Ordinary People as Monks and Mystics*

The trip to Crestone, Colorado, from Kalamazoo, Michigan, was a real adventure. The alarm went off at 5:00 A.M., and I woke to a damp, dark October sky. After my husband helped me load my gear in the car, we heard a swish, crack and huge thud. The dead oak branch we had watched all summer finally fell off after the night rain. My prayer as I left for the airport was that this week-long trip would remove some of my "dead wood" as well.

I flew out of Grand Rapids to the Denver airport. I was happy that I had put my belongings in a backpack, because the Denver airport was mind-boggling. After some checking, lots of walking, and a shuttle service, I arrived at a hanger that housed the airline that flew into Alamosa. Pat McGowan, my soul friend and a member of the community, was to pick me up.

The flight to Alamosa in the twin otter plane through the Sangre de Cristo mountains was a religious experience for me. Having grown up in northwestern Ohio's rich, flat farmland, I know why the Jews called God a mountain. Most of the hour-long plane ride, I was glued to the window in awe of His Mountain Majesty. The physical sensation of flying above the tree line added to the effect. It was something I'll never forget or be able to describe adequately.

When I landed in Alamosa, Pat was not there. The airport looked obscure enough to be on a movie set, and I began to ask myself why I was there instead of back home at my son's soccer game. Shortly, Pat arrived; she apologized for being late. She had gotten into a long line at the grocery store. It was just what I needed to hear to feel at home and back on the earth again. Being a housewife and mother, long grocery store lines are familiar territory.

Before beginning the drive to Crestone one hour away, Pat suggested that we get something to eat at a small Mexican restaurant in Alamosa. I was delighted, since it was dinner time and in the excitement of travel I had not eaten well.

My friendship with Pat McGowan had begun five years ago. I had learned about the Spiritual Life Institute through some tapes on Saint Teresa of Avila by Mother Tessa Bielecki. Hearing these tapes was a turning point in my life. Although raised a Catholic, I had some vague notions that a deep prayer life belonged in monasteries, that it was for people with pious tendencies that I seemed to lack, and worse yet, that praying that way would turn me into a spooky introvert. Yet, I had an incredible longing to know God in a deep way. After hearing Mother Tessa talk about Theresa of Avila, I realized that this Theresa who knew so well how to pray was hardly a spooky introvert! She was a human, fun-filled, vital woman of prayer. Suddenly, I was freed to learn how to pray.

Then, coincidentally, I met Pat McGowan through a mutual friend, Father James O'Leary. A member of the Spiritual Life Institute, she became my "soul friend," a term used by the community instead of spiritual director. Through her letters, books she recommended, *Desert Call* and *Nada Network* (community publications), I had grown tremendously. To me, Pat was a spiritual midwife, always there, helping "birth" my little efforts to know God.

After a good visit, we began the last and most beautiful part of the journey. The countryside was desolate, its inhabitants very poor and Hispanic. Through my Midwestern eyes, everything looked dry and brown. The ranches on the road to Crestone had a few cows, dried-up weeds everywhere and very sandy soil. Pat told me the only crop is potatoes.

But the mountains! They completely surround the land there.

It's as if the road were at the bottom of a huge bowl and the mountains formed the sides. It was getting to be dusk; Pat suggested I look to my right to see the "Blood of Christ" on the mountaintops. This is the meaning of Sangre de Cristos. Sure enough, from the peaks this reddish glow ran downward to the mountains' midsections. The light looked like something I had seen in *Arizona Highways* as a child. It was almost surreal. I felt as if I were on holy ground. If a retreat is meant to lift us out of our ordinary way of doing and being, this was a fine beginning.

As we got closer to Crestone, I saw what looked like goats roaming the streets. The closer we came, I realized they weren't goats, but deer. There must have been fifty of them. It was incredible. Pat said they always stay in town during the hunting season.

We drove through Crestone slowly, careful not to hit the grazing deer. We finally saw the sign for "Nada" and "Carmelite Way," marking the entrance to the monastery. It was beautiful beyond words. The gravel entrance road opened up onto miles of desert, white-capped mountains and an indigo sky. The square-topped mountain called Kit Carson, which the monks have renamed Mount Carmel, seemed to dominate the entire land. Everything seemed to meet here: desert, sky, mountain and silence.

The silence that greeted me that evening is still with me. Sometimes in my harried daily existence, I remember the silence of those mountains and immediately I am brought back to some peace. I remember that God is like that mountain, secure, powerful, and unchanging. I feel grounded again; God is here in charge and I can let go and stop trying to run the universe. Remembering that landscape reminds me of the verse: "Be still and know that I am God." (Psalms 46:10).

The monastery architecture is incredibly mixed: Southwestern, Spanish, medieval, Celtic. It's wildly dramatic and playful at the same time. The monastery reflects the monks who live there. It is not an easy life. They chop wood, raise vegetables, construct their own buildings, produce two publications and still have time to share with the constant flow of retreatants. As hard as their life is, they never seemed to take themselves too seriously. I found them surprisingly fun to be with.

Each monk and retreatant has his own hermitage nestled on the mountain. Pat quickly led me to my hermitage, which was closest (gratefully) to the main buildings that included their chapel and Agape, which is their living-dining-library building.

My hermitage was called Lindbergh after Anne Morrow Lindbergh, who wrote *Gift From the Sea*. I am not sure what I expected, but I was surprised by its beauty and simplicity: plants, stucco, rocks, and aspen. Deep womanly touches were everywhere without sentimentality or austerity. A hot plate, small refrigerator and sink in one corner, a wood stove, a long writing desk topped by bookshelves on the other wall. Under the huge picture window was a double bed with a beautiful handmade Carmelite quilt (browns and white) made by a friend of the community. What was to become my favorite spot in the room was a small window seat tucked into the east wall. I ate my breakfast there each morning, watching the sun come up behind Mount Carmel. On the table was a basket of fresh fruit. I could see the kitchen had been stocked with cheese, salsa, rice, beans, peanut butter and staples. Someone had spent a lot of time getting this place ready for me, I remember thinking. I felt very cared for and welcomed.

Pat said we should hurry because the bell for night prayer would ring soon. Every Saturday evening, the monks begin their Sabbath celebration with evening prayers and an all-night vigil in front of the Blessed Sacrament. Retreatants are free to sign up for a vigil hour if they wish. I decided to sign up for 4:00 A.M., since it would be something I'd never do at home. I wanted to break free from some of the routine and responsibilities of my life.

Mother Tessa often quotes Zorba the Greek, saying, "Everyone needs a little bit of madness, otherwise we'll never be able to cut the rope and be free." Getting up in the middle of the night, walking by flashlight was a good way to cut the rope of routine, I thought.

It is easy for me to get so bogged down in responsibilities that I lose touch with my center. I get so caught up in the details of running a house and raising a family that I find myself living on my edges instead of from the center. When I lose touch with my center, I lose touch with God. What I needed to do was to work those edges through my center. A friend described it well when she said it's like kneading bread: we keep taking the outer edges and working them through the middle.

What I prayed for during Sabbath vigil was a return to my center and the central relationship of my life, my relationship with God. I asked for the light to see, during that week in the desert, what in myself and my surroundings prevents that centering. I asked for the grace to see what I needed to change and then the courage to do it. With hindsight, I know God heard my prayer.

Walking out into the night air after the Sabbath vigil, I was undone by the beauty. It was pitch black except for the starlight and a sliver of moon over Mount Carmel. I could hear the wind whistling through the sand and desert grass. It was a little cold since sundown, and even with the flashlight in hand it was dark on the well-worn path to my hermitage. There was wind and cold and silence all around me. "How did I ever get to a desert in the mountains of Colorado?" I asked myself. I wondered why I didn't feel strange or afraid, but at home and so alive.

Time in a Trappist Monastery
Mary Alice Strom

It was Christ the King Sunday 1987. I had repacked twice. Bob was still shaking his head and saying that I was taking too much, that I'd never be able to carry it all, when he delivered me to the King Street Station in Seattle, where I would take the Amtrak to Glenwood Springs, Colorado.

I was going to Father Thomas Keating's Snowmass Intensive Retreat, and I was full of anticipation. I'd been telling friends that it was one of *the* events of my life, and it was. The trip was supposed to take thirty-six hours, and I would be gone for twelve days.

When I arrived at Snowmass, I learned that, because I had requested a bedroom of my own, I was to stay in a building called the School House. Three other women were housed there: Sister Bernadette, Sister Dominique, and Nancy. I was invited to call the nuns, who came from the Sisters of Charity of Leavenworth, Kansas, simply Bernadette and Dom.

Since the School House was more than a short walk from the Ranch House, I was assured of transportation by Bernadette and Nancy, both of whom had driven from Denver. Dom had come from Spokane and, like myself, had no car.

The cuisine was vegetarian. The main meal of the day, we were told, would be at noon. The main course at supper would be soup. But all the meals proved to be more than adequate, and delicious, too. Breads, salads, and soups were superbly created and served. The staff, true to their statement of intention on the orientation sheet, were ever present, attending spoken, whispered, nodded, or silently communicated needs.

All meals after the first shared that evening were taken at the large table in the kitchen. For breakfast and the noon meal, one of the staff would read from Father Keating's newest book, *The Mystery of Christ—Liturgy as Spiritual Experience.* At the evening meals there was no lack of lively conversation, and I did not observe anyone who seemed to wish for more quiet. I think we might have been a talkative group, as groups go, though none of the staff ever expressed that.

For a long time I had experienced peace and spiritual nourishment from my practice of centering prayer. But now, would the long periods of prayer, broken only by the contemplative walk, allow some emotional material, perhaps of a cataclysmic nature, to surface?

Also, I had come to the retreat with some concerns about my

Personal Retreat Experiences 69

health that could be resolved neither quickly nor easily. So far, anxiety, an old enemy, had not plagued me. But now, with silence, and apart from the busy-ness to which I was so accustomed, would I become aware of an overwhelming fear that I had, until now, repressed?

But there was no time to mull these things. There was a stir in the kitchen, and I realized, with some excitement, that Father Keating was arriving for a post-supper discussion. That first evening, the structures of the retreat were reviewed.

Father Keating would join us on alternate evenings during the retreat. On the evenings that "we didn't have Father," we would attend vespers at the monastery.

The people who slept at the Ranch House could observe the regular (for retreatants) rising time of 4:40 A.M. Those who slept at the School House would need to rise earlier in order to get to the Ranch House in time for vigils and centering prayer at 5:00 A.M. The schedule, which might have been a tall order for all but those already acclimated to the rigors of monastic living, was greeted good-naturedly by the group.

Mary Ann told us that we could speak at our own discretion at such times as the afternoon break between lunch and centering prayer at 3:20 P.M. If conversation seemed desirable during a walk at that time, or during the trip to and from Mass, this was permissible. We were asked to exercise sensitivity, never to thoughtlessly break into another's silence. Talking indoors, unless very quiet and away from the others, would break everybody's silence, so it was not permitted.

Mass was at the monastery, about a mile away from the Ranch House.

Centering prayer periods were often referred to as "sits." Sitting was sometimes called meditation. Sits always began with the reading of Holy Scripture. At the morning sit, there was a psalm, followed by a reading from one of St. Paul's letters, then another psalm. The midday and afternoon sits began with the reading of one psalm. Later in the retreat, after a few in the group had attended lauds at the monastery with the monks, the morning sit was begun with taped hymn-singing by monks, the tape lent to us by Father Keating.

There was a volunteer sheet so that we could all share in the duties of Scripture reading, bell ringing to announce sits, meals, and conferences, and saying the blessing before meals. Next to it was a sign-up sheet for interviews with Father Keating.

Father Keating instructed us and encouraged us. He was ever interested in hearing our questions, reactions, and experiences. When the matter of Thanksgiving Day came up because it fell on the coming Thursday, three days away, Father Keating said there would be no special observance for retreatants. It would be too early in the retreat to break in with exceptional activities that could threaten the developing momentum of the retreat journey. "After all, every day is Thanksgiving in a monastery," he pointed out.

On the first morning, I observed myself struggle with the silence. Confident that the discomfort would pass, I asked myself what it was about abstinence from speech that made me uneasy.

I turned to my journal, as if to a friend, to share the discovery. I wrote, "Speech is a defense for me. I feel so vulnerable, naked, transparent without it.

"Isn't that strange? Speech is for making things known, and yet, I feel more known without it." This, I think, was the first major "I learned" from the retreat. Speech, like thought, becomes a tool for what Father Keating has named the "false self." How often have I used speech for every purpose under the sun, other than to simply reveal what is? And how unnecessary it is, so often, even to do that!

The meditation room was where we sat in prayer. We were encouraged to select a chair or spot on the floor for our own use throughout the retreat. I picked a somewhat isolated spot near the front of the room, and a straight-backed chair. I was tempted to try the floor but afraid that my back might give out.

The first meditation was at 6:00 A.M., an hour later than all other days of the retreat, except Sunday. A votive candle in front of the staff member who led the meditation was the only light in the room. At this first period of the not-yet-dawning day, the psalmist and the reader used flashlights to read by.

I began to relax after the first sit, although during breakfast the silence was still awkward for me. I noticed myself wanting to communicate with nods, gestures, expressions, and the like. What a noisy person I found myself to be, even in this wordless environment. Also, I noticed myself searching the demeanor of the others for signs of what they might be thinking. Noisy and nosey, too! If any of the others were having similar reactions, I didn't detect it. I've concluded that each person's experience of deep silence is very personal and ultimately influenced by their spiritual condition at the time.

That morning I rode to Mass with Bernadette, Dom and Nancy. I wasn't sure whether I could walk the distance and still be on time. I postponed my first walk for a time when punctuality was more of a certainty.

The ride to church in the dawning light was like a journey homeward to a place I'd never been. Snow covered the road through the plateau country, and the sun's first rays made bold contrast of light and dark on the surrounding mountains.

St. Benedict's is situated at the base of the mountains. Viewed from a distance, it seems almost a continuation of the foothills. The tiny cluster of buildings is almost obscured by a few trees and stands in gentle contrast to its magnificent backdrop.

We entered the church through a heavy wooden door. A spacious anteroom provided a place for books, for visiting. Another heavy wooden door led to a corridor that brought us to the sanctuary doors.

We entered, and facing us at the far end of the church was a tall, narrowly arched stained glass window depicting the Blessed Virgin Mary and the Infant Jesus. The colors were mainly blues with red accents. There was no time to gawk. I followed the others, bowing from the waist down at the top of three small steps, and then descending into the main part of the chapel. I took a place, with the others, on one of the benches that lined the walls on both sides. The monks sat on chairs, backs against the walls. The small altar of carved wood stood beneath the window of Our Lady and the Baby Jesus. Now I could really look at the window. It said welcome. It said home.

The monks chanted a psalm, then sang a hymn, and Mass began. I experienced a feeling of being reunited with something primary. It was an experience of death and resurrection, together. I felt myself releasing a hold on my life, so that something else might come in.

Lay people, other than the retreatants and staff members, were there. On subsequent days I noticed a number of regulars in addition to some drop-ins who joined the monks for morning Mass, despite the earliness of the hour, the weather, and the distance from town.

There was no homily on weekdays, and there was a welcome sensitivity evident in the provision of pauses and silences during Mass.

Guests joined the monks around the altar during the Liturgy of the Eucharist. After a reverent and unhurried exchange at the Sign of Peace, Communion under both Species was given. Monks distributed an altar bread that was whole-grained and substantial, and then the chalice was passed. Following this, all returned to their original places for the conclusion of the Mass.

I left the church with a feeling of elation. As the day wore on, I realized that whatever residual anxiety I might have had concerning the retreat, the silence, the others, had been fully lifted. I was left with a rare sense of freedom in which to participate fully in this banquet for the spirit.

Conferences were held in the meditation room. There was a time when Father Thomas gave all the conferences in person, but now, thanks to technology, seventeen were on videotape. He gave the eighteenth in person on the last evening of the retreat.

Thus, the cycle of days was set into motion: prayer, meals, reading, journaling, liturgy, conferences, interviews with Father Keating, walks, silence, and fellowship during the evening meal.

For me, a significant dimension of the retreat was provided by the presence of the others. They shared the retreat, and to some extent, their journey and their love, with me. This is what made it complete.

If there is such a thing as getting an answer at a retreat, any more than one gets them daily, moment by moment, if one is alert, I received one on the last evening.

It wasn't unique. I'd even heard of a similar experience. A man traveled around the world in an attempt to find his "place." When he returned home to his own kitchen, and his grandmother offered him a cup of soup, he realized that his place (purpose? meaning?) had been there all along.

It was in just such a moment that Dave, a staff member, offering me a cup of coffee, became a speaking symbol for me. Until that moment, my attention had been scattered. Then, instantly, his gesture of offering was an icon.

As I received the coffee, I felt a sense of empowerment to serve, like Dave, in a kitchen, a home, in any environment. At the same time, I was aware that I had had this power all along. But at that moment, it was as if I had been recommissioned. This was one of the benedictions I received in the last hours of the retreat.

I turned to my journal often in the silence. There were thoughts I couldn't develop unless I put them down. It was almost as if I had to relieve my mind of the weight of half of the thought, the question part, so that I could pick up the other part, the answer. Another way that my journal helped was in answering inner promptings to make a commitment. The memory of having made a promise to my journal helps me to be faithful.

The snapshots of Snowmass I brought back have come to mean more to me than I expected they would. They help me to remember the work of the retreat and to transplant the seedling aspirations from there to here.

One of my favorites was taken after the retreat. Nancy had taken me to the Amtrak station in Glenwood Springs. Sister Elizabeth was also along. For a while I remained in the retreat cocoon.

Suddenly I was alone in the station. It was a sunny day, very springlike for December 3. I closed my eyes, welcoming this opportunity to pray before beginning my journey homeward. But the waiting room became filled with people and sounds. I picked up my gear and found a warm spot in the sun on the station platform. I sat on one of my bags and leaned against the station wall. This was an even better spot than before.

I closed my eyes. I lost track of time and even place until noises roused me from my peaceful state. Suddenly aware of my situation, I opened my eyes. Right in front of me were four cases of beer, two coolers, two travel packs, and a pair of western boots. "Welcome to the real world," they seemed to say. I took a picture of the scene, as I sat with my back against the station wall.

Directory of Retreat and Renewal Centers

Detachment from the things perceived by the senses means the vision of things spiritual.
—St. John Climacus

The purpose of this directory is to provide a catalog in which would-be retreatants may browse and get an idea of what is offered where. The best course is then to write or call the retreat centers of interest and request their brochures. Most of the centers in this book have excellent and informative brochures available.

Please note that, where office hours are listed, they are within the time zone of that particular center. Prices have not been given, because they are often subject to change; prices are always listed in the brochures. Although most centers indicate how far in advance you should book, nearly every center states that, if space is available, retreatants will be taken up to the last minute. The key is communication—if you really want to make a retreat at a specific center, call them!

Listings are organized by state, then alphabetically within the states by the names of the centers. Canada is listed after the United States.

Although every effort has been made to obtain the most up-to-date information about the centers, it is inevitable that changes will occur between the time the final manuscript is submitted and the book is printed. If in any doubt about a directory entry, invest in a telephone call to the center that interests you to verify the information.

Alabama

Benedictine Sisters' Conference Center
Order of St. Benedict

This is a beautiful spot in God's creation and we love to share it with others. The fact that this is our home gives it a unique atmosphere conducive to spiritual growth. We have 2 accommodations buildings: Benet Hall, a ranch-type house overlooking Lake Maurus with semiprivate rooms and 4 central baths; and Mary Hall with both private and semiprivate rooms, 2 dorms, and central baths. The main chapel seats 300 and is equipped with a pipe organ. Guests are welcome to join the sisters for the daily Liturgy of the Hours and the Eucharist. Primary spiritual practice is Lectio Divina in the Eastern mode. Closed Holy Week and December 20 through January 2.

Types of Retreats/Programs Offered: Directed/Group; Directed/Private; Hermitage/Solitary; Ecumenical; Prayer Days; Engaged Encounter; Special; Miscellaneous Programs
Open to: Everyone
Person to Contact: Sister Mary Lourdes Michel, Office Manager
Address: 916 Convent Road, Cullman, AL 35055
Mailing Address: P.O. Box 488, Cullman, AL 35056-0488
Telephone: 205-734-4622
Office Hours: 8:30–11:30 A.M.; 12:30–4:00 P.M.
Notice Required: Preferably 1 week

Blessed Trinity Shrine Retreat
Missionary Servants of the Most Blessed Trinity

Our threefold mission is to provide an environment of peace and solitude, to strengthen and renew faith, and to offer opportunities to develop spiritual leadership among the laity. This mission is carried out through our presence as a center of prayer and hospitality, retreat programs addressing the needs of people today, spiritual direction opportunities, outreach to parishes for spiritual programs, involvement of the laity

Blessed Trinity Shrine, Holy Trinity, Alabama

(adults and youth) in giving retreats, and the assistance of volunteer personnel. Directed and private retreats are available and may be arranged on an individual basis by calling the retreat house and making a reservation. Spiritual direction is also available. Closed Thanksgiving weekend and 2 weeks at Christmas.

Types of Retreats/Programs Offered: Directed/Group; Directed/Private; Conference; Hermitage/Solitary; Ecumenical; Charismatic; Prayer Days; Engaged Encounter; Cursillos; Special; Miscellaneous Programs
Open to: Everyone
Person to Contact: Sister Virginia Morris, Director; Sister Judith Jones, Reservationist
Address: Holy Trinity, AL 36859
Telephone: 205-855-4474
Office Hours: 9:00 A.M. to 5:00 P.M.
Notice Required: Groups—6 months to a year; individuals—6 weeks to 2 months

Monastery of the Visitation
Society of Jesus (Jesuit)

Visitation Monastery, established in 1832, is one of the historic monuments in old Mobile. It initiated retreats in 1956 and has since welcomed thousands of retreatants and married and engaged Encounter couples. The retreat house is completely modernized, with air-conditioned rooms, tiled baths, and a restaurant-equipped kitchen offering delicious food. The weekend retreats begin Friday evening with registration from 5:00 P.M., dinner at 6:00 P.M. and Mass at 7:30 P.M. Retreats end Sunday after noon.

Types of Retreats/Programs Offered: Directed/Group; Encounters; Cursillos
Open to: Everyone
Person to Contact: Director
Address: 2300 Spring Hill Avenue, Mobile, AL 36607
Telephone: 205-473-2321

Directory of Retreat and Renewal Centers

Arizona

Franciscan Renewal Center
Order of Friars Minor, St. Barbara Province

Our Center, founded in 1951 by Franciscan Friars, is named Casa de Paz y Bien—House of Peace and All Good. We are in scenic Paradise Valley between Camelback and Mummy mountains. Phoenix Sky Harbor and Scottsdale Municipal Airports are each about a 20-minute drive from the Casa. We are a desert oasis with a central area of extensive lawns and gardens, Southwestern Spanish-style buildings, a large swimming pool, and a separate therapy spa. All rooms include private bath and individually controlled heat and air-conditioning. Piper Hall is a completely equipped conference and meeting center. Handicapped accessible.

Types of Retreats/Programs Offered: Directed/Group; Directed/Private; Conference; Hermitage/Solitary; Ecumenical; Charismatic; Prayer Days; Parent-Teen; Encounters in Spanish; Special; Miscellaneous Programs
Open to: Everyone
Person to Contact: Father Raymond Bucher, Director
Address: 5802 East Lincoln Drive, Scottsdale, AZ 85253
Telephone: 602-948-7460
Office Hours: 8:00 A.M. to 9:00 P.M. by phone
Notice Required: Average 2 to 5 weeks

Our Lady of Solitude House of Prayer
Diocesan

Our Lady of Solitude is the Phoenix diocesan House of Prayer with a contemplative-solitary thrust. Its reason for existence is to give praise and glory to the Father by providing a place apart for prayer. We are five miles north of Phoenix, surrounded by mountains and the Sonoran Desert, on a desert mesa overlooking Black Canyon City. The main building at the top of the prayer mountain houses an oratory, 7 private retreat rooms, a

Franciscan Renewal Center, Scottsdale, Arizona

spacious meditation-reading room with fireplace and library, a kitchen and a dining room. An adjacent knoll offers opportunity for more solitude and a spectacular vista. It is graced by a laura of hermitages and a meditation chapel. Outside of a fellowship meal, all is in solitude and quiet.

Types of Retreats/Programs Offered: Directed/Private; Hermitage/Solitary; Prayer Days
Open to: Everyone except youths, families, and couples
Person to Contact: Sister Mary Therese Sedlock, Director
Address: P.O. Box 1140, Black Canyon City, AZ 85324
Telephone: 602-374-9204
Office Hours: 1:00–4:00 P.M.
Notice Required: 2 weeks

Arkansas

Abbey Retreat Coury House
Benedictine

Coury House is the center for the spiritual ministry for retreats conducted by the Benedictine monks of New Subiaco Abbey. Our facilities include a chapel and a large meeting room; rooms have twin beds, towels and linens, and private baths. A retreat here offers time alone, time to relax, conference time with the retreat master, praying with the monks at vespers, a walk to the Lourdes Grotto and the Abbey cemetery, and meditation at our outdoor Way of the Cross.

Types of Retreats/Programs Offered: Directed/Group; Directed/Private; Conference; Hermitage/Solitary; Ecumenical; Prayer Days; Marriage Encounter; Cursillos; Special
Open to: Everyone. Have facilities for families.
Person to Contact: Father Hilary Filiatreau, Director of Retreats
Address: Highway 22, Subiaco, AR 72865
Telephone: 501-934-4411
Office Hours: 8:00 A.M. to 5:00 P.M.
Notice Required: Groups—6 months to a year; individuals—1 month

California

Angela Center
Ursuline Sisters

Angela Center is named for Angela Merici, founder of the Ursuline community. We are an Ecumenical Christian Center sponsored by the Ursuline Sisters. In our programs we seek to integrate spirituality, psychology, social responsibility, and the arts, believing that religious experience can best be understood through its expression in our daily lives. We are located in a country hillside setting with acreage for walking, private and semiprivate rooms, dining room, chapel, lounges, and an inner garden courtyard.

Types of Retreats/Programs Offered: Directed/Group; Directed/Private; Conference; Hermitage/Solitary; Ecumenical; Charismatic; Prayer Days; Encounters; Cursillos; Special; Miscellaneous Programs
Open to: Everyone except youths

Angela Center, Santa Rosa, California

Person to Contact: Sister Christine, Director; Tricia Schexnaydre, Office Manager
Address: 535 Angela Drive, Santa Rosa, CA 95403
Telephone: 707-528-8578
Office Hours: 9:00 A.M. to 5:00 P.M. Monday through Friday
Notice Required: Variable

Center For Spiritual Development
Sisters of St. Joseph of Orange

Through our programs and serene environment, we strive to provide a place where individuals and groups can nourish their spiritual lives. Special emphasis in programming is directed toward care givers in ministry. We extend a continuing invitation to prayer, renewal and deepening of ministry skills, as well as to the personal growth and development of the minister. Facilities include a solitude wing designed especially for private retreatants.

Types of Retreats/Programs Offered: Directed/Group; Directed/Private; Conference; Solitary; Ecumenical; Prayer Days; Marriage Encounter; Special; Miscellaneous Programs
Open to: Everyone except youths and families
Person to Contact: Sister Eileen McNerney, Executive Director
Address: 434 South Batavia Street, Orange, CA 92668
Telephone: 714-744-3175
Office Hours: 8:30 A.M. to 4:30 P.M.
Notice Required: 1 week

El Carmelo Retreat House
Discalced Carmelites

El Carmelo is at the foot of the San Bernadino Mountains in the midst of an orange grove. We conduct our weekend retreats according to the traditional format of a silent, preached retreat. There is no special emphasis on "processing" or group interaction. The emphasis is on quiet reflection. Open year-round.

Types of Retreats/Programs Offered: Directed/Group; Engaged Encounter; Special
Open to: Everyone except youths and families
Person to Contact: Father Stephen Watson
Address: P.O. Box 446, 926 E. Highland Avenue, Redlands, CA 92373
Telephone: 714-792-1047
Office Hours: 9:00 A.M. to 5:00 P.M.
Notice Required: 2 weeks

Immaculate Heart Hermitage
Camaldolese Benedictines

We are on the Pacific Coast, and all our nine guest rooms have views of the ocean. Our physical quiet is special. Many who come—whether Catholic or not—find the monastic liturgy helpful and inspiring and our simple church conducive to prayer and meditation. But we are very explicitly nondirective, though we are glad to give counsel if asked. In this way, many find their way to what they really want. Location is remote, with no public transportation; people can be picked up in Monterey on Fridays only by special arrangement. Vegetarian diet.

Types of Retreats/Programs Offered: Solitary retreats only
Open to: Everyone except youths, families, and couples
Person to Contact: Father Aelred Squire, Guestmaster
Address: Big Sur, CA 93920
Telephone: 408-667-2456
Office Hours: 8:30–11:15 A.M.; 1:30–8:00 P.M.
Notice Required: 6 to 8 weeks, preferably by phone

La Casa de Maria
Immaculate Heart Community

La Casa de Maria is a nonprofit, ecumenical retreat and conference center of Christian origin governed by a multidenomi-

La Casa de Maria, Santa Barbara, California

national board of trustees. The goal of La Casa is to provide, through its environment and its programs, a place of peace where individuals of all faiths can search for truth, engage in dialogue, realize their own self-worth, experience the sacred, and then, refreshed and renewed, participate more effectively in the creation of a just and peaceful world. Sharing the grounds with La Casa is the Center for Spiritual Renewal, a retreat house for those who wish to make private retreats.

Types of Retreats/Programs Offered: Directed/Group; Conference; Hermitage/Solitary; Ecumenical; Charismatic; Prayer Days; Parent-Teen; Special; Miscellaneous Programs
Open to: Everyone
Person to Contact: Don George, Director; Steph Glatt, Associate Director
Address: 800 El Bosque Road, Santa Barbara, CA 93108
Telephone: 805-969-5031
Office Hours: 8:00 A.M. to 5:00 P.M.
Notice Required: 60 to 90 days

Manresa Retreat House
Society of Jesus (Jesuit)

Our Retreat House is named after a small town in northeast Spain, where St. Ignatius Loyola, the founder of the Society of Jesus, spent 11 months at the start of his conversion to a life dedicated to God's service. Our Manresa Retreat House stands on lands inhabited originally by Shoshone Indians and later owned by a succession of ranchers. In addition to the main retreat buildings, there are hermitages. Retreats are on weekends, beginning with dinner at 7:00 P.M. on Friday and ending on Sunday around 2:45 P.M.

Types of Retreats/Programs Offered: Directed/Group; Directed/Private; Conference; Hermitage/Solitary; Prayer Days; Special
Open to: Everyone except youths and families, but mostly men
Person to Contact: Father Terrance Mahan, Superior-Director
Address: 18337 East Foothill Blvd., P.O. Box K, Azusa, CA 91702-1330
Telephone: 818-969-1848
Office Hours: 9 A.M. to 4 P.M.
Notice Required: Variable

Mercy Center
Sisters of Mercy

Mercy Center is on 40 acres of oak-clad grounds and is a place where we love to believe people can come "and be joyful in this house of prayer." A retreatant can expect hospitality, privacy, beauty, and an opportunity (depending on time of year) for different prayer experiences, such as Taize and Christian sitting prayer. Spiritual direction is available from well-trained directors, but it must be requested in advance. There are 89 rooms, all private. Practices taught include Eastern-Christian meditation, Ignatian exercises, guided imagery, and Taize prayer.

Directory of Retreat and Renewal Centers 87

Types of Retreats/Programs Offered: Directed/Group; Directed/Private; Ecumenical; Prayer Days; Meditation Intensives and other Special; Miscellaneous Programs
Open to: Everyone except youths and families
Person to Contact: Mary Waskowiak, Director; Sharon Almeida, Information Coordinator
Address: 2300 Adeline Drive, Burlingame, CA 94010
Telephone: 415-340-7474
Office Hours: 8:00 A.M. to 4:00 P.M.
Notice Required: 6 months minimum for summer; 2 months for balance of year

Mount Calvary Monastery and Retreat House
Episcopal, Order of the Holy Cross (Benedictine)

We are located in a large Spanish house situated dramatically on a ridge 1,250 feet above Santa Barbara, with a commanding view of the seacoast and Pacific Ocean. Central to each day at Mount Calvary is the "work" of prayer, or opus dei, as St. Benedict called it. The 4 services of the Divine Office are both an act of praise to God and an intercession for the needs of the world. Matins is said at the break of day, diurnum is a brief midday pause, vespers is sung at the close of the work day, and compline is the final prayer at night. The principal liturgical service of each day is the Eucharist. Guests are welcome and encouraged to participate in these services with the monastic community. Closed late August.

Types of Retreats/Programs Offered: Directed/Group; Directed/Private; Conference; Hermitage/Solitary; Special
Open to: Everyone except youths and families
Person to Contact: Guestmaster
Address: P.O. Box 1296, Santa Barbara, CA 93102
Telephone: 805-962-9855
Office Hours: 9:30 A.M. to 4:30 P.M.
Notice Required: 1 month to 1 year for weekends; 1 week for weekdays

Presentation Center
Sisters of the Presentation of the Blessed Virgin Mary

We are a religious retreat and educational conference center characterized by Christian hospitality. Situated on 264 acres of magnificent Santa Cruz Mountains, our facilities include conference rooms for large and small groups, a self-contained conference-dining building, single and double occupancy bedrooms, and cottages (some with kitchens) that accommodate 4 to 8 persons each. We have a large swimming pool, tennis and volleyball courts, a nature trail and other hiking areas, a fireplace lounge, and a beautiful lake surrounded by redwoods.

Types of Retreats/Programs Offered: Directed/Group; Directed/Private; Conference; Hermitage/Solitary; Ecumenical; Prayer Days; Encounters; Cursillos; Special
Open to: Everyone
Person to Contact: Sister Doris Cavanaugh, Administrator

Presentation Center, Los Gatos, California

Address: 19480 Bear Creek Road, Los Gatos, CA 95030
Telephone: 408-354-2346
Office Hours: 8:00 A.M. to 5:00 P.M.
Notice Required: Variable

Prince of Peace Abbey
Order of St. Benedict

Located on a hill overlooking the San Luis Rey River Valley and the Pacific Ocean, Prince of Peace Abbey is a Benedictine monastery in which the monks seek God through the traditional Benedictine blend of prayer and work. The monks invite their guests to seek God with them through sharing their silence, prayer, and reflection in an atmosphere of contemplative peace. Individuals may come in the traditional monastic way to spend time at the monastery. They are invited to participate in the monastic prayer, Eucharist, contemplative silence and work as they wish. Retreats may be brief (minimum 3 days) or as long as one week and normally begin with evening Vespers at 5:00 P.M., followed by dinner. Closed in July.

Types of Retreats/Programs Offered: Hermitage/Solitary; Days of Recollection; Special
Open to: Everyone except youths and families
Person to Contact: Guestmaster
Address: 650 Benet Hill Road, Oceanside, CA 92054
Telephone: 619-430-1305
Office Hours: 8:00–10:30 A.M.; 1:00–5:00 P.M.
Notice Required: 2 months for weekends; 1 month for weekdays

Sacred Heart Renewal Center
Diocesan

The center is an oasis in the high desert of California's Mohave Desert. Because of its remote setting, it is quiet and serene. The grounds have trees and grass even though located on 79 acres

Sacred Heart Renewal Center, Victorville, California

of beautiful desert. This provides ample room to walk, spending time with God. The facility also has a swimming pool from April through October, as well as horseshoes, volleyball, and basketball.

Types of Retreats/Programs Offered: Directed/Group; Directed/Private; Conference; Solitary; Prayer Days; Encounters; hosts Special Retreats and other programs
Open to: Everyone except families
Person to Contact: Carol Olin, Reservation Secretary
Address: 13333 Palmdale Road, Victorville, CA 92392
Telephone: 619-241-2538
Office Hours: 9:00 A.M. to 3:00 P.M. Tuesdays and Fridays
Notice Required: Variable

St. Andrew's Priory
Benedictine

Valyermo is a Benedictine monastery in the northern foothills (altitude 3,600 feet) of the San Gabriel Mountains on the edge of the Mojave Desert. A converted ranch house and other buildings make up St. Andrew's Priory, making possible a large program of hospitality for individuals and groups. Guest house facilities include double rooms with twin beds and private baths. Linens and towels are provided, and some meals are shared with the monastic community. Guests are invited to join in the prayer services of the monks. Private retreats can be made from Monday (after 3 P.M.) through Friday (until 9 A.M.); *please,* no Sunday overnights. High school students and young adults are welcome for retreats, workshops and spiritual seminars at our Youth Center, an informal but comfortable facility with two large dormitories.

Types of Retreats/Programs Offered: Conference; Hermitage/Solitary; Ecumenical; Charismatic; Prayer Days; Special; Miscellaneous Programs

Open to: Everyone except families; have separate Youth Retreat Center

Person to Contact: Guestmaster

Address: P.O. Box 40, Valyermo, CA 93563

Telephone: 805-944-2178

Office Hours: 8:00–11:45 A.M.; 1:30–5:30 P.M.

Notice Required: More than 2 months for weekends; approximately 2 weeks for weekdays

Santa Sabina Center
Dominican Sisters of San Rafael

Santa Sabina is a retreat and conference center located adjacent to the wooded, 100-acre Dominican College. From the quiet of Santa Sabina's inner courtyard garden and adjoining chapel, the spirit of tranquility and simplicity permeates the center. Santa Sabina offers a place of quiet and beauty for groups and individuals who come for center retreats or for their own programs. Santa Sabina Center, Catholic in its history and heritage, is ecumenical in its philosophy and outreach. The center welcomes men and women of all faiths to participate in programs or to spend individual time in quiet and reflection. The focus is on a contemplative way of being in the style of Thomas Merton, James Finley, centering prayer, etc.

Types of Retreats/Programs Offered: Directed/Group; Hermitage/Solitary; Ecumenical; Prayer Days; Encounters; Miscellaneous Programs including paper making as meditation
Open to: Everyone except youths and families
Person to Contact: Sister Susannah Malarkey, Director
Address: 1520 Grand Avenue, San Rafael, CA 94901
Telephone: 415-457-7727
Office Hours: 8:45 A.M. to 5:00 P.M. Monday through Friday
Notice Required: 1 month, sometimes less

Vallombrosa Center
Archdiocesan

Vallombrosa Conference and Retreat Center occupies 10 beautifully landscaped acres and includes a mansion built in the Civil War era. We are conveniently located between San Francisco and San Jose. Vallombrosa provides facilities for retreats, seminars, conferences, and workshops, lasting one or more days, tailored to the needs of individuals or groups. Accommodations include single and double rooms, all with private baths. The spacious lawns and variety of rare and beautiful trees from around the world create peaceful and reflective surroundings.

Types of Retreats/Programs Offered: Directed/Group; Conference; Charismatic; Prayer Days; Special Programs
Open to: Everyone except families
Person to Contact: Vera Davis, Coordinator of Sponsored Programs
Address: 250 Oak Grove Avenue, Menlo Park, CA 94025
Telephone: 415-325-5614
Office Hours: 7:30 A.M. to 4:30 P.M.
Notice Required: 1 week

Villa Maria Del Mar
Sisters of the Holy Names, California Province

Overlooking Monterey Bay, Villa Maria Del Mar is a center for retreats (private or group), seminars, conferences, and meetings of various kinds. Accommodations include double and single rooms, all with private baths, in the Main House and in Siena Hall.

Types of Retreats/Programs Offered: Directed/Group; Directed/Private; Hermitage/Solitary; Special
Open to: Everyone except youths and families
Person to Contact: Sister Regina Ann, Director
Address: 2 - 1918 E. Cliff Drive, Santa Cruz, CA 95062
Telephone: 408-475-1236
Office Hours: 9:00 A.M. to 5:00 P.M.
Notice Required: 1 year

Villa Maria House of Prayer
Sisters of St. Joseph of Carondelet

Description not available

Types of Retreats/Programs Offered: Directed/Private; Hermitage/Solitary; Prayer Days
Open to: Everyone except youths, families, and couples
Person to Contact: Any staff member
Address: 1252 N. Citrus Drive, La Habra, CA 90631
Telephone: 213-691-5838
Notice Required: 2 to 3 months for summer; rest of year variable

Colorado

Benet Hill Center
Benedictine

Retreats through Benet Hill Center are offered within a monastic setting of prayer in community, solitude, and hospitality. Benet

Hill's chapel, private rooms, and monastery grounds, located in the Austin Bluffs (altitude 6,200 feet) with a view of Pikes Peak, provide the space and atmosphere conducive to that inner journey to God. Centering prayer is among the practices taught.

Types of Retreats/Programs Offered: Directed/Group; Directed/Private; Conference; Hermitage/Solitary; Programs include 4-year Scripture Program, Contemplative Prayer, and Spiritual Direction
Open to: Everyone except youths, families, and couples
Person to Contact: Sister Rose Ann Barmann, Director
Address: 2577 N. Chelton Road, Colorado Springs, CO 80909
Telephone: 719-473-6184
Office Hours: 8:30 A.M. to 5:00 P.M. Monday through Friday
Notice Required: 2 to 3 weeks

Benet Pines Retreat Center
Benedictine

Benet Pines Retreat Center offers a place of retreat year-round. Two cabins and three hermitages, on thirty acres of pine forest (altitude 7,000 feet) in view of Pikes Peak, provide space for silence and solitude which is conducive to a prayer-filled experience of God. Retreatants have the opportunity to enter into the monastic rhythm of the day, and the staff offers individual and group experiences within the intimacy of small community life. Practices taught include centering prayer and the Ignatian exercises.

Types of Retreats/Programs Offered: Directed/Group; Directed/Private; Conference; Hermitage/Solitary; Ecumenical; Prayer Days; Special; ongoing Centering Programs
Open to: Everyone. Families may set up tents.
Person to Contact: Sister Colette Neigel or Sister Anne Stedman, Co-Directors
Address: 15780 Highway 83, Colorado Springs, CO 80921

Telephone: 719-495-2574
Office Hours: 9:00 A.M. to 5:30 P.M.
Notice Required: 1 month

Bethlehem Retreat Center
Bethlehem Missionary Fathers

The Bethlehem Center is a nonprofit retreat and conference center offering customized services for conferences, seminars, and retreats for corporations, institutions, and churches. We are in a 30-acre country setting with a spectacular view of the Rocky Mountains, a winding tree-lined creek, and hilltop shrines. We are between Denver (altitude 5,280 feet) and Boulder, 30 minutes from the Denver airport. Rooms may be single, double, or family size. The staff is also available for retreats, conference facilitation, and workshops.

Types of Retreats/Programs Offered: Directed/Group; Conference; Hermitage/Solitary; Ecumenical; Prayer Days; Liberation Theology, Global Justice, and other programs
Open to: Everyone. Have large family rooms with 4 beds each.
Person to Contact: Mr. Noel Dunne, Administrator
Address: 12550 Zuni St., Northglenn, CO 80234
Telephone: 303-451-1371
Office Hours: 8:30 A.M. to 4:00 P.M.
Notice Required: Approximately 2 months

Monastery of St. Walburga
Benedictine

We are a community of 20 women, living a traditional monastic life according to the Rule of St. Benedict. We live on and run a 150-acre farm at the base (altitude 5,600 feet) of the Rockies. We chant the entire Divine Office; approximately four and a half hours a day are spent in chapel. Guests are welcome to join us in chapel for any or all of the hours. The greatest gift that we have, and that we can share with our guests, is the atmosphere of prayer and peace that permeates the monastery.

Types of Retreats/Programs Offered: Hermitage/Solitary. Will host groups.
Open to: Everyone
Person to Contact: Sister Simone Conlin, Guestsister
Address: 6717 South Boulder Road, Boulder, CO 80303
Telephone: 303-494-5733
Office Hours: 8:30–11:30 A.M.; 2:30–5:15 P.M.
Notice Required: 1 week

Nada Hermitage/Spiritual Life Institute
S.L.I. Community

Nada Hermitage is outside Crestone, one hour north of Alamosa, at an altitude of 7,600 feet in the majestic Sangre de Cristo Mountains. We are a small monastic community of hermits founded for men and women in 1960 by Father William McNamara with a mandate from the visionary Pope John XXIII. We live like the early Carmelites, who followed the example of the prophet Elijah and lived on Mount Carmel under a common monastic rule characterized by simplicity and minimal structure to enable them to offer God a pure and undivided heart. We live in separate hermitages, and our monastic life is a rhythm of work and play, solitude and togetherness, fast and feast, discipline and wildness, sacrifice and celebration, contemplation and action. Retreatants participate in our monastic rhythms or choose solitude in their own hermitages. Each hermitage is self-contained with a small kitchen. Mondays and Tuesdays are days of complete solitude, Wednesday through Saturday are days with some community activity and some solitude, and Sundays are holy days of leisure "wasted" in praying and playing.

Types of Retreats/Programs Offered: Hermitage/Solitary
Open to: Everyone except youths and families

Nada Hermitage, Crestone, Colorado

Person to Contact: Mark letters "Retreat Request"
Address: Box 119, Crestone, CO 81131
Telephone: 719-256-4778
Notice Required: 6–8 months in summer, 2–3 months in winter

Sacred Heart Retreat House
Jesuits

Sacred Heart Retreat House is in the foothills (altitude 6,200 feet) of the Rocky Mountains, approximately 20 miles south of Denver. Spacious and beautiful landscaping overlooks a natural valley on 4 sides with a view of the mountains to the west. The retreat house is operated by Jesuit priests and brothers; all of the priests have had training in giving retreats and spiritual direction. Private rooms with central baths. Weekend retreats begin at 8:00 P.M. Friday and conclude with a 5:30 P.M. supper Sunday evening. The full 30-day *Spiritual Exercises* of St. Ignatius are offered, usually during July. Closed for 2 weeks at Christmas.

Types of Retreats/Programs Offered: Directed/Private; Conference; Hermitage/Solitary; Ecumenical; Prayer Days; Special
Open to: Everyone except youths and families
Person to Contact: Father Robert Houlihan, Director
Address: P.O. Box 185, 4801 Highway 67, Sedalia, CO 80135

Telephone: 303-688-4198
Office Hours: 9:00 A.M. to 4:30 P.M.
Notice Required: Variable

St. Benedict's Monastery
Cistercian (Trappist)

St. Benedict's did not return a questionnaire for this book, but this is where Father Thomas Keating lives and teaches centering prayer to retreatants. For a vivid description of an intensive centering prayer retreat here, see the personal narrative chapter in this book.

(Author's note: The monks of St. Benedict's support themselves in part by baking wonderful cookies. Send for their price list and try the orange almond butter. Makes a great and unusual gift!)

Types of Retreats/Programs Offered: Directed/Group
Open to: Everyone except youths and families
Person to Contact: Guestmaster
Address: 1012 Monastery Road, Snowmass, CO 81654
Telephone: 303-927-3311
Notice Required: Variable

Connecticut

Archdiocesan Spiritual Life Center
Archdiocesan

Interfaith in its outreach, the Spiritual Life Center seeks to assist people in the awareness and development of their spiritual life. Located in a wing of St. Thomas Seminary, the center is only 10–15 minutes from downtown Hartford. The seminary grounds, acres of rolling meadows, tree-lined driveways and walks, make it an ideal place for quiet reflection and prayer. The interior of the center also provides a setting for solitude and prayer. Staffed

Directory of Retreat and Renewal Centers 99

by professionals whose academic training and experience make them competent to assist people in their spiritual development, the center offers spiritual direction, provides programs for spiritual enrichment and training for this ministry.

Types of Retreats/Programs Offered: Hosts programs of groups; offers a spiritual direction internship program
Open to: Everyone except youths and families
Person to Contact: Sister Maureen McMahon, Director
Address: 467 Bloomfield Avenue, Bloomfield, CT 06002
Telephone: 203-243-2374
Office Hours: 9:00 A.M. to 5:00 P.M.

Mercy Center at Madison
Sisters of Mercy of Connecticut

Mercy Center is a center for renewal and human development. Its ministry is hospitality encompassed in both the renewal and

Mercy Center, Madison, Connecticut

personal growth it sponsors and in the groups hosted in renewal, education, training, and community development. The center was established in 1973 as a center for renewal and human development. Formerly the W.T. Grant Summer Estate, it has 40 acres reaching down to 1,100 feet of beachfront on Long Island Sound. Directed retreatants are accommodated in private rooms with general bathrooms. Participants in other programs are accommodated in double rooms with general bathroom facilities. Because of changeable shoreline temperatures, warm informal clothing is advised.

Types of Retreats/Programs Offered: Directed/Group; Directed/Private; Conference; Hermitage/Solitary; Prayer Days; Special; Miscellaneous Programs
Open to: Everyone except youths
Person to Contact: Program Registrar
Address: Box 191, 167 Neck Road, Madison, CT 06443-0191
Telephone: 203-245-0401
Office Hours: 8:30 A.M. to 4:30 P.M.
Notice Required: Several months for summer; 2 weeks to 1 month for weekends

Our Lady of Calvary Retreat
Sisters of the Cross and Passion

Our Lady of Calvary, a diocesan retreat house for women, is in the colonial town of Farmington, a peaceful and beautiful suburb 12 miles west of Hartford. Facilities include both single and double rooms (some with private baths), chapel, library, gift shop, and 18 acres of pleasant grounds. Our Lady of Calvary Retreat is easily accessible for the disabled. Sisters of the Cross and Passion (Passionist Sisters) who staff the retreat house aim to be "people for the people," providing for others a place where life and growth are shared, fostered and celebrated. The retreat house, on occasion, will host study groups, adult programs, workshops, seminars, ministry conferences, and ecumenical gatherings, when these do not interfere with regularly scheduled retreat programs. Closed in August.

Types of Retreats/Programs Offered: Directed/Group; Directed/Private; Conference; Hermitage/Solitary; Prayer Days; Parent-Teen; Special
Open to: Everyone, but primarily women
Person to Contact: Mrs. Roberta J. Cote, Administrator
Address: 31 Colton Street, Farmington, CT 06032
Telephone: 203-677-8519
Office Hours: 10:00 A.M. to 3:00 P.M.
Notice Required: Average 2 weeks

Visitation Center
Congregation of Notre Dame

Visitation Center is a human development and reflection center owned and operated by the Sisters of the Congregation de Notre Dame. Located on a beautiful mountain in Ridgefield, the center is primarily a rental facility. The center offers the unique advantages of a large, fully equipped facility, enclosed within 50 acres of woodland overlooking the rolling hills of New York State. Accommodations include double rooms for workshops and weekend retreats, and single rooms for directed and extended retreats. Suites with kitchens available. Closed in August.

Types of Retreats/Programs Offered: Directed/Group; Directed/Private; Ecumenical; Prayer Days; Encounters; Tres Dias; Special
Open to: Everyone
Person to Contact: Sister Eileen Kelly, Director. Sister Carolyn Kinnamon, Assistant Director
Address: 223 West Mountain Road, Ridgefield, CT 06877
Telephone: 203-438-9071
Office Hours: 9:00–11:30 A.M.; 1:00–5:00 P.M.
Notice Required: 1 to 1 ½ years for weekend space

Wisdom House
Daughters of Wisdom (Catholic Nuns)

Wisdom House is an ecumenical retreat and conference center in the beautiful rolling hills of Litchfield, on 58 acres of woods and meadows suitable for cross-country skiing, hiking, nature walks, or meditation. There is a swimming pool for summer. A two-story, 200-year-old farmhouse offers a completely self-contained setting for small groups. A larger building with both private rooms and dormitories is available and is handicapped accessible. There are rooms with extra beds for families. We prefer no smoking in the buildings.

Types of Retreats/Programs Offered: Directed/Group; Directed/Private; Conference; Hermitage/Solitary; Ecumenical; Charismatic; Prayer Days; Parent-Teen; Encounters; Cursillos; Special; Miscellaneous Programs
Open to: Everyone
Person to Contact: Ivan O. Hawk, Administrator/Deacon
Address: Clark Road, RFD #3, Litchfield, CT 06795
Telephone: 203-567-3163
Office Hours: 8:30 A.M. to 4:30 P.M.
Notice Required: As soon as possible

District of Columbia

Washington Retreat House
Franciscan Sisters of the Atonement

The Washington Retreat House was established by Mother Luana White, founder of the Franciscan Sisters of the Atonement, and opened its doors in 1930. Although its initial primary thrust was the spiritual development of women, it has been used by other groups as well. Women and men come from their daily lives to hear the Word of God, to listen and reflect on that Word, and through prayer come to a new life. Closed in July and August.

Directory of Retreat and Renewal Centers 103

Types of Retreats/Programs Offered: Directed/Group; Directed/Private; Conference; Hermitage/Solitary; Ecumenical; Prayer Days; Special
Open to: Everyone except families
Person to Contact: Sister Consiline Flynn, Director
Address: 4000 Harewood Road, N.E., Washington, D.C. 20017
Telephone: 202-529-1111
Notice Required: 2 weeks for individuals; 1 year for groups

Florida

Dominican Retreat House
Dominican Sisters

Dominican hospitality offers friendship without binding the guest, and freedom without loneliness. It is the creation of a free space into which a stranger can enter and become a friend, a space in which one can change. It creates a space for healing, peace and detachment from the ordinary claims of daily life. The Dominican Sisters are here for you, trained in the work of retreats, religious education and other forms of the pastoral ministry. In addition to the Sisters, a priest completes the retreat team. We share in a common enthusiasm and talent for bringing the word of God and His love to you through prayer services, conferences and availability for private consultation and direction.

Types of Retreats/Programs Offered: Directed/Group; Directed/Private; Conference; Hermitage/Solitary; Charismatic; Prayer Days; Special; Miscellaneous Programs
Open to: Everyone except families
Person to Contact: Sister Mary Meenan, Director
Address: 7275 S.W. 124th Street, Miami, FL 33156
Telephone: 305-238-2711
Office Hours: 8:00 A.M. to 5:00 P.M.
Notice Required: Minimum 1 year

Franciscan Center
Franciscan Sisters

The Franciscan Center is a modern retreat facility on the Hillsborough River in Tampa on an 8-acre tract of spacious and scenic grounds that are conducive to prayer and reflection. The Franciscan Center provides an atmosphere of hospitality, peace, and acceptance, rooted in the spirit of Franciscan tradition, which allows people to come away from daily activities and find spiritual nourishment, growth, and direction for their lives. Also available is Sabbath House, a small dwelling set apart at one end of the center property affording separation for a day or several days of quiet spiritual repose. Limited activity in July and August.

Types of Retreats/Programs Offered: Directed/Private; Conference; Hermitage/Solitary; Ecumenical; Charismatic; Prayer Days; Encounters; Special
Open to: Everyone except families
Person to Contact: Sister Eva M. Di Camillo, Director of Public Relations/Retreat Coordinator
Address: 3010 Perry Avenue, Tampa, FL 33603
Telephone: 813-229-2695
Office Hours: 9:00 A.M. to 4:00 P.M.
Notice Required: 1 month

Holy Name Priory
Benedictine Sisters

We are not a retreat center, we are a convent motherhouse. We welcome guests for private, directed or special retreats. They will share daily in the Eucharist, the Liturgy of the House, and meals with us. We offer special retreats for those discerning a religious vocation. We have laypersons affiliated as Oblates who come bimonthly for spiritual programs. Facilities are limited from September through May. In the summer, large groups can use nearby college residence halls. Alcoholics Anonymous has a number of weekend retreats with us in the summer. We are 35 miles northeast of Tampa in the rural rolling hills of central Florida.

Types of Retreats/Programs Offered: Directed/Private; Special; Oblate Program
Open to: Everyone except families and couples
Person to Contact: Sister Mary David or Sister Irma
Address: Dr. H, St. Leo, FL 33514
Telephone: 704-588-8320
Notice Required: Prefer 2 to 4 weeks

Our Lady of Florida Spiritual Center
Passionists

The constant danger is that our lives can become absurd. The word absurd includes the Latin *surdus,* which means deaf. An absurd life is one in which we have become deaf and can no longer hear the calling voice of our Loving Lord. Our Lady of Florida Spiritual Center is that hospitable space where we can move out of absurd living, away from deafness—to listening to God's special call to us. Overlooking beautiful Lake Worth, facilities include single and double rooms, a spacious chapel, outdoor shrines and gardens for meditation, and a gift shop and book store.

Types of Retreats/Programs Offered: Directed/Group; Conference; Cursillos; Miscellaneous Programs
Open to: Everyone
Person to Contact: Retreat Secretary
Address: 1300 U.S. Highway #1, North Palm Beach, FL 33408
Telephone: 407-626-1300
Notice Required: Variable

San Pedro Center
Franciscans, T.O.R.

Set on 450 acres on the shores of Lake Howell, our center is close to the airport and major highways. Programs at the center provide a place away from the busy world for reflection, prayer, retreats, and workshops. We run an excellent Summer Scripture Camp for Youth where they can live in community—learning and experiencing more about the Catholic faith while participating in activities like swimming, canoeing, drama, music, liturgy. We have an ongoing centering prayer program. There are no restaurants within walking distance for private retreatants, but cabins are efficiencies.

Types of Retreats/Programs Offered: Directed/Group; Directed/Private; Conference; Hermitage/Solitary; Charismatic; Prayer Days; Parent-Teen; Encounters; Cursillos; Special; Miscellaneous Programs
Open to: Everyone
Person to Contact: Mary Mericle, Business Manager, or Linda Beauregard, Program Coordinator
Address: 2400 Dike Road, Winter Park, FL 32792
Telephone: 407-671-6322
Office Hours: 8:30 A.M. to 4:30 P.M.
Notice Required: Variable

Hawaii

Spiritual Life Center
Roman Catholic

Those who come to the Spiritual Life Center enjoy the beauty of the St. Francis High School grounds on which it is located and the spaciousness of the University of Hawaii campus adjacent to Marianne Hall. A view of the soaring mountains, the sound of Manoa Stream, the songs of many birds, and the flowering bushes and trees create an atmosphere conducive to prayer, reflection, rest, and renewal. Accommodations include single rooms (double on request), a small chapel, a library, and a swimming pool. Proximity to the Franciscan Sisters chapel and to the Newman Center offers a choice of Mass times and optional spaces for prayer.

Types of Retreats/Programs Offered: Directed/Group; Directed/Private; Conference; Hermitage/Solitary; Ecumenical; Prayer Days; Special; Miscellaneous Programs including centering prayer
Open to: Everyone except families
Person to Contact: Sister Katherine Theiler, Director
Address: 2717 Pamea Road, Honolulu, HI 96822
Telephone: 808-988-7800
Notice Required: Variable

Illinois

Cabrini Retreat Center
Missionary Sisters of the Sacred Heart
Description not available.

Types of Retreats/Programs Offered: Directed/Group; Directed/Private; Conference; Hermitage/Solitary; Ecumenical; Charismatic; Engaged Encounter; Special; Miscellaneous Programs
Open to: Everyone except families
Person to Contact: Sister Ilaria Povero, Director
Address: 9430 Golf Road, Des Plaines, IL 60016
Telephone: 312-297-6530
Notice Required: Variable

Cardinal Stritch Retreat House
No religous affiliation

Our center offers 52 private rooms with bath. We are part of a seminary campus, encompassing 900 acres. Our building is more than a mile from any other building, ensuring privacy and quiet. We are on a large lake, with mostly wooded area surrounding us. We are primarily for priests and ordained deacons. We offer preached, directed, and private retreats. Closed in July.

Types of Retreats/Programs Offered: Directed/Group; Directed/Private; Hermitage/Solitary; Special

Open to: Priests
Person to Contact: Father Robert Ferrigan, Director
Address: P.O. Box 455, Mundelein, IL 60060
Telephone: 312-566-6060
Office Hours: 8:00 A.M. to 4:00 P.M.
Notice Required: No time limit

Cenacle Retreat House
Religious of the Cenacle

The Cenacle in Chicago is a quiet and peace-filled place in the midst of the city. We are a city house with a garden; Lincoln Park, the Conservatory, the Zoo, and Lake Michigan are only a few blocks away. Our facilities are conducive to prayer and restful reflection, with spacious rooms and a peaceful atmosphere. We are easily reached by public transportation. The Cenacle Sisters are here for you, trained in the work of retreats, religious education and other forms of the pastoral ministry. We are available to help you as you listen to the Lord. Closed 2½ weeks in the summer.

Types of Retreats/Programs Offered: Directed/Group; Directed/Private; Conference; Hermitage/Solitary; Ecumenical; Prayer Days; Special; Miscellaneous Programs
Open to: Everyone except youths and families
Person to Contact: Sister Rosemary Duncan, Ministry Coordinator
Address: 513 Fullerton Parkway, Chicago, IL 60614
Telephone: 312-528-6300
Office Hours: 8:30 A.M. to 5:00 P.M.
Notice Required: Variable

Divine Word International
Divine Word Missionaries

Divine Word International is a conference center rather than a retreat house in the conventional sense. We sponsor mainly youth retreats (75–80 per year). All kinds of religious and educational groups use our facilities for various kinds of meetings.

Types of Retreats/Programs Offered: Directed/Group; Directed/Private; Conference; Hermitage/Solitary; Prayer Days; Special Lent and Advent educational programs
Open to: Everyone except families
Person to Contact: Father Robert J. Flinn, Director
Address: 2001 Waukegan Road, Techny, IL 60082
Telephone: 312-272-1100
Office Hours: 8:30 A.M. to 5:00 P.M.
Notice Required: 6 months to a year

Franciscan Apostolic Center
Hospital Sisters of the Third Order of St. Francis

We are primarily a place of spiritual ministry where healing and liberation of soul and body can be achieved in an atmosphere of serenity. Activities include retreats, days of renewal, prayer meetings, and various workshops and seminars concerned with

Franciscan Apostolic Center, Springfield, Illinois

spiritual and human development. Since most of our bedrooms are not air-conditioned, we do not encourage groups to attend in July and August. Centering prayer is taught as part of quiet weekends.

Types of Retreats/Programs Offered: Directed/Group; Directed/Private; Conference; Hermitage/Solitary; Prayer Days; Cursillos; Special
Open to: Everyone except families
Person to Contact: Sister Joan Case, Director
Address: P.O. Box 19431, Springfield, IL 62794-9431
Telephone: 217-522-2695
Notice Required: 2 weeks

King's House of Retreats and Renewal
Oblates of Mary Immaculate

King's House is on 47 acres of rolling hills, with expansive lawns and thick woods. The main building is a 3-story red brick edifice with a 64-room dormitory and chapel at one end, a dining hall, and a large conference room. The atmosphere is very homey and friendly. Outdoor Stations of the Cross, gardens, and a 5-acre campground are part of the facility. The mission of the King's House of Retreats is to be a welcoming place where people can find an atmosphere of prayer, support, and encouragement.

Types of Retreats/Programs Offered: Directed/Group; Directed/Private; Conference; Hermitage/Solitary; Ecumenical; Charismatic; Prayer Days; Special; Miscellaneous Programs
Open to: Everyone
Person to Contact: Kathleen J. Aubuchon, Director of Development
Address: N. 66th Street, Belleville, IL 62223
Telephone: 618-397-0584
Office Hours: 8:00 A.M. to 5:00 P.M.
Notice Required: Prefer 1 month, but variable

King's House of Retreats
Oblates of Mary Immaculate

King's House of Retreats is set above the Illinois River in a quiet wooded area. Single and double rooms are air-conditioned, with bath/shower. Meals are served family-style in the attractive dining room. Our capacity is 96.

Types of Retreats/Programs Offered: Directed/Group; Directed/Private; Conference; Hermitage/Solitary; Ecumenical; Charismatic; Prayer Days; Encounters; Special
Open to: Everyone except families
Person to Contact: Father Wayne Like, Director
Address: P.O. Box 165, Henry, IL 61537
Telephone: 309-364-3084
Office Hours: 8:30 A.M. to 4:00 P.M.
Notice Required: Variable

Oasis Place of Prayer
Covenant member Wheaton Franciscan — Lay

Oasis provides a comfortable home with private rooms, a kitchen and eating area, and a communal room. Oasis is located in woods with trails, a creek, and a pond. Camping is available. A quiet and reflective atmosphere provides a place where individuals and groups can continue to grow and respond to Jesus' invitation to "live on in me, as I do in you" (John 15:4). Centering prayer is taught. Closed in December.

Types of Retreats/Programs Offered: Directed/Private; Conference; Hermitage/Solitary; Ecumenical; Prayer Days; Special
Open to: Everyone except youths and families
Person to Contact: Ann Kuhn, Director
Address: 17175 Galena Road, Plano, IL 60545
Telephone: 312-552-8201
Office Hours: 9:00 A.M. to 5:00 P.M.
Notice Required: 2 months

Our House of Prayer
Sisters of Mercy, Chicago

Our House of Prayer, so named by the black community in which it is located, offers an inexpensive, readily available center to people interested in prayer and faith-sharing experiences. It is open to all religious groups. Most groups bring their own agenda and director. Meals are planned in dialogue with the group, which carries the major responsibility for them. Closed in July and August.

Types of Retreats/Programs Offered: Directed/Group; Directed/Private; Conference; Hermitage/Solitary; Prayer Days
Open to: Everyone except youths and families
Person to Contact: Sister Norella or Sister Evangeline, Co-Directors
Address: 8718 S. Paulina Street, Chicago, IL 60620
Telephone: 312-233-5609
Office Hours: Most anytime
Notice Required: 2 months

St. Francis Retreat House, Oak Brook, Illinois

Directory of Retreat and Renewal Centers 113

St. Francis Retreat House at Mayslake
Franciscan

St. Francis Retreat House at Mayslake is a place of retreat in the Roman Catholic tradition. Its primary ministry, reflecting the life of Francis of Assisi, is to rebuild the church in the spirit of renewal begun by the Second Vatican Council. This it does through programs challenging the Christian faithful to deepen their personal and communal relationship with God and creation. Common prayer and liturgical worship of a high quality form an essential component of all the programs. We are open to all who seek a deepening of the spirit, and participation by believers of other faiths is welcome. In keeping with St. Francis' great awareness of the presence of God in all creation, we maintain a natural environment requisite for the quiet and solitude of our guests. The center is also available to nonprofit groups for their own programs, as long as these are compatible with our primary ministry.

Types of Retreats/Programs Offered: Directed/Group; Directed/Private; Conference; Hermitage/Solitary; Prayer Days; Special; Miscellaneous Programs
Open to: Everyone except youths and families
Person to Contact: Jonathan Foster, OFM, Director
Address: 1717 31st Street, Oak Brook, IL 60521
Telephone: 312-323-1687
Office Hours: 8:00 A.M. to 4:30 P.M. Monday through Friday; 8 A.M. to noon Saturday
Notice Required: Variable for individuals; 6 months to 1 year for groups

Siloam
Privately owned

Siloam is a place for retreat and prayer, a small arboretum. Individuals are welcomed for a day of prayer, or a longer retreat, for spiritual direction, or a reflective walk along the many trails. Church staffs and other small groups often come for a day. The house and cottage contain beds for 7 persons. The cottage has its own kitchen, with a limited pantry, and a private bath. Retreatants prepare their own meals. Churches of several denominations are located within 3 miles, and daily Mass is offered nearby.

Types of Retreats/Programs Offered: Varies
Open to: Everyone
Person to Contact: David or Martha Bartholomew
Address: 18 N. 600 West Hill Road, Dundee, IL 60118
Telephone: 312-428-6949
Notice Required: Variable

The Villa—Center for Renewal
Sisters of Mercy

This facility is temporarily closed for evaluation of its future direction and mission. It is a 64-acre farm, with quiet woods, meadows of wildflowers, rustic buildings, wooded paths along the Fox River, and an island.

Types of Retreats/Programs Offered: Directed/Group; Directed/Private; Conference; Hermitage/Solitary; Ecumenical; Charismatic; Prayer Days; Parent-Teen; Encounters; Cursillos; Special; Miscellaneous Programs
Open to: Everyone
Person to Contact: Sisters of Mercy
Address: 35 W. 076 Villa Maria Road, St. Charles, IL 60174
Telephone: 312-742-6419
Notice Required: Normally, a few weeks; several months for September, October, and May

Indiana

Alverna Retreat Center
Franciscan Order of Friars Minor

Established in 1930 as the estate of a prominent Indianapolis financier, the four buildings and 35 acres of grounds (with lawns, evergreen grove, paths, creek, grotto) of Alverna Retreat Center make a uniquely reflective and peaceful setting. The Carriage House offers a completely separate facility for family and youth retreats. The Alverna Counseling Center offers marriage, family, and individual counseling. Portiuncula Chapel sits as a special gem nearby. Named after a mountain in Italy where St. Francis of Assisi prayed, Alverna has been owned and operated by Franciscans since 1947. The Retreat Center serves those who wish to draw aside from the world for a time of reflection, prayer, and reassessment of personal life. The staff conducts a variety of programs and hosts many diverse groups for their own activities.

Types of Retreats/Programs Offered: Directed/Group; Directed/Private; Conference; Hermitage/Solitary; Ecumenical; Charismatic; Prayer Days; Encounters; Special; Miscellaneous Programs
Open to: Everyone
Person to Contact: Sheila Gilbert, Administrator
Address: 8140 Spring Mill Road, Indianapolis, IN 46260
Telephone: 317-257-7338
Office Hours: 8:30 A.M. to 5:00 P.M. weekdays
Notice Required: 1 to 2 weeks

Beech Grove Benedictine Center
Sisters of St. Benedict

Some of the comments we have received from our retreatants sum up what we are and what we have to offer: "The Benedictine hospitality made me feel at home, and the Madonna Chapel was inspiring." "The accommodations are all that is necessary. Places to sit comfortably for reading and to enter into private/communal worship are available." "The center seems to have everything a person would need for a thoughtful, prayerful retreat experience. The greatest resource, I believe, is the staff." Only single bedrooms are available.

Types of Retreats/Programs Offered: Directed/Group; Directed/Private; Conference; Hermitage/Solitary; Prayer Days; Cursillos; Miscellaneous Programs
Open to: Everyone
Person to Contact: Sister Juliann Babock, Program Director
Address: 1402 Southern Avenue, Beech Grove, IN 46107
Telephone: 317-788-7581
Office Hours: 8:30 A.M. to 5:00 P.M.
Notice Required: 3 months

Fatima Retreat House
Diocesan

Consistent with the Mission of Jesus, Fatima Retreat House offers an environment of hospitality conducive to reflection, and programs for spiritual enrichment. A center of the Archdiocese of Indianapolis, it is primarily committed to serving the needs of individuals, parishes, and agencies of the Catholic community. Fatima also welcomes people of other religious traditions, and groups seeking a place to conduct programs consistent with its spirit. It is in a wooded area, which gives a secluded feeling in the heart of Indianapolis.

Types of Retreats/Programs Offered: Directed/Group; Directed/Private; Conference; Hermitage/Solitary; Ecumenical; Prayer Days; Encounters; Special; Miscellaneous Programs
Open to: Everyone
Person to Contact: Kevin DePrey, Director
Address: 5353 E. 56th Street, Indianapolis, IN 46226
Telephone: 317-545-7681
Office Hours: 9:00 A.M. to 5:00 P.M.
Notice Required: 6 months to 1 year

John XXIII Center
Diocesan

John XXIII Center is a retreat and study center sponsored by the Diocese of Lafayette-in-Indiana. It is a place where hospitality lives. It is a retreat center in a setting of peace and tranquility. John XXIII is a home—cozy, comfortable, and community oriented. Facilities include single and double rooms, a chapel with open space, a large discussion room, smaller visiting areas, a spacious and colorful basement for larger group activities, and a small library and reading room. Closed in July and August.

Types of Retreats/Programs Offered: Directed/Group; Directed/Private; Conference; Hermitage/Solitary; Ecumenical; Charismatic; Prayer Days; Parent-Teen; Marriage Encounter; Special; Miscellaneous Programs
Open to: Everyone
Person to Contact: Father Keith Hosey, Director, or Sister Maureen Mangen, Co-Director
Address: 407 W. McDonald, Hartford City, IN 47348
Telephone: 317-348-4008
Office Hours: 9 A.M. to 5 P.M.
Notice Required: 2 to 3 weeks

Kordes Enrichment Center
Benedictine

Kordes Enrichment Center, nestled in the scenic hills of rural southern Indiana one mile off Interstate 64 at Ferdinand, lies in the shadow of the majestic Benedictine Convent Chapel. A colonnade affords a panoramic view of the countryside. The Center provides an ideal environment in which to retreat while experiencing the 1,500-year old tradition of Benedictine hospitality. Hiking, fishing, swimming in summer, and tennis are available. Climbing stairs is required. The retreat center is on the lovely grounds of the Motherhouse. Bedrooms have twin beds, and bathrooms are not private. Practices taught include centering prayer and the Ignatian Exercises. No facilities for families.

Types of Retreats/Programs Offered: Directed/Group; Directed/Private; Conference; Hermitage/Solitary; Ecumenical; Prayer Days; Special; Miscellaneous Programs including centering prayer
Open to: Everyone
Person to Contact: Sister Joella Kidwell, Director
Address: R.R. #3, Box 200, Ferdinand, IN 47532
Telephone: 812-367-2777
Office Hours: 8:00 A.M. to 4:30 P.M.
Notice Required: 1 week for individuals

Lindenwood, A Ministry and Retreat Center
Poor Handmaids of Jesus Christ

Lindenwood is a ministry and retreat center located on the beautiful and peaceful rural campus of Convent Ancilla Domini and Ancilla College, 100 miles east of Chicago and north of Indianapolis. We offer 96 beds and meeting rooms for up to 250. Most bedrooms include two single beds, shower and bathroom facilities and individually controlled heat and air-conditioning units. All spaces are handicapped accessible. Lindenwood provides retreats, conferences, seminars, and workshops designed to enhance human excellence and develop leadership skills. It is dedicated to sharing resources through cooperation and collaboration in the planning and facilitating of all programs. No facilities for families.

Types of Retreats/Programs Offered: Directed/Group; Directed/Private; Conference; Hermitage/Solitary; Ecumenical; Prayer Days; Encounters; Cursillos; Miscellaneous Programs including creation spirituality
Open to: Everyone
Person to Contact: Adrienne Clark, Executive Director

Address: Convent Ancilla Domini, P.O. Box 1, Donaldson, IN 46513
Telephone: 219-935-1780
Office Hours: 8:30 A.M. to 5:00 P.M.
Notice Required: Variable

Sarto Retreat House

Description not available

Types of Retreats/Programs Offered: Directed/Group; Conference; Ecumenical; Charismatic; Prayer Days; Encounters; Cursillos; Special
Open to: Everyone
Person to Contact: Donald F. Lahay, Director
Address: 4200 N. Kentucky Ave., P.O. Box 4169, Evansville, IN 47724-0169
Telephone: 812-424-5536
Office Hours: 8:00 A.M. to 5:00 P.M.
Notice Required: Variable

The Solitude of St. Joseph or St. Joseph Solitude
Brothers of Holy Cross

Created as a center for people of all backgrounds and faith experiences to be still and nourish their relationship with God, themselves, and others, the Solitude of St. Joseph exists as a space apart, dedicated to the Sacred. Guests are welcome for a few hours, overnight, a weekend, or longer. Located on the west edge of the University of Notre Dame, the Solitude of St. Joseph occupies the East Annex of Columba Hall. Situated between St. Mary's and St. Joseph's lakes and near the Notre Dame woods, ample space exists for quiet reflection and walking. In order to allow guests to develop their own rhythm of rest, reflection, and prayer, there are no scheduled events at the solitude. Meals are prepared by the guests from the food provided. Liturgy is celebrated weekly. At other times, guests are free to select one of the many Eucharistic celebrations held daily on the Notre Dame campus.

Types of Retreats/Programs Offered: Directed/Private; Hermitage/Solitary
Open to: Everyone except youths and families
Person to Contact: Brother John Kuhn, Director
Address: P.O. Box 983, Notre Dame, IN 46556
Telephone: 219-239-5655
Office Hours: 9:00 A.M. to 5:00 P.M.
Notice Required: Variable. Peak periods are Holy Week, Easter Week, and June, July, and August.

Yokefellow Institute
Nondenominational

The Yokefellow Institute and Retreat Center was built in 1964 as a practical expression of the Yokefellow Movement, dedicated to the renewal of individuals, churches, and society. Partially hidden behind a beautiful hill at the end of a long lane, Yokefellow Institute and Retreat Center nestles into the bend of a gently flowing stream and the bosom of an encircling woods. Our very setting prompts the renewal so needed in our individual and corporate life. Over the past 2 decades it has gained an international reputation as a center of real spiritual growth and vitality. Accommodations include air-conditioned rooms with twin beds and private baths.

Types of Retreats/Programs Offered: Conference; Ecumenical; Miscellaneous Programs
Open to: Men and women
Person to Contact: James R. Newby, Executive Director
Address: 920 Earlham Drive, Richmond, IN 47374
Telephone: 317-983-1575

Office Hours: 8:30 A.M. to 4:30 P.M.
Notice Required: Maximum 6 months

Iowa

Shalom Retreat Center
Sisters of St. Francis of Dubuque

The Shalom Center, a short distance from Mount St. Francis, is a quiet space at the north end of the city, a holy place in a peaceful environment of natural and historic beauty. The building itself has a rich heritage, and the center has room to walk and enjoy the outdoors.

Types of Retreats/Programs Offered: Directed/Group; Directed/Private; Conference; Hermitage/Solitary; Prayer Days; Marriage Encounter; Miscellaneous Programs
Open to: Everyone
Person to Contact: Sister Marie Therese Kalb, Director
Address: 1001 Davis Avenue, Dubuque, IA 52001
Telephone: 319-582-3592 or 583-2255
Office Hours: 9:00 A.M. to 5:00 P.M.
Notice Required: Variable

Kansas

ACUTO
Adorers of the Blood of Christ

ACUTO is a center of renewal and prayer maintaining an environment for listening and responding to God's word within the individual's heart; a center for prophetic voices speaking of new visions of community and Church; a center promoting persons of wholeness and integrity. Representing the charism of the Adorers of the Blood of Christ and responding to the spiritual needs of the people of Wichita, the ACUTO Center for Renewal and

Prayer seeks to provide spiritual growth opportunities for all interested Christians.

Types of Retreats/Programs Offered: Directed/Private; Hermitage/Solitary; Ecumenical; Prayer Days; Special; Miscellaneous Programs including creation spirituality
Open to: Everyone except youths and families
Person to Contact: Rita Robl, Director
Address: 1165 Southwest Boulevard, Wichita, KS 67213
Telephone: 316-945-2542
Office Hours: 9:00 A.M. to 9:00 P.M.
Notice Required: 1 week

Spiritual Life Center (currently Villa Christi Retreat House)
Redemptorist Community

The Spiritual Life Center will open in January 1990, replacing Villa Christi Retreat Center, which has been in operation since 1962. The new center will be a state-of-the-art facility with 60 private rooms with baths, chapel, meeting rooms, and adoration chapel. The center is staffed by the Redemptorist Community and owned by the Diocese of Wichita. Centering prayer, Ignatian Exercises, and contemplation methods are among the practices which are taught.

Types of Retreats/Programs Offered: Directed/Group; Directed/Private; Conference; Hermitage/Solitary; Ecumenical; Charismatic; Prayer Days; Encounters; Cursillos; Special; Miscellaneous Programs
Open to: Everyone
Person to Contact: Father Thomas M. Santa, Director
Address: After January 1990: Woodlawn and 45th Street East, Wichita, KS
Current Mailing *Address:* 424 N. Broadway, Wichita, KS 67202
Telephone: 316-943-2108
Office Hours: 8:30 A.M. to 4:30 P.M.
Notice Required: Variable

Kentucky

Abbey of Gethsemani
Cistercian (Trappist)

The Abbey of Gethsemani offers a monastic setting that may be shared by lay people who reside in a guest house and spend a few days of quiet and prayer with us. Retreats are open to men and women separately. Nondirected, personal retreats are held from Monday to Friday and from Friday to Sunday year-round. There are thousands of acres of woods for walking and meditation. Guest house accommodations are private rooms with showers. Guests are encouraged but not required to attend the monastic office, which is held 7 times daily. Retreatants dine in separate quarters, with talks offered at meals through tapes. Silence and solitude are encouraged, but time is allowed after lunch and dinner for socializing. A priest is available for those who wish. The abbey is 50 miles south of Louisville, and there is no public transportation to it.

Types of Retreats/Programs Offered: Directed/Private; Hermitage/Solitary
Open to: Everyone except youths, families, and couples
Person to Contact: Father Damien, Guestmaster
Address: Trappist, KY 40051
Telephone: 502-549-3117
Notice Required: Variable

Catherine Spalding Center
Sisters of Charity of Nazareth, Kentucky

Description not available. A guest house is available for families.

Types of Retreats/Programs Offered: Directed/Group; Directed/Private; Conference; Hermitage/Solitary; Ecumenical; Charismatic; Prayer Days; Special; Miscellaneous Programs
Open to: Everyone
Person to Contact: Sister Carol Clasgens, Director

Address: Box 24, Nazareth, KY 40048
Telephone: 502-348-1515
Office Hours: 8:30 A.M. to 4:30 P.M.
Notice Required: 2 to 3 months

Flaget Center for Spirituality and Ministry Formation
Archdiocesan

It would be easy to describe Flaget Center simply as a retreat center with ministry offices on the first floor. In the traditional vision of a retreat center, a place of solitude and stillness, the activity of the ministry offices would seem out of place. Yet it is genuine outreach that is the hallmark of Christian love. The fruits of our prayer, reflection, and solitude should be a call to minister in our lives. Therefore it is fitting that ministry formation offices should share one space with this retreat center. Admittedly, it does give Flaget a unique atmosphere. If you are seeking a place for an extended private retreat, you would not come here. Yet there are few who offer better locations for communal retreats. Single and double rooms are available, and the center is handicapped accessible.

Types of Retreats/Programs Offered: Directed/Group; Conference; Ecumenical; Charismatic; Prayer Days; Encounters; Cursillos
Open to: Everyone
Person to Contact: Steven Wirth, Director
Address: 1935 Lewiston Place, Louisville, KY 40216
Telephone: 502-448-8581
Office Hours: 8:30 A.M. to 5:00 P.M. weekdays
Notice Required: 2 to 3 months

Marydale Retreat Center
Diocesan

Marydale Retreat Center is 9 miles south of Cincinnati, situated above a large scenic lake and surrounded by acres of well-kept grounds, walkways, and trees. The retreat house is a one-floor building that is air-conditioned and handicapped accessible. There are also several other lodges available. Families accommodated in a camping program. Most retreats at Marydale are conducted on weekends, beginning with dinner on Friday evening and ending on Sunday shortly after noon.

Types of Retreats/Programs Offered: Conference; Ecumenical; Youth; Special; Miscellaneous Programs
Open to: Everyone
Person to Contact: Ed Stieritz, Director, or Eric Vones, Business Manager
Address: 945 Donaldson Highway, Erlanger, KY 41018
Telephone: 606-371-4224
Office Hours: 8:00 A.M. to 4:30 P.M.
Notice Required: Prefer 1 month, but flexible

Louisiana

Abbey Christian Life Center
Benedictine Monks

The Benedictines of St. Joseph Abbey in St. Benedict, 4 miles north of Covington, host retreats for those who seek the peace and recollection of a monastic setting to forward their spiritual and religious goals. Almost all retreats are booked to capacity. Retreatants are housed in a separate building a few hundred yards from the abbey church. The building, designed by the late John Lawrence, head of the Tulane School of Architecture, has 40 private rooms, chapel, lounge and library, dining room and kitchen, and counseling/reconciliation rooms. There are 6 conferences given during the course of the typical retreat weekend, which begins Friday evening and ends early Sunday afternoon. The daily midday liturgy with the monks of the abbey is held in the serenely majestic abbey church with its magnificent, inspired artwork.

Types of Retreats/Programs Offered: Conference; Ecumenical; Charismatic; Prayer Days; Special; Miscellaneous Programs

Abbey Christian Life Center, St. Joseph Abbey, St. Benedict, Louisiana

Open to: Everyone except youths and families
Person to Contact: Father William MacCandless, Director
Address: Saint Joseph Abbey, Saint Benedict, LA 70457
Telephone: 504-892-1800
Office Hours: Switchboard open 8:00 A.M. to 10:00 P.M. daily
Notice Required: 90 days

Directory of Retreat and Renewal Centers

Archdiocesan Spirituality Center
Archdiocesan

Our center was founded for the ongoing renewal of the priests and religious of our diocese and area. The focus is on ongoing spiritual direction, individual and within support groups. Directed retreats may be made at the center upon request. We are not a retreat center per se, though we do give directed retreats. We are a spirituality center for priests and religious focusing on spiritual direction. The center offers the space and quiet atmosphere for personal time away, whether for a few hours, a day, or a weekend.

Types of Retreats/Programs Offered: Directed/Private; Prayer Days; Miscellaneous Programs
Open to: Priests, nuns, religious brothers, seminarians
Person to Contact: Sister Noel Toomey, Director
Address: 12951 Morrison Road, New Orleans, LA 70128
Telephone: 504-242-1155
Office Hours: 9:00 A.M. to 5:00 P.M. Mon.–Fri.
Notice Required: Not applicable

Ave Maria Retreat House
Oblates of Mary Immaculate

Ave Maria Retreat House is on the banks of Bayou Barataria, on 20 acres of land with many trees draped with Spanish moss. The atmosphere is serene and peaceful. Those coming here find the facility, the surroundings, and the programs to be very conducive to prayer, reflection, and renewal. Ave Maria consists of five separate buildings: a large conference hall, two dormitories with a total of fifty rooms with private baths, and an administration building, which also contains another conference hall and the dining room. These buildings are fully carpeted, air-conditioned and joined by covered walkways. The contemplative practices taught follow those of St. John of the Cross and St. Theresa of Avila.

Types of Retreats/Programs Offered: Directed/Private; Hermitage/Solitary; Charismatic; Prayer Days; Encounters; Special for the Handicapped
Open to: Everyone except families
Person to Contact: Father Dan Schuckenbrock, Director
Address: Rt. 1, Box 0368AB, Marrero, LA 70072
Telephone: 504-689-3837
Office Hours: 9:00 A.M. to 4:30 P.M.
Notice Required: Variable

Cenacle Retreat House
Religious of the Cenacle

Our retreat house is in Metairie, a suburb of New Orleans, on Lake Pontchartrain. There are approximately 50 private rooms with a shared bath between two rooms. Most of the weekends are silent preached retreats open only to women. We offer some specialized programs to men and women. We are always open to having directed retreatants and private retreatants. There is a large meeting room where group sessions are held. The chapel is open at all times, and there is a small prayer room where people can pray sitting on the floor. There are grounds around the house and access to the lake over the levee in front of the house. The Cenacle Sisters are trained as spiritual directors and are assigned each retreatant for a session during the weekend retreats. We have a smoke-free environment, with smoking permitted only in the large parlor. No shorts may be worn in the meetings, the chapel, or the dining room. Closed 2 weeks in June, 1 week in August, and a few days at Christmas and Easter.

Types of Retreats/Programs Offered: Directed/Group; Directed/Private; Conference; Hermitage/Solitary; Ecumenical; Prayer Days; Special; Miscellaneous Programs
Open to: Everyone except youths and families; mostly women
Person to Contact: Sister Barbara Menard, Ministry Coordinator
Address: 5500 St. Mary Street, P.O. Box 8115, Metairie, LA 70011

Telephone: 504-887-1420
Office Hours: 8:30 A.M. to 4:30 P.M.
Notice Required: Variable

Jesuit Spirituality Center
Society of Jesus

The Jesuit Spirituality Center is in the heart of Acadian country, 150 miles west of New Orleans and 11 miles north of Lafayette. The natural beauty of rural Louisiana, the historic setting of St. Charles College, and the year-round mild climate make it an ideal setting for prayer and discernment. All the scheduled retreats, unless otherwise indicated, are individually directed. A directed retreat at the spirituality center is a personal guided prayer experience of 5, 8, or 30 days, in which the retreatant follows the dynamics of the spiritual exercises of St. Ignatius. Each is assigned a director with whom the retreatant meets daily for reflection and spiritual discernment. Silence, both interior and exterior, is a necessary condition for the efficacy of a directed retreat.

Types of Retreats/Programs Offered: Directed/Private; Special; Miscellaneous Programs
Open to: Everyone except youths, families, and couples
Person to Contact: Father Thomas J. Madden, Director
Address: St. Charles College, Grand Coteau, LA 70541-1003
Telephone: 318-662-5251
Office Hours: 8:00 A.M. to 5:00 P.M.
Notice Required: Variable; 1 month for June and July

Maryhill Renewal Center
Diocesan

Maryhill Renewal Center is on a scenic and peaceful 184-acre woodland tract north of Pineville. It provides space, time, and environment for the recognition, enhancement, and

Maryhill Renewal Center, Pineville, Louisiana

implementation of lifelong religious learning, formation, and spiritual development. Facilities include some modern motel-like double bedrooms with private baths, 4 suites for private retreats or family get-aways, conference and meeting rooms, and several rustic buildings. Owned and operated by the Diocese of Alexandria, Louisiana, it is available to churches of all denominations, civic clubs, and nonprofit organizations for retreats, meetings, seminars, and overnight programs.

Types of Retreats/Programs Offered: Directed/Group; Directed/Private; Conference; Hermitage/Solitary; Ecumenical; Charismatic; Prayer Days; Parent-Teen; Marriage Encounter; Special
Open to: Everyone
Person to Contact: Sister Ann Lacour, Executive Director
Address: 600 Maryhill Road, Pineville, LA 71360
Telephone: 318-640-1378
Office Hours: 8:00 A.M. to 5:00 P.M.
Notice Required: 1 month

Our Lady of the Oaks
Jesuit

Description not available.

Types of Retreats/Programs Offered: Conference
Open to: Everyone except youths and families
Person to Contact: Father Babb, Director
Address: P.O. Drawer D, Grand Coteau, LA 70541
Telephone: 316-662-5410
Office Hours: 8:00 A.M. to 4:00 P.M. weekdays
Notice Required: Women, 1 year; men, 3 months

Rosaryville Spirit Life Center
St. Mary's Dominican Sisters

Located an hour from New Orleans, Rosaryville is a place for renewal of life—for the reflection, creativity and integration that the demands of everyday time and space make difficult. Rosary Hall houses the chapel, 2 dining rooms, gift shop, conference room, library, and staff offices. St. John's Hall next door houses conference rooms, and private and double occupancy bedrooms. Kateri Hall, a gym converted to dormitories with bunk beds, is primarily for use by youths groups; it also has a spacious recreation/conference area. There are a swimming pool and picnic area on the grounds. Rosaryville sponsors and hosts individual and group programs for clergy, religious, and laity. It also hosts youth retreats and summer camps in separate facilities.

Types of Retreats/Programs Offered: Directed/Group; Directed/Private; Ecumenical; Charismatic; Prayer Days; Parent-Teen; Special
Open to: Everyone
Person to Contact: Sister M. Paulette Paille, Director
Address: 400 Rosaryville Road, Ponchatoula, LA 70454
Telephone: 504-294-5039

Office Hours: 9:00 A.M. to 5:00 P.M.
Notice Required: 3 to 6 months

St. Mary's Dominican Conference Center
Dominican

St. Mary's is in a university area of New Orleans one block from a streetcar line and two blocks from beautiful Audubon Park. Our grounds include a patio and courtyard, and a walking/jogging path is nearby in the park. We are a conference center for sponsored or hosted retreats, conferences, seminars, workshops, days of renewal, etc. We also offer individuals spiritual direction, counseling, sabbatical housing, and respite from family demands. The conference center has 5 separate areas of varying capacity, 2 chapels, and each air-conditioned bedroom is adjacent to a shower/restroom. We are a non-smoking facility; smoking areas are provided outside.

Types of Retreats/Programs Offered: Directed/Group; Directed/Private; Conference; Hermitage/Solitary; Ecumenical; Prayer Days; Special for Grief; Miscellaneous Programs
Open to: Everyone except youths and families
Person to Contact: Sister Mary Ann Culotta, Director
Address: 540 Broadway, New Orleans, LA 70118
Telephone: 504-861-8711
Office Hours: 9:00 A.M. to 5:00 P.M.
Notice Required: 2 weeks to a year for weekends

Maine

Marie-Joseph Spiritual Center
Presentation of Mary

Once a grand old resort hotel, the Marie-Joseph Spiritual Center sits in quiet seclusion on a sandy point jutting into the Atlantic Ocean on the coast of Maine. Surrounded by stretches of salt marsh, clean sandy beaches, rock-lined coastal areas, and a

Marie Joseph Spiritual Center, Biddeford, Maine

wildlife sanctuary, the setting is beautiful, peaceful, serene, and occasionally awesome in its grandeur. The resident Sisters personally guide retreats and give days of renewal, as well as providing an environment and services that encourage individuals or groups to spend one day or many in personal reflection. Practices taught include the Ignatian Exercises. June, July, and August are limited to Sisters only.

Types of Retreats/Programs Offered: Directed/Group; Directed/Private; Conference; Hermitage/Solitary; Charismatic; Prayer Days; Engaged Encounter; Special; Miscellaneous Programs
Open to: Everyone except youths
Person to Contact: Sister Marie May Lausier, Director of Center Activities
Address: R.F.D. #2, Biddeford, ME 04005
Telephone: 207-284-5671
Office Hours: 9:00 A.M. to 4:30 P.M.
Notice Required: Minimum 1 week

Maryland

Bon Secours Spiritual Center
Sisters of Bon Secours

Set in rolling hills amidst 300 acres of Maryland countryside, Bon Secours Spiritual Center is a perfect setting for reflection, prayer, and work. The center building is a large stone structure, rich with simplicity and offering a diversity of meeting rooms. Bon Secours facilities include single rooms, conference and dining rooms for large and small groups, and a chapel and oratory. There are a swimming pool, a meditation garden, and nature walks in a nearby forest. In addition to hosting a variety of meetings, conferences, and workshops, we offer our facility and the services of our retreat staff to persons who desire solitude for prayer and reflection.

Types of Retreats/Programs Offered: Directed/Private; Conference; Ecumenical; Prayer Days; Special
Open to: Everyone except youths and families
Person to Contact: Mrs. Shirley W. Hawes, Administrator
Address: P.O. Box 278, Marriottsville, MD 21104
Telephone: 301-442-1320
Office Hours: 9:00 A.M. to 4:30 P.M.
Notice Required: 6 months to 1 year for weekends; 3 months for weekdays

Loyola-on-the-Potomac Retreat House
Society of Jesus (Jesuit)

Description not available.

Types of Retreats/Programs Offered: Directed/Group; Directed/Private; Conference; Hermitage/Solitary; Charismatic; Prayer Days; Special
Open to: Everyone except families
Person to Contact: Jo Ann Queen, Executive Secretary
Address: Faulkner, MD 20632

Telephone: 301-870-3515
Office Hours: 9:30 A.M. to 3:30 P.M.
Notice Required: Variable

Manresa-on-Severn
Society of Jesus (Jesuit)

On the Severn River overlooking historic Annapolis and the beautiful Chesapeake Bay, Manresa-on-Severn is a retreat and renewal center staffed by the Jesuits of the Maryland Province, a Religious Sister, and a married couple. The house has 3 floors and no elevator, but all of the retreat rooms have individually controlled heat and air-conditioning. Although the work is based on the spiritual exercises of St. Ignatius, from September to May the most common retreats at the center are weekend retreats or single days of recollection. Summer is primarily devoted to six-to-eight-day retreats and workshops.

Types of Retreats/Programs Offered: Directed/Group; Directed/Private; Conference; Hermitage/Solitary; Ecumenical; Charismatic; Prayer Days; Parent-Teen; Encounters; Special; Miscellaneous Programs
Open to: Everyone
Person to Contact: Lucille Oliver, Office Manager, or Father Joseph A. Currie, Director
Address: 85 Manresa Drive, Annapolis, MD 21401
Telephone: 301-974-0332
Office Hours: 8:30 A.M. to 6:00 P.M.
Notice Required: 1 month

St. Anthony's Wood
Secular Franciscan Order

St. Anthony's Wood, a contemplative nondirected hermitage in the Franciscan tradition, is on a 54-acre farm in the north central woods of Maryland. It is owned and operated by the Lay Women's Association of Maryland, Inc., a nonprofit organization of Secular Franciscans, with the approval of the Baltimore Archdiocese. Two overnight guests may be accommodated in the farmhouse, and may use the two hermitages in the woods during the day. An additional five individuals may utilize the farm for one day of recollection, to preserve the stillness essential to the eremitical experience. Retreatants set their own daily routine, which usually begins with a 6:00 A.M. rising for 7:00 A.M. Mass at the local parish. Because fasting is essential to the eremitical experience, meals are very light. Closed October through April.

Types of Retreats/Programs Offered: Hermitage/Solitary
Open to: Women and nuns
Person to Contact: Sue Fischer, Director/Owner
Address: 3938 Backwoods Road, Westminster, MD 21157
Telephone: 301-876-2689
Office Hours: 2:00–7:00 P.M.
Notice Required: 1 to 3 months

Massachusetts

Center for Spiritual Direction
Roman Catholic

Our primary work is individual spiritual direction. Although we do conduct weekend, 8-day, and even 30-day retreats at other centers, we do not have overnight facilities. Using space provided by the Mercy Hospital, the center opened in 1976 under the supervision of the Center for Religious Development of Cambridge, Massachusetts; approval was given by Bishop Christopher J. Weldon in 1978. The center realizes that a consistent relationship with another person is helpful in understanding the movement of God in our lives. Services are provided by a team of professionally qualified men and women in the ministry of spiritual direction. Closed June, July, and August.

Types of Retreats/Programs Offered: Directed/Group; Directed/Private; Conference; Prayer Days; Miscellaneous Programs
Open to: Everyone except youths and families
Person to Contact: Sister Barbara Farrell, Coordinator
Address: Memorial House: Mercy Hospital, Carew Street, Springfield, MA 01101-9012
Telephone: 413-734-8843 or 788-0195
Office Hours: As needed
Notice Required: Variable

The Jesuit Center
Society of Jesus (Jesuit)

All our retreats are given within the movement of daily life; we offer no enclosed retreats. There is a 12-week group retreat in which participants meet one evening a week for 12 weeks. The 12-week individual retreat is for those who are able and willing to pray each day for 12 weeks and also to meet with a member of our staff once a week at the center. A 30-week individual retreat based on the full Ignatian Exercises and requiring a serious commitment of time and energy for daily prayer and a weekly meeting at the center is also offered.

Types of Retreats/Programs Offered: Directed/Group; Directed/Private
Open to: Everyone except youths and families
Person to Contact: Father John Surette, Director
Address: Sullivan Square, Charlestown, MA 02129
Telephone: 617-242-2550
Office Hours: 9:00 A.M. to 2:00 P.M.
Notice Required: 1 month

LaSalette Center for Christian Living
LaSalette Missionary

Do you need a space for quiet and reflection in the overwhelming busyness of your life? Do you need to slow down and experience the goodness of the Lord? Come and rest awhile . . . spend the day . . . stay overnight . . . seek out direction on your own, or take part in one of our many retreat offerings. In whatever way you feel the Spirit calling you to reflection and renewal, please come! We open our doors and our hearts to you in Christian hospitality. May you go away refreshed, having experienced once more the peace and reconciliation of our gracious God. Five family retreats per year.

Types of Retreats/Programs Offered: Directed/Group; Directed/Private; Conference; Charismatic; Prayer Days; Parent-Teen; Marriage Encounter; Cursillos; Special; Miscellaneous Programs
Open to: Everyone
Person to Contact: Father Gilles Genest, Co-Director
Address: Attleboro, MA 02703
Telephone: 508-222-8530
Office Hours: 9:00 A.M. to 5:00 P.M.
Notice Required: 2 to 3 weeks

Marian Center
Daughters of the Heart of Mary

Formerly a large family home nestled in a wooded area, Marian Center was a flourishing traditional retreat center from the time of its purchase by the Daughters of Mary in 1954 to 1984, when much of the house, including a new wing, was converted to meet the changing needs of the religious community. At present, only the first floor of Marian Center is used for retreat events, which precludes any overnight functions. Nevertheless, the center runs a full schedule of day and evening spiritual direction and education programs. It has also hosted regional and national meetings of various church and service groups, with overnight accommodations provided by nearby motels. Marian Center is lovely, peaceful, and known for its hospitality.

Types of Retreats/Programs Offered: Directed/Group; Conference; Hermitage/Solitary; Ecumenical; Charismatic; Prayer Days; Parent-Teen; Special; Miscellaneous Programs

Open to: Everyone
Person to Contact: Sister Virginia Towner, Ministry Coordinator
Address: 1365 Northampton Street, Holyoke, MA 01040
Telephone: 413-533-7171
Office Hours: 9:00 A.M. to 5:00 P.M.
Notice Required: Prefer at least 2 to 3 days

Miramar Retreat Center
Divine Word Missionaries

Miramar Retreat Center is on the South Shore overlooking Duxbury and Cape Cod bays from fields where the Wampanoag Indians once lived and where the Pilgrims settled. Miramar (a Spanish word meaning "view of the sea") was opened as a seminary by Divine Word Missionaries in 1922 and as a retreat center in 1948. We provide retreats for lay people, clergy and religious, single persons and married couples, all ages and groups, youths, religious educators, parish councils, special programs for separated, widowed, or divorced. Miramar has single or double rooms with private baths; its extensive grounds provide areas for reflection.

Types of Retreats/Programs Offered: Directed/Group; Directed/Private; Conference; Hermitage/Solitary; Prayer Days; Miscellaneous Programs
Open to: Everyone except families
Person to Contact: Father Paul J. Connors, Director
Address: Box M, Duxbury, MA 02331
Telephone: 617-585-2460
Office Hours: 9:00 A.M. to 5:00 P.M.
Notice Required: 1 week

St. Joseph's Abbey Retreat House
Cistercian (Trappist)

We have a small retreat house in which we provide retreats twice every week for laymen and priests. The weekend retreat begins on Friday afternoon and ends on Sunday after lunch. The midweek retreat extends from Monday afternoon until Friday morning. Our retreat schedule is arranged to afford ample time for prayer, rest, and reading. While our guests are not in direct contact with the monastic community, we try to keep the retreat house in close conformity with our own contemplative way of life. Meditation, reading and a spirit of contemplative quiet are encouraged. There is one conference a day given by a retreat master from the abbey, who is also available for confessions and private talks. The retreatants are encouraged to attend the daily community Eucharist and the Liturgy of the Hours in the abbey church.

Types of Retreats/Programs Offered: Directed/Group
Open to: Men and priests
Person to Contact: Father Damian Carr, Guestmaster
Address: St. Joseph's Abbey, Spencer, MA 01562
Telephone: 508-885-3010
Office Hours: 9:00 A.M. to 8:00 P.M.
Notice Required: Reservations not accepted more than 6 months in advance

St. Stephen Priory Spiritual Life Center
Dominican Order of Men; staffed by Sisters of Notre Dame

Twenty miles southwest of downtown Boston, the center offers 76 acres of suburban woodlands bordering the Charles River. The property houses the original turn-of-the-century manor, with its additional wing built in 1950, a second retreat building called Siena House, and Julie House, the ministry house for women staff persons. Single and double rooms are available. There are a large swimming pool for the summer, tennis, handball, and basketball courts, an exercise area, a stereo room, a canoe, and bicycles. Trails through the woods and along the river are inviting for walking or hiking. The center is the home of a Dominican community of men, and 3 Sisters of Notre Dame de Namur staff persons live in the ministry house.

Types of Retreats/Programs Offered: Directed/Group; Directed/Private; Hermitage/Solitary; Prayer Days; Encounters; Special; Miscellaneous Programs
Open to: Everyone except youths and families
Person to Contact: Father John Burchill, Program Director
Address: 20 Glen Street, P.O. Box 370, Dover, MA 02030
Telephone: 508-785-0124
Office Hours: 9:00 A.M. to 4:30 P.M.

Society of St. John the Evangelist: Emery House
Anglican

The Society of St. John the Evangelist is a community of lay and ordained men who take life vows of poverty, celibacy, and obedience. Founded by Richard Meux Benson in Oxford, England, in 1866, the society is the oldest Anglican religious order for men. Emery House is our home and is opened to guests for daylong workshops and conferences, and for individual and group retreats from one day to one week. All services of worship, celebrated from the Book of Common Prayer, are open to our guests and to the public. Emery House is a retreat center of the society about one hour's drive north from Boston. It is set in more than 120 acres of field and woodland bounded by the Merrimack and Artichoke rivers and adjacent to a beautiful 400-acre state park. The main house dates from the eighteenth century. In 1987 the Chapel of the Transfiguration, with meeting rooms below, was added to the house. There are also the Coburn Hermitages, a cluster of 5 houses designed for solitary and group use. Facilities include only one double room.

Types of Retreats/Programs Offered: Directed/Group; Directed/Private; Hermitage/Solitary; Special
Open to: Everyone except youths and families
Person to Contact: Guestmaster
Address: Emery Lane, West Newbury, MA 01985
Office Hours: 9:00 A.M. to 5:00 P.M. weekdays
Notice Required: Variable

Society of St. John the Evangelist: Guest House
Anglican

The Society of St. John the Evangelist is a community of lay and ordained men who take life vows of poverty, celibacy, and obedience. Founded by Richard Meux Benson in Oxford, England, in 1866, the society is the oldest Anglican religious order for men. The guest house is our home and is opened to guests for daylong workshops and conferences and for individual and group retreats from one day to one week. All services of worship, celebrated from the Book of Common Prayer, are open to our guests and to the public. The guest house is on the Charles River just a short walk from Harvard University and the Episcopal Divinity School. Only one double room. Closed June through August.

Types of Retreats/Programs Offered: Directed/Group; Directed/Private; Hermitage/Solitary; Special
Open to: Everyone except youths and families
Person to Contact: Leith Speiden, Guest House Assistant
Address: 980 Memorial Drive, Cambridge, MA 02138
Telephone: 617-876-3037
Office Hours: 9:00 A.M. to 5:00 P.M. weekdays
Notice Required: Variable

Michigan

Augustine Center
Diocesan

At the site of the Sacramentine Monastery, our center overlooks Crooked Lake, a popular resort area in northern Michigan. Public access to the lake is one block from the center, and we are six miles from Alpine ski areas. Offering 22 acres of woods for walking, hiking, or cross-country skiing, we provide an ideal setting with a tranquil atmosphere for reflection, recreation, renewal, and decision making. Single and double rooms available, all with private baths.

Augustine Center, Conway, Michigan

Types of Retreats/Programs Offered: Directed/Group; Directed/Private; Conference; Hermitage/Solitary; Ecumenical; Charismatic; Prayer Days; Marriage Encounter; Special; Miscellaneous Programs
Open to: Everyone except families

Person to Contact: Sister Barbara Hubeny, Administrative Director
Address: P.O. Box 84, Conway, MI 49722-0084
Telephone: 616-347-3657
Notice Required: Variable

Colombiere Retreat—Conference Center
Society of Jesus (Jesuits)
Colombiere Center is on 400 wooded acres just outside the historic village of Clarkston, 50 miles north of the Detroit airport and 20 miles south of the Flint airport. Rolling hills and fields provide a quiet setting. The grounds feature tennis courts, an exercise trail, a baseball field, and an indoor gymnasium. There are an indoor swimming pool, a picnic area with grills for summer, trails for cross-country skiing, and a pond for ice skating in winter. Single and double rooms available, as well as a limited number of suites with private bath and study.

Colombiere Center, Clarkston, Michigan

Types of Retreats/Programs Offered: Directed/Group; Directed/Private; Conference; Special; Miscellaneous Programs, including a 2-year program to train lay retreat/spiritual directors
Open to: Everyone except families
Person to Contact: Father Robert J. D'Amico, Director
Address: 9075 Big Lake Road, P.O. Box 139, Clarkston, MI 48016
Telephone: 313-625-5611
Office Hours: 8:00 A.M. to 5:00 P.M.
Notice Required: Prefer 1 month

Emmaus Monastery
The Emmaus Community

Committed to enabling and to celebrating the contemplative dimension of every Christian vocation, the Emmaus Community offers retreatants the silence and empty space of 80 acres of fields and wooded hills in which to explore intimacy with the triune God. With open hands, we welcome you to encounter your God in the winter solitude, in the busy germination of the planting season, in the lushness of summer's growth, and in the ripening that is autumn. A member of Retreats International, we provide space for those longing for solitude or for some involvement in our monastic, contemplative prayer life during their retreat. We are organic farmers living 60 miles from any major city.

Types of Retreats/Programs Offered: Directed/Private; Conference; Hermitage/Solitary; Ecumenical; Prayer Days; Special; Associate Program
Open to: Everyone
Person to Contact: Sister Diane L. Stier, Director
Address: 7001 Tamarack Road, Vestaburg, MI 48891
Telephone: 517-268-5494
Office Hours: Before 8:00 P.M.
Notice Required: Prefer at least 1 month

The Hermitage Community, Inc.

Mennonite

Sixty-four rolling acres with a homestead, farmland, plus 40 acres of woods with trails provide an appropriate setting to calm the soul and focus the experience of spiritual growth. The main floor of the remodeled 1899 bank barn is beamed with hand-hewn logs from a nearby tamarack swamp. This rustic but cozy center has a library, a chapel, a meeting room, a kitchen-dining area, and 8 sleeping rooms close to bathrooms. There is an apartment for longer term use and a hut about a ten-minute walk into the woods. Simple, nutritious meals are provided, as much as possible from our garden. The kitchen is open to all guests for breakfast and lunch on a self-serve basis. The evening meal is usually a time of conversation with retreatants and staff. The remainder of the time, those on retreat are encouraged to maintain silence for themselves and others.

Types of Retreats/Programs Offered: Directed/Private; Hermitage/Solitary; Prayer Days; Special; Formation Program
Open to: Everyone except youths and families
Person to Contact: H. Eugene and Mary Herr, Co-Directors and Founders
Address: 11321 Dutch Settlement, Three Rivers, MI 49093
Telephone: 616-244-8696
Office Hours: 1:00–5:00 P.M.
Notice Required: Prefer 1 month, but variable

Homes of Providence—House of Prayer

We are an ecumenical center for spiritual and personal growth, founded by Rose Marie Garvie, a woman led by God responding to the needs of the times in a very radical and creative way. We offer private retreats, days of prayer, Bible sharings, seminars, workshops, group meetings, as well as the desert experience of a hermitage. We are open to all those committed to a search for self, for their truth, to live a fuller life in response to the call of what they are meant to be and do. This is a beautiful old farmhouse in the country, situated on 60 acres, 15 of which are woods, and bordered by a river. There are a large pond with fish and a hermitage on the property. Accommodations for one family. Closed in July.

Types of Retreats/Programs Offered: Directed/Private; Hermitage/Solitary; Prayer Days; Special
Open to: Everyone
Person to Contact: Rose Marie Garvie, Founder, or Theresa Doran, Director
Address: 2475 S. Fowlerville Road, Fowlerville, MI 48836, and 3847 Old Homestead Road, Howell, MI 48843
Mailing Address: P.O. Box 1184, Fowlerville, MI 48836
Telephone: 517-223-8200 or 546-1137
Office Hours: Anytime
Notice Required: At least 1 month

Marygrove Retreat Center
Diocesan

Located on 40 acres of wooded land on picturesque Garden Bay near Lake Michigan on the Upper Peninsula, Marygrove is a retreat center that seeks to offer a quiet place. On the grounds there are many shrines plus the Stations of the Cross and walking paths. Facilities include double and single rooms. A retreat at Marygrove, whether for a day, a weekend, or a week, whether offered by others or designed by the individual, can be a time of deep renewal in faith.

Types of Retreats/Programs Offered: Directed/Group; Directed/Private; Conference; Hermitage/Solitary; Ecumenical; Charismatic; Prayer Days; Parent-Teen; Marriage Encounter; Cursillos; Special; Miscellaneous Programs
Open to: Everyone
Person to Contact: Father Timothy H. Desrochers, Director
Address: P.O. Box 38, Garden, MI 49835

Telephone: 906-644-2771
Office Hours: 9:00 A.M. to 5:00 P.M.
Notice Required: Prefer 1 month

Queen of Angels
Capuchin Franciscan

Queen of Angels Retreat Center is on 17 parklike acres, including a woods of old oak trees. The building is one-story and handicapped accessible. Facilities include private rooms, chapel, large conference room and smaller meeting rooms, library, and lounge with fireplace. Inner peace is a cry of the human heart. Each person entering Queen of Angels Retreat enjoys this peace. For a few days, the center can provide an opportunity to truly meet God and one's own inner spirit.

Types of Retreats/Programs Offered: Directed/Group; Directed/Private; Hermitage/Solitary; Ecumenical; Charismatic; Prayer Days; Special
Open to: Everyone except families
Person to Contact: Father William Alcuin, Director
Address: 3400 S. Washington Road, P.O. Box 2026, Saginaw, MI 48605
Telephone: 517-755-2149
Office Hours: 9:00 A.M. to 5:00 P.M.
Notice Required: A few weeks

St. Augustine's House
Lutheran Benedictine

St. Augustine's House is a small Lutheran religious community following the Benedictine tradition. Retreatants are invited to share in our quiet life and to participate with us in the monastic Liturgy of the Hours and also in the Holy Eucharist. Only five guest rooms are available for overnight stays. Small groups of up to 20 may make a daytime retreat with us.

Directory of Retreat and Renewal Centers 149

Types of Retreats/Programs Offered: Directed/Private; Hermitage/Solitary; Ecumenical; Prayer Days
Open to: Men, priests, religious men, non-Catholics
Person to Contact: Father Richard G. Herbel, Prior
Address: 3316 East Drahner Road, P.O. Box 125, Oxford, MI 48051
Telephone: 313-628-5155
Office Hours: 9:00 A.M.–12:00 noon; 3:00–6:00 P.M.
Notice Required: None

St. Clare Capuchin Retreat House
O.F.M. Capuchin

St. Clare Capuchin Retreat House is a Tudor mansion with 4 acres of land 50 miles north of Detroit on the St. Clair River. We work mainly with high school juniors and seniors. Retreats are offered weekly from Tuesday evening to Thursday afternoon and from Friday evening to Sunday afternoon. Closed in August. St. Clare is staffed by 3 Capuchins who are experienced in youth ministry.

Types of Retreats/Programs Offered: Directed/Group; Ecumenical; Youth; programs for handicapped and young adults
Open to: Everyone except families and couples; specialize in youths
Person to Contact: Brother Michael Graf, Director
Address: 1975 N. River Road, St. Clair, MI 48079
Telephone: 313-329-9011
Office Hours: 9:00 A.M. to 3:00 P.M. Monday through Thursday
Notice Required: 1 year

St. Paul of the Cross Retreat Center
Passionist Community

We, the Passionist retreat team, pattern our ministry on the model of St. Paul of the Cross, the founder of the Passionists and after whom this retreat center is named. We are dedicated to offering the retreat center as a resource place for all manner of Christian apostolate and ministry. Whatever advances the Kingdom of God is welcome to our facility. We are a one-level, peaceful center easily accessible off a major expressway. Facilities include rooms with private baths, a beautiful chapel, a large meeting room, and a beautiful setting for fresh air and exercise.

Types of Retreats/Programs Offered: Directed/Group; Directed/Private; Conference; Hermitage/Solitary; Ecumenical; Prayer Days; Parent-Teen; Special; Miscellaneous Programs
Open to: Everyone except families
Person to Contact: Father Patrick Brennan, Retreat Director
Address: 23333 Schoolcraft, Detroit, MI 48223
Telephone: 313-535-9563
Office Hours: 8:00 A.M. to 8:00 P.M.
Notice Required: 6 months to 1 year

Visitation—The Lord's Barn
Sisters, Servants of the Immaculate Heart of Mary

Visitation facilities are in a spacious wooded area. The Lord's Barn, a place for quiet prayer and reflection, is open to all from early morning to evening every day. Books and tapes on prayer and related topics are available in the loft. A den in the staff residence can be used for conferences and shared prayer by small groups. A small retreat house has overnight accommodations for individuals or groups up to 4. Two hermitages offer an experience of radical solitude. A room offering space and materials for creative prayer expression through art and music is available for retreatants. In the small retreat house, food is provided but retreatants cook their own meals; in the hermitages, retreatants bring their own food and cook it.

Types of Retreats/Programs Offered: Directed/Group and Conference offered off site; on-site Directed/Private; Hermitage/Solitary; Prayer Days; Special, including 30-day Ignatian Retreats;

Miscellaneous Programs including Creation and Whole Earth Spirituality
Open to: Everyone except youths and families
Person to Contact: Sister Eva Schoell, Coordinator
Address: 529 Stewart Road, Monroe, MI 48161
Telephone: 313-242-5520
Notice Required: As soon as possible; hermitages are especially in demand

Weber Center
Adrian Dominican Sisters

Weber Center, a retreat/conference center in Adrian (75 minutes from Detroit airport; 45 minutes from Toledo airport) offers a quiet environment for retreatants to "enter their center." In a reflective, hospitable atmosphere, retreatants enjoy the advantages of single bedrooms, staff spiritual directors,

Weber Center, Adrian, Michigan

comfortable and pleasant meeting space, convenient laundry and kitchen areas, book and gift shop, women's resource center, and scenic rural-setting campus. Family accommodations are available, but family groups are no longer emphasized at this center.

Types of Retreats/Programs Offered: Directed/Group; Directed/Private; Conference; Hermitage/Solitary; Ecumenical; Prayer Days; Special; Miscellaneous Programs
Open to: Everyone except youths and families
Person to Contact: Sister Jodie Screes, Director
Address: 1257 E. Siena Heights Drive, Adrian, MI 49221
Telephone: 517-263-7088
Office Hours: 8:30 A.M. to 5:00 P.M.
Notice Required: 1 month

Minnesota

Assisi Community Center
Sisters of St. Francis—Congregation of Our Lady of Lourdes

Assisi Community Center serves a variety of people, both religious and laypersons of all faiths. The short-term retreats and days of prayer are planned around the Great Commandment to serve God, self, and neighbor. The longer-term retreats are mainly for the Sisters in our community but are open to others. Our center also rents space to ecumenical groups that meet our educational, cultural, or spiritual criteria.

Types of Retreats/Programs Offered: Directed/Group; Directed/Private; Conference; Hermitage/Solitary; Ecumenical; Prayer Days; Encounters; Special; Miscellaneous Programs
Open to: Everyone
Person to Contact: Sister Colleen Byron, Coordinator of Programs
Address: Box 4900, Rochester, MN 55903
Telephone: 507-289-0821

Office Hours: 8:30 A.M. to 4:30 P.M.
Notice Required: Variable

Benedictine Center
Benedictine

We, the Benedictines of St. Paul's Priory, offer the warmth of our monastic home and peaceful grounds to persons of all faiths and cultural traditions and races to "listen with the ears of your heart" to where God is calling you. All are welcome to worship with our Benedictine community in Eucharist and Liturgy of the Hours, as well as to use our two chapels for quiet prayer. Facilities include single and double rooms, and over 90 acres of wooded land and meadow are available for walks and other outdoor activities.

Types of Retreats/Programs Offered: Directed/Group; Directed/Private; Conference; Hermitage/Solitary; Prayer Days; Special
Open to: Everyone
Person to Contact: Sister Mary White, Center Director
Address: 2675 E. Larpenteur Avenue, St. Paul, MN 55109
Telephone: 612-777-7251
Office Hours: 9:00 A.M. to 4:30 P.M.
Notice Required: Minimum 2 days

Cenacle Retreat House
Religious of the Cenacle

Founded in 1949, the Cenacle offers retreats and days of prayer for groups, directed retreats and days for individuals, spiritual direction, and workshops on many topics related to the inner journey. The Cenacle is a Christian community grounded in the fidelity of a loving God. It is also a place providing an atmosphere of prayer and welcome, in which all who come may connect with God and one another. Listening to and more fully knowing the reality of God in their lives, those who come are enabled to give to others of what they have received.

Types of Retreats/Programs Offered: Directed/Group; Directed/Private; Conference; Hermitage/Solitary; Ecumenical; Charismatic; Prayer Days; Special; Miscellaneous Programs
Open to: Everyone except youths and families
Person to Contact: Sister Mary Sharon Riley, Coordinator of Ministry
Address: 1221 Wayzata Boulevard, Wayzata, MN 55391
Telephone: 612-473-7308
Office Hours: 8:00 A.M. to 4:30 P.M.
Notice Required: Variable; 1 month advised

Christian Brothers Retreat Center
F.S.C.

Cut back in the woodlands along the St. Croix River, just ten miles north of Stillwater, the center's 50 acres provide an ideal setting for reflection, spiritual renewal, and deliberation. The center offers, under one roof, single guest rooms, large and small meeting rooms, a fellowship room, a dining room, and chapels. For outdoor recreation, there are a swimming pool and a tennis court in warm weather. Guests can stroll around the 4-acre lake or enjoy the beautiful St. Croix River. Trails for biking and cross-country skiing are available at nearby O'Brien State Park. At present we host groups almost exclusively, and we are working toward offering family support programs. Once a month we offer a prayer day called "Celebrating Women."

Types of Retreats/Programs Offered: Directed/Group; Directed/Private; Conference; Prayer Days; Parent-Teen; Special
Open to: Everyone
Person to Contact: Brother Laurence Walther, Administrator
Address: 15525 St. Croix Trail North, Marine on St. Croix, MN 55047
Telephone: 612-433-2486

Office Hours: 9:00 A.M. to 5:00 P.M. daily
Notice Required: 1 year

The Dwelling Place
Franciscan Sisters of Little Falls

The Dwelling Place offers a quiet atmosphere where it is easy to reflect on one's own life and relationship with God and others. There are private rooms, a prayer room, and library. It is located on our Motherhouse campus with adequate space for walking and a nature trail. There are an indoor swimming pool, sauna, hot tub, and exercise room. Full body massage is also available. Located about one-half mile from us, but still on campus and linked with The Dwelling Place, are two hermitages in our pine forest. These also are available to the retreatants. We usually ask our retreatants to bring only themselves, notebook and pencil, and relaxing clothes. Bibles are supplied. Next door is St. Francis Center, which offers a wide variety of specialized retreats and programs. Together, we offer something for everyone.

Types of Retreats/Programs Offered: Directed/Group; Directed/Private; Conference; Hermitage/Solitary; Special
Open to: Everyone except youths and families
Person to Contact: Sister Lillian Kroll, Director
Address: 116 8th Avenue S.E., Little Falls, MN 56345
Telephone: 612-632-2981
Office Hours: 8:00 A.M.–12:00 noon; 2:00–4:00 P.M.
Notice Required: Minimum 2 weeks

Maryhill Renewal Center
Daughters of the Heart of Mary

Description not available.

Types of Retreats/Programs Offered: Directed/Group; Directed/Private; Conference; Hermitage/Solitary; Prayer Days; Special; Miscellaneous Programs

Open to: Everyone
Person to Contact: Sister Theresa Pasquarello, Program Director
Address: 260 Summit Avenue, St. Paul, MN 55102
Telephone: 612-224-8566
Office Hours: 9 A.M. to 4 P.M. weekdays
Notice Required: Variable

McCabe Renewal Center
Benedictines from St. Scholastica Priory in Duluth

McCabe Renewal Center is an ecumenical retreat and renewal center for persons of all ages, sponsored by the Benedictine Sisters of St. Scholastica Priory in Duluth. Programs sponsored and hosted by the center integrate spiritual development with personal growth, psychology, and social responsibility in an environment which is aesthetically pleasing, comfortable, and peace-filled. Our center is on spacious grounds in the Hunter's Park area of Duluth. The area is scenic and beautiful at all seasons and lends itself to leisure, relaxation, and reflection. McCabe Renewal Center provides a smoke-free environment for your comfort.

Types of Retreats/Programs Offered: Directed/Group; Directed/Private; Conference; Hermitage/Solitary; Ecumenical; Prayer Days; Engaged Encounter; Special; Miscellaneous Programs
Open to: Everyone except families
Person to Contact: Sister Martha Bechtold, Director
Address: 2125 Abbotsford Avenue, Duluth, MN 55803
Telephone: 218-724-5266
Office Hours: Anytime
Notice Required: 1 week

St. Francis Center
Franciscan Sisters of Little Falls

The mission of St. Francis Center is to serve the spiritual, educational, health, social, aesthetic, and psychological needs of persons in a holistic, Christian manner. The center includes: the St.

Clare Resource Center, a religious library; the St. Francis Christian Development Center for evangelization and lay ministry; the St. Francis Health and Recreation Center; St. Francis Hospitality Services for workshops, seminars, meetings, conventions, and retreats; the St. Francis Music Center; and Wholistic Growth Resources, a 9-month residential program for holistic living. Located 2 hours from the airport, facilities include pool and sauna, massage, hot tub, and exercise trail. Affiliated with The Dwelling Place (see separate entry) located adjacent to it.

Types of Retreats/Programs Offered: Directed/Group; Directed/Private; Conference; Hermitage/Solitary; Ecumenical; Prayer Days; Encounters; Special; Miscellaneous Programs
Open to: Everyone
Person to Contact: Larry Engholm, Chief Executive Officer; Lillian Kroll, Director of Retreats; Bob Barnes, Director of Outreach; Roberta Zimmer, Director of Hospitality
Address: 116 8th Avenue S.E., Little Falls, MN 56345
Telephone: 612-632-2617
Office Hours: 8:00 A.M. to 5:00 P.M.
Notice Required: 1 month

Spiritual Journey Ministries
Franciscan Sisters

Spiritual Journey Ministries is a day renewal center operating out of St. Joseph's Convent as a part of the Franciscan Sisters of Little Falls outreach program. Spiritual Journey Ministries is the name given to a variety of spiritual, educational, and holistic activities designed to assist, refresh, encourage, and guide persons to walk the journey of life in a deep and meaningful way. As well as days of retreat and recollection, Spiritual Journey Ministries offers workshops and seminars in theology, spirituality, human development, and wellness. No overnight accommodations.

Types of Retreats/Programs Offered: Conference; Prayer Days; Miscellaneous Programs
Open to: Everyone except youths and families

Person to Contact: Sister Alexandra Gamades, Director
Address: 106 N. 7th Avenue, Waite Park, MN 56387
Telephone: 612-253-8850
Office Hours: 9:00 A.M. to 9:00 P.M.
Notice Required: 24 hours

Tau Center
Sisters of St. Francis

Tau Center is in the beautiful Hiawatha Valley region of the Mississippi River in southeastern Minnesota, adjacent to a women's college, in the west end of the city about a half hour from the LaCrosse airport. Franciscan hospitality is a tradition expressed through retreats and programs sponsored and hosted by the center for various individuals, church groups, and community agencies desiring time and space for prayer, work, and study. The Sisters of St. Francis desire that all who come to Tau Center receive the gift of Christ's peace.

Types of Retreats/Programs Offered: Directed/Group; Directed/Private; Conference; Hermitage/Solitary; Ecumenical; Charismatic; Prayer Days; Parent-Teen; Encounters; Special; Miscellaneous Programs
Open to: Everyone
Person to Contact: Sister Mary Ann Hoffmann, Co-Director
Address: 511 Hilbert, Winona, MN 55987
Telephone: 507-454-2993
Office Hours: 9:00 A.M. to 5:00 P.M. Monday through Saturday
Notice Required: 1 week to several months

Villa Maria Ecumenical Retreat Center
Ursuline Sisters

Villa Maria Center is on 169 acres of woodlands near the shores of Lake Pepin and completely surrounded by Frontenac State

Park. A resident community of Ursuline Sisters extends to guests warm hospitality, welcome, and a spirit of prayerfulness. Retreatants may enjoy daily liturgy, quiet, long walks amid natural surroundings, swimming in an indoor pool, recreating in the gymnasium or on the tennis courts, and delicious country style buffet meals. Spiritual direction is available for those who wish. Housing includes family and youth camp facilities, a fifty-three room conference center, and a solitary hermitage. Closed Holy Week and Christmas Day.

Types of Retreats/Programs Offered: Directed/Group; Directed/Private; Conference; Hermitage/Solitary; Ecumenical; Charismatic; Prayer Days; Engaged Encounter; Special; Miscellaneous Programs
Open to: Everyone
Person to Contact: Sister Chabanel Mathison, Director
Address: Frontenac, MN 55026
Telephone: 612-345-3455
Office Hours: 9:30 A.M. to 12:30 P.M. daily; 1:00–3:00 P.M. weekdays
Notice Required: Individuals, 24–48 hours; groups, 1 year

Mississippi

The Dwelling Place
Dubuque Franciscan

The Dwelling Place is a Franciscan prayer center on the site of a former Trappist monastery. Situated on a 17-acre pine-studded tract in east central Mississippi, the prayer center contains a retreat house, hermitage, chapel, library, and spacious grounds. Five private retreat rooms are available in the retreat house; for those who so desire, there is the option of the hermitage (trailer). The Portiuncula chapel and library offer space for prayer, study, and reflection. Adjacent grazing land with woods and ponds is available for walking and exploring.

Types of Retreats/Programs Offered: Directed/Group; Directed/Private; Hermitage/Solitary; Ecumenical; Prayer Days; Miscellaneous Programs
Open to: Everyone except youths and families
Person to Contact: Sister Clare Van Lent, Director
Address: Star Route Box 126, Brooksville, MS 39739
Telephone: 601-738-5348
Office Hours: 8:30 A.M. to 4:30 P.M. daily
Notice Required: At least 1 week

Missouri

Caroline Hall Retreat and Conference Center
School Sisters of Notre Dame

Caroline Hall, a modern retreat and conference facility, is in South St. Louis County overlooking the Mississippi River just north of historic Jefferson Barracks Park. The facility adjoins the School Sisters of Notre Dame Motherhouse, which is surrounded by acres of rolling hills, beautifully landscaped and spacious, an ideal setting for personal and spiritual growth. Caroline Hall is a hosting facility, and its staff members are dedicated to offering an atmosphere of warm hospitality and presence to the needs of all guests. Facilities include a variety of meeting rooms, private bedrooms, dormitory space, a large dining room, prayer room, lounges, recreational space, a gym and indoor swimming pool. Closed end of August to near end of September.

Types of Retreats/Programs Offered: Directed/Group; Conference; Ecumenical; Charismatic; Prayer Days; Engaged Encounter; Miscellaneous Programs
Open to: Everyone
Person to Contact: Sister Joseph Miriam Nemec, Coordinator
Address: 320 E. Ripa Avenue, St. Louis, MO 63125
Telephone: 314-544-4756
Office Hours: 9:00 A.M. to 12:00 noon weekdays
Notice Required: Variable

Center for Spirituality, St. Louis, Missouri

Center for Spirituality
Sisters of St. Joseph of Carondelet

The Center for Spirituality is a unit within the Provincial House of the Sisters of St. Joseph of Carondelet. Located in one of the oldest neighborhoods in St. Louis, the brick and stone complex sits on a high spot of land with a view of the Mississippi River from its quiet enclosed yard. The center includes a beautiful chapel, 6 guest rooms for female retreatants, a large meeting room, a tape and book library, and a private kitchen area. (Meals may be taken privately or in the main dining room of the Provincial House.) There is also a serene cloistered courtyard, which is a lovely spot for meditation. Through retreats, days of prayer, and special programs, the center provides a quiet atmosphere for listening to the Lord as he speaks to your life.

Types of Retreats/Programs Offered: Directed/Private; Hermitage/Solitary; Prayer Days; Special; Miscellaneous Programs
Open to: Everyone except families
Person to Contact: Sister Doris Mattingly, Coordinator
Address: Sisters of St. Joseph, 6400 Minnesota, St. Louis, MO 63111
Telephone: 314-481-8573

Office Hours: 8:30 A.M. to 4:30 P.M.
Notice Required: Variable

Christina House Hermitages
Olivetan Benedictines of Pecos, New Mexico

Christina House is a product of the charismatic renewal that is part of the broader renewal of the Roman Catholic Church mandated by Vatican Council II. For those seeking deep communion with the Lord through prolonged prayer and solitude, Christina House provides underground hermitages—earth homes—that overlook the Mississippi River. These units are built forty feet from each other and provide maximum privacy and silence for the hermits. The setting is one of peaceful and scenic beauty. The hermitages are available for use year-round. Each is equipped with appliances and utensils for light cooking and has its own bath. Basics are supplied. Morning prayer, the Eucharist, and evening prayer are usually celebrated daily in the Christina House chapel.

Types of Retreats/Programs Offered: Directed/Private; Hermitage/Solitary
Open to: Everyone except families
Person to Contact: Father Wilfrid Tunink, Director
Address: Abbey Lane, P.O. Box 619, Pevely, MO 63070-0619
Telephone: 314-479-3697
Office Hours: Anytime
Notice Required: Anytime

Franciscan Prayer Center
Sisters of St. Francis of the Holy Eucharist

The Franciscan Prayer Center is on the grounds of the Motherhouse of the Sisters of St. Francis of the Holy Eucharist. The campus includes 82 acres of natural surroundings, including secluded woods, walking trails, open fields, and a fish pond, and access to bicycling, jogging areas, tennis courts, parks, and a swimming pool. In addition to traditional retreat facilities, the center also includes a hermitage. The staff offers a variety of retreats and programs that may be presented at the center or in homes or parishes, depending on the needs of the group or individual. Set a day or more aside and come walk our grounds, share our home, enjoy our friendship, spend time in our hermitage, celebrate the Sacrament of Peace, pray with us.

Types of Retreats/Programs Offered: Directed/Group; Directed/Private; Conference; Hermitage/Solitary; Ecumenical; Charismatic; Prayer Days; Marriage Encounter; Cursillos; Special; Miscellaneous Programs
Open to: Everyone
Person to Contact: Sister Josephine Boyles, Administrator
Address: 2100 North Noland Road, Independence, MO 64050
Telephone: 816-252-1703
Office Hours: 8 A.M. to 4:30 P.M.
Notice Required: Variable

II Ritiro (Little Retreat)
Servants of the Paraclete

Less than an hour from downtown St. Louis, II Ritiro was founded in the late 1970s as a retreat facility for priests and brothers who are seeking time for quiet prayer within an affirming community. The center is situated on nearly 100 acres of beautiful wooded rolling hills in the foothills of the Ozarks, with swimming facilities and hiking trails. In addition to the main facilities, there is a beautiful hermitage on a wooded hillside. Completely self-contained with its own kitchen, heat and air-conditioning, it provides an ideal environment for a private retreat, with a rustic chapel nearby for reflection. Retreatants are invited to join the II Ritiro Community in morning prayer, Liturgy, afternoon adoration and evening prayer.

Types of Retreats/Programs Offered: Directed/Private; Conference; Hermitage/Solitary; Ecumenical; Prayer Days; Special
Open to: Priests and male religious
Person to Contact: Father Bertin Miller, Retreat Director
Address: P.O. Box 281, Dittmer, MO 63023
Telephone: 314-677-5140
Office Hours: 7:30 A.M. to 4:00 P.M.
Notice Required: 1 month

Maria Fonte Solitude
Society of Our Mother of Peace

Separate hermitages in a wooded environment emphasize the spiritual benefits of solitude—separation from diversions, socializing, and affluence—in order to experience radical need for God and desire for a more intimate relationship with Him. Beginners are helped to make good use of solitude, and spiritual direction is available for anyone desiring it. Hermitages are very simple but equipped with light, heat, air-conditioning, shower, sink, and toilet, and blankets, towels, and linens are provided. All three meals are provided and taken privately. Daily Mass and Divine Office are available in the chapel, and there is a large library. Grounds are rugged but spacious. Rainwear is essential. Located about 30 minutes outside St. Louis in woods with some rugged terrain and steep paths.

Types of Retreats/Programs Offered: Directed/Private; Hermitage/Solitary
Open to: Everyone except youths, families, and couples
Person to Contact: Sister Mary Catherine, Retreat Director, or Father John Hansen, Assistant
Address: 6150 Antire Road, P.O. Box 322, High Ridge, MO 63049
Telephone: 314-677-3235
Office Hours: 9:15 A.M. to 3:00 P.M.; 7:00–7:45 P.M.
Notice Required: Variable

Marianist Apostolic Center
Society of Mary

Marianist Apostolic Center is one of the few Catholic retreat centers in the United States actively promoting and providing retreats for high school students on a full-time basis. The center is on the Meramec River near Eureka, Missouri, about 25 miles west of St. Louis. It has 40 private bedrooms and baths, a large chapel, a lounge, and is situated on 130 wooded, gently rolling acres for walking, playing, and praying. When students come to our center, they give time to God. They take the time to look again, to retreat from the pressure of the world and re-treat what is going on in life. Part of our uniqueness can be attributed to the fact that we have a paid professional staff of youth ministers that directs each retreat.

Types of Retreats/Programs Offered: Directed/Group; Directed/Private; Conference; Hermitage/Solitary; Charismatic; Prayer Days; Parent-Teen; Engaged Encounter
Open to: Everyone except families, but mostly youths
Person to Contact: Father Donald H. Schepers, Administrator
Address: 1280 Highway 109, P.O. Box 718, Eureka, MO 63025
Telephone: 314-938-5390
Office Hours: 8:30 A.M. to 4 P.M.
Notice Required: Variable

Nazareth House
Roman Catholic; private lay ownership

Description not available.

Types of Retreats/Programs Offered: Directed/Group; Conference; Miscellaneous Programs
Open to: Everyone
Person to Contact: Peggy L. Montgomery, Director
Address: 716 Geyer Avenue, St. Louis, MO 63104

Telephone: 314-231-8979
Notice Required: Variable

Our Lady's Retreat House
Passionist Community

Our Lady's Retreat House is an inviting center for ongoing spiritual renewal, located on 2½ acres of quiet secluded property in northwestern St. Louis County, close to the University of Missouri at St. Louis and the St. Louis airport. The Passionist Community of priests and brothers staff the comfortable facility designed to foster peace-filled reflection and prayer, faithful to the ideals of hospitality, prayer, and missionary activity characteristic of the founder, St. Paul of the Cross. By word and example, the Passionists strive to help the retreatants apply the teachings and suffering of Jesus to their own lived situation. Year-round programs are presented and hosted for men, women, married couples, youths, clergy, religious, and other special groups.

Types of Retreats/Programs Offered: Directed/Group; Directed/Private; Hermitage/Solitary; Ecumenical; Prayer Days; Special
Open to: Everyone except families
Person to Contact: Father John Schork, Director
Address: 3036 Bellerive Drive, St. Louis, MO 63121-4622
Telephone: 314-389-5100
Office Hours: 9:00 A.M. to 4:00 P.M. weekdays
Notice Required: 1 month

Pallottine Renewal Center
Sisters of the Pallottine Missionary Society

Pallotine Renewal Center is in a quiet, rural area north of St. Louis, just 20 minutes from the airport and 35 minutes from downtown St. Louis. Facilities include a spacious chapel-in-the-round, 83 acres of woodlands, a gymnasium, and a swimming pool heated for year-round use. Single and double rooms are available. Pallottine Renewal Center has hosted and sponsored retreats and workshops for individuals and organizations since 1969. Pallottine has served health and educational institutions, religious affiliations, secular businesses, the disabled, special interest groups, and self-help organizations.

Types of Retreats/Programs Offered: Directed/Group; Directed/Private; Conference; Hermitage/Solitary; Ecumenical; Charismatic; Prayer Days; Parent-Teen; Marriage Encounter; Special; Miscellaneous Programs
Open to: Everyone except families
Person to Contact: Sister Carmencita Brown, Director
Address: 15270 Old Halls Ferry Road, Florissant, MO 63034
Telephone: 314-837-7100
Office Hours: 8:00 A.M. to 4:00 P.M.
Notice Required: Variable

Queen of Heaven Solitude
Society of Our Mother of Peace

Separate hermitages in a wooded environment emphasize the spiritual benefits of solitude—separation from diversions, socializing, and affluence—in order to experience radical need for God and desire for a more intimate relationship with Him. Beginners are helped to make good use of solitude, and spiritual direction is available for anyone desiring it. Hermitages are very simple but equipped with light, heat, air-conditioning, shower, sink, and toilet, and blankets, towels, and linens are provided. All three meals are provided and taken privately. Daily Mass and Office are available in the chapel, and there is a large library. Grounds are rugged but spacious. Rainwear is essential. Located near Springfield in woods with some rugged terrain and steep paths.

Types of Retreats/Programs Offered: Directed/Private; Hermitage/Solitary
Open to: Everyone except youths, families, and couples
Address: Route 1, Box 107A, Marionville, MO 65705
Telephone: 417-744-2011

Office Hours: 9:15 A.M. to 3:00 P.M.; 7:00–7:45 P.M.
Notice Required: Variable

Retreat and Conference Center
Benedictine

The Retreat and Conference Center at Conception Abbey and Conception Seminary College is in a rural setting about one hundred miles north of Kansas City. It is conducted by the Benedictine Monks of Conception Abbey, founded in 1873. It offers a quiet setting for reflection and prayer, and ample space for quiet walks. Many retreatants also enjoy taking part in the public prayer and liturgies celebrated in the abbey church. Most of the groups that come to the center provide their own retreat director. Many individuals come in order to spend just a few days or a week in quiet reflection and prayer without a director. For groups, the living quarters are separate from the conference room and dining room. There is some distance between the buildings.

Types of Retreats/Programs Offered: Directed/Private; Conference; Hermitage/Solitary; Special
Open to: Everyone except families
Person to Contact: Father Kenneth Reichert, Director
Address: Conception Abbey and Conception Seminary College, Conception, MO 64433
Telephone: 816-944-2211
Office Hours: 8:30 A.M. to 4:30 P.M. weekdays
Notice Required: One month for individuals; 4 to 6 months for group

Seton Center
Daughters of Charity of St. Vincent de Paul

Seton Center is a wing of Marillac Provincial House, the headquarters of the West Central Province of the Daughters of Charity of St. Vincent de Paul. Seton is sponsored by the Daughters of

Charity and, after research into the needs of the area, was established about ten years ago as a hosting facility for groups whose purposes are religious, educational, or charitable. There are 68 private rooms with central bath facilities, meeting rooms of various sizes, food services, and extensive grounds. Participants have remarked on the peaceful, prayerful atmosphere and the well-maintained physical plant. Closed last 2 weeks of August, and between Christmas and New Year's.

Types of Retreats/Programs Offered: Almost any type of retreat may be given by a sponsoring group
Open to: Everyone except families
Person to Contact: Sister Carol Hoelscher, Hospitality Coordinator
Address: 7800 Natural Bridge Road, St. Louis, MO 63121
Telephone: 314-382-2800
Office Hours: 8:30 A.M. to 5:00 P.M.

Thompson Center
Ecumenical

Thompson Center is set amid thirty acres of lawns and woodlands and has facilities for 44 persons overnight. The center is readily accessible by highways and is close to St. Louis airport, yet is characterized by a quality of serenity and peacefulness. The central building is an old mansion, and a dormitory, meeting hall, and chapel have been added. The center is ecumenical in sponsorship and participation.

Types of Retreats/Programs Offered: Directed/Group; Miscellaneous Programs
Open to: Everyone except youths and families
Person to Contact: The Reverend Martin Seeley, Executive Director
Address: 12145 Ladue Road, St. Louis, MO 63141
Telephone: 314-434-3633
Office Hours: 8:30 A.M. to 4:45 P.M.

White House Retreats
Society of Jesus (Jesuit)

Carved in stone above the main entrance of White House Retreats are the words, "Thou shalt love the Lord thy God." Love of God has been drawing laymen and, since 1980, laywomen to make regular spiritual retreats in the Ignatian style here since its founding in 1922. White House Retreats has grown into a complex of native limestone buildings situated on 75 acres of wooded and landscaped grounds high on the bluffs overlooking the Mississippi River. The grounds include outdoor Stations of the Cross, a grotto, and a nature trail for meditation. Built into the side of the Gothic chapel is a replica of the cave at Manresa, Spain, in which St. Ignatius conceived his spiritual exercises. Facilities include private rooms and baths. Weekend retreats begin with dinner at 7:00 P.M. Thursday and end after dinner at 6:00 P.M. on Sunday. Midweek retreats begin with lunch at 1:00 P.M. Monday and end at noon Thursday following brunch.

Types of Retreats/Programs Offered: Directed/Group
Open to: Everyone except youths and families
Person to Contact: Father Denis Daly, Director
Address: 7400 Christopher Drive, St. Louis, MO 63129
Mailing Address: Jesuit Hall, Suite 204, 3601 Lindell Boulevard, St. Louis, MO 63108
Telephone: 314-533-8903
Office Hours: 9 A.M. to 4:30 P.M. weekdays
Notice Required: Variable

Montana

Sacred Heart Renewal Center
Diocesan

Sacred Heart Renewal Center was originally a convent and is close to downtown and next to a Catholic high school. In 1980 it was reopened as the renewal center. SHRC is owned by our dioceses, and since 1987 it has been run by the lay community. We have no live-in staff. We remain a hospitality center for many user groups, and we offer at least one center retreat or other program each month. Convent-style rooms only. Closed in July and August.

Types of Retreats/Programs Offered: Directed/Group; Conference; Directed/Private and Hermitage/Solitary for one day only; Ecumenical; Prayer Days; Encounters; Cursillos; Special; Miscellaneous Programs
Open to: Everyone
Person to Contact: Bev Gormley, Center Director
Address: 26 Wyoming Avenue, Billings, MT 59101
Telephone: 406-252-0322
Office Hours: 9:00 A.M. to 4:00 P.M. weekdays
Notice Required: Variable

Ursuline Center
Ursuline

Description not available.

Types of Retreats/Programs Offered: Directed/Group; Directed/Private; Conference; Hermitage/Solitary; Ecumenical; Charismatic; Prayer Days; Encounters; Cursillos; Special; Miscellaneous Programs
Open to: Everyone except families
Person to Contact: Sister Marietta Devine, Superior and Retreat Director
Address: 2300 Central Avenue, Great Falls, MT 59401
Telephone: 406-452-8585
Office Hours: 8:30 A.M. to 1:30 P.M. weekdays
Notice Required: Minimum 4 to 6 weeks

Nebraska

Crosier Renewal Center
Crosier Fathers

Started in the early 1970s, the Crosier Renewal Center is part of the Crosier Monastery. We serve as a host for all denominations to hold their own conferences, and we provide workshops and retreats with our own staff or with outside noted speakers. Facilities include single and double rooms, meeting rooms, tennis court, gym, large dining room and spacious chapel. We have a no-smoking policy except in the coffee room and in the dining room (immediately after meals). Double rooms available for families.

Types of Retreats/Programs Offered: Directed/Group; Directed/Private; Conference; Hermitage/Solitary; Ecumenical; Charismatic; Prayer Days; Parent-Teen; Marriage Encounter; Cursillos; Special; Miscellaneous Programs
Open to: Everyone
Person to Contact: Mary Ann Warner, Assistant Director
Address: 223 E. 14th Street, Box 789, Hastings, NE 68902
Telephone: 402-463-3188
Office Hours: 9:00 A.M. to 4:30 P.M.
Notice Required: Variable

St. Columban's Center
Columban Fathers

St. Columban's Center, in the middle of Bellevue, is only 20 minutes from downtown Omaha. The spacious 40-plus acres on the semi-wooded property of the Columban Fathers Mission ensure privacy and tranquility. The Center is available for use by day, week, or weekend. The center was redesigned in 1980 for the growing needs of nonprofit, educational, and spiritual groups that sometimes have difficulties finding space at a reasonable cost for seminars, meetings, and retreats.

Types of Retreats/Programs Offered: Directed/Group; Directed/Private; Conference; Ecumenical; Charismatic; Prayer Days; Encounters; Special
Open to: Everyone except families
Person to Contact: Anthony Hassett, Director of Retreats
Address: 2810 N. Calhoon, St. Columban's, NE 68056
Telephone: 402-291-1920
Notice Required: 2 weeks

New Hampshire

The Common
Discalced Carmelite Friars

The Common is a hilltop mansion built in 1898 and situated on 173 acres of meadows and woodlands in the Monadnock Mountain region of southern New Hampshire. The Common is a retreat center for people of all beliefs. Facilities include single, double, and triple rooms, conference rooms, a chapel, a meditation room, and a library. There is an outdoor swimming pool, and cross-country skiing is available in winter. The spirituality taught is based on that of St. Teresa of Avila and St. John of the Cross, the sixteenth century reformers of the Carmelite Order, and emphasizes meditation and solitude. Anyone may come for a private retreat whenever space is available; whenever a retreat or seminar is not scheduled, the facilities are available to groups.

Types of Retreats/Programs Offered: Directed/Private; Conference; Hermitage/Solitary; Ecumenical; Charismatic; Prayer Days; Parent-Teen; Special; Miscellaneous Programs, including 2 Jungian seminars annually
Open to: Everyone
Person to Contact: Father Paul Fohlin, Director
Address: 174 Old Street Road, Peterborough, NH 03458
Telephone: 603-924-6060
Office Hours: 9:00 A.M. to 1:00 P.M. weekdays
Notice Required: Variable

Oblate Retreat House
Missionary Oblates of Mary Immaculate

The Oblate Retreat House is in a secluded, natural setting in southern New Hampshire. It is 50 minutes from Boston's Logan Airport, with transportation service available to nearby Nashua. Facilities include private rooms, 2 large conference halls, spacious chapel and dining room. The Oblate Retreat House specializes in weekend retreats, but also offers individuals an opportunity to make a private retreat with or without direction. The retreat house facilities are open to not-for-profit religious and/or educational groups. Closed in July.

Types of Retreats/Programs Offered: Directed/Group; Directed/Private; Charismatic; Prayer Days; Encounters; Special
Open to: Everyone except families
Person to Contact: Father George Capen, Director
Address: 200 Lowell Road, Rte 3-A, P.O. Box 158, Hudson, NH 03051
Telephone: 603-882-8141
Office Hours: 9:00 A.M. to 5:00 P.M. weekdays
Notice Required: 1 week

St. Francis Retreat Center
Order of Friars Minor (Franciscan)

Located on the New Hampshire seacoast 55 miles north of Boston, St. Francis Retreat Center is one block from the ocean on 6 acres of land. The center is a spacious and comfortable facility that can accommodate individuals, small groups, and large groups in a reflective and prayerful setting. The main building has two large conference rooms, three smaller meeting rooms, facilities for shared and silent dining, a main chapel, and a prayer room. Single and double bedrooms are available. In a separate area of the center's grounds is a facility we call The Hermitage. The first floor of The Hermitage has a spacious living/meeting room, a large dining room, a fully equipped kitchen, a simple chapel, a reading room, and two lavatories. The second floor has 10 single bedrooms and 2 full bathrooms with showers.

Types of Retreats/Programs Offered: Directed/Group; Directed/Private; Conference; Hermitage/Solitary; Ecumenical; Charismatic; Prayer Days; Engaged Encounter; Cursillos; Special; Miscellaneous Programs
Open to: Everyone
Person to Contact: Brother Michael Harlan, Administrative Coordinator
Address: 860 Central Road, Rye Beach, NH 03871
Telephone: 603-964-5559
Office Hours: 9 A.M. to 5 P.M.
Notice Required: 6–8 months for summer, 4–6 months other times

New Jersey

Cenacle Retreat House
Congregation of Our Lady of the Retreat in the Cenacle

Within metropolitan New York, the Highland Park Cenacle overlooks the Raritan River. The white-shingled colonial building is set among pines offering a tranquil setting. Those coming on retreat especially notice the warmth and comfort of the house and its peaceful, prayerful atmosphere. Most rooms are single and include a sink. No rooms with private bath, and no elevator. Ample area for walking, enjoying the outdoors in good weather. Closed July 1 through August 10.

Types of Retreats/Programs Offered: Directed/Group; Directed/Private; Conference; Hermitage/Solitary; Ecumenical; Charismatic; Prayer Days; Parent-Teen; Special; Miscellaneous Programs
Open to: Everyone except youths and families
Person to Contact: Sister Mary Lou Heffernan, Retreat Office Director

Address: 411 River Road, Highland Park, NJ 08904
Telephone: 201-249-8100
Notice Required: Variable

Queen of Peace Retreat House
Benedictine Monks

The Retreat House is part of St. Paul's Abbey. Located on a 500-acre tract of woodlands and fields, part of the atmosphere of the house is silence. The Retreat House at St. Paul's Abbey is really a pastoral work of the monastic community. For nearly forty years the monks have accepted groups to come for weekends to share in the peace of the monastery. The groups are shown Benedictine hospitality and welcome. Over the years the monks have given conferences and offered individual sessions with their retreatants and invited them to share in some of the Liturgy of their community. For the most part the retreat house has focused on a group experience on its weekend retreats. Today the bulk of our ministry is concerned with retreats for the chemically dependent.

Types of Retreats/Programs Offered: Conference; Cursillos; Special
Open to: Everyone except families
Person to Contact: Father Basil Wallace, Manager
Address: St. Paul's Abbey, Newton, NJ 07860-0007
Telephone: 201-383-2470 or 0660
Office Hours: 9 A.M. to 4 P.M.
Notice Required: 2 weeks to 1 month

San Alfonso Retreat House
Redemptorist Fathers

San Alfonso is a Redemptorist Spiritual Center on 8 beautiful acres right on the ocean. Facilities include private rooms, large chapel, spacious meeting rooms, reading room, and religious article and bookstore. In addition to the scheduled retreats, San Alfonso offers days and evenings of recollection for adults, for school faculties, for young people, and for parish societies and parish councils. Father Rudolph Harvey, a weekly columnist in the Buffalo, New York Diocesan newspaper, has said: "It would be hard to imagine a spot more conducive to prayerful meditation than this beautiful building by the sea."

Types of Retreats/Programs Offered: Directed/Group; Charismatic; Prayer Days; Special; Miscellaneous Programs
Open to: Everyone except families
Person to Contact: Father Paul V. Beyan, Rector
Address: P.O. Box 3098, 755 Ocean Avenue, Long Branch, NJ 07740
Telephone: 201-222-2731
Office Hours: 9:00 A.M. to 4:00 P.M.
Notice Required: Variable

The Upper Room Spiritual Center
Diocesan

The Upper Room, established in 1978, is a Diocesan spiritual center that supports and nourishes the spiritual lives of the laity, religious, and clergy of the Trenton Diocese through spiritual direction, retreats, days and evenings of recollection, courses on prayer and Christian living, and service to the charismatic prayer groups. Spacious and comfortable surroundings make it an inviting place of prayer, worship, and service to others. In addition to the more traditional retreat efforts, the Upper Room lists the following among its goals: to provide leadership training, teaching and pastoral care to the charismatic renewal in the diocese; and to develop competent spiritual directors for this ministry through an intensely supervised, ongoing direction and retreat program.

Types of Retreats/Programs Offered: Directed/Group; Directed/Private; Conference; Hermitage/Solitary; Prayer Days; Special; Miscellaneous Programs
Open to: Everyone except youths under 18 and families
Person to Contact: Sister Maureen Conroy, Sister Carol Conly, Father Joseph Tedesco, Co-Directors
Address: P.O. Box 1104, Neptune, NJ 07753
Telephone: 201-922-0550
Office Hours: 9:00 A.M. to 4:00 P.M.
Notice Required: 1 month

New Mexico

Dominican Retreat House
Dominican

Description not available.

Types of Retreats/Programs Offered: Directed/Group; Conference; Prayer Days; Special; Miscellaneous Programs
Address: 5825 Coors Road SW, Albuquerque, NM 87105
Telephone: 505-877-4211
Notice Required: Variable

Holy Cross Retreat
Order of Friars Minor Conventual

Holy Cross Retreat, an adobe ranch house built in 1913, is situated in a large grove of pecan trees, affording a peaceful and restful atmosphere. Located 3 miles south of Las Cruces and 40 miles north of El Paso, Texas (site of the nearest airport), Holy Cross is, practically speaking, the only open retreat facility for all religious denominations within a radius of 200 miles or more. The retreat house is staffed by Conventual Franciscan Friars and is available for religious, educational, and cultural retreats and conferences in addition to its own offerings of programs and spiritual retreats. Facilities include single, double, and triple occupancy motel-style rooms with private baths, a large conference room, meeting rooms, a library, and spacious grounds. Although open all year, most of the lay staff members—including the cooks—are on vacation for two weeks at Christmas.

Types of Retreats/Programs Offered: Directed/Group; Directed/Private; Conference; Hermitage/Solitary; Ecumenical; Charismatic; Prayer Days; Encounters; Special; Miscellaneous Programs including Franciscan Spirituality Retreats
Open to: Everyone
Person to Contact: Father Noel Kramer, Director of Retreats
Address: P.O. Box 158, Mesilla Park, NM 88047
Telephone: 505-524-3688
Office Hours: 9 A.M. to 5 P.M. weekdays
Notice Required: Variable

Monastery of Christ in the Desert
Benedictine

Our monastery is in a beautiful canyon, about 6,500 feet above sea level, in northwestern New Mexico. It is surrounded by miles of federal wilderness, accessible only by a 12-mile dirt road, so solitude and quiet are assured. Our guest house is a place where individuals can take part in the prayer and work of the monastery. Our day is divided between times of prayer in common, blocks of time for private prayer and reading, the daily manual labor, and some relaxation. The heart of our community life is our prayer in common. We meet 7 times a day for the canonical offices as well as for the daily Eucharist (Mass). We provide private retreats for individuals, but cannot provide regular spiritual direction during the retreat. If a guest wishes to speak with one of the monks during a stay here, that can be arranged through the Guestmaster. We do not provide directed retreats, but encourage our guests to participate in the common prayer, meals, and work of the monastery. Closed first 2 weeks of May.

Monastery of Christ in the Desert, Abiquiu, New Mexico

Types of Retreats/Programs Offered: Hermitage/Solitary
Open to: Everyone except youths and families
Person to Contact: Guestmaster
Address: Abiquiu, NM 87510
Telephone: 505-756-2188
Notice Required: 1 month to 6 weeks

Our Lady of Guadalupe Abbey, Pecos Benedictine Community
Benedictine

Twenty-five miles from Santa Fe, the abbey, commonly referred to as "the Pecos Community," is a 1,000-acre property that started as a dude ranch, evolved into a Trappist farm, and is now a Benedictine monastery and charismatic retreat center. Pecos has been the focus of much attention because of its mixed community of men and women living as one community, and because of the holistic spirituality associated with this lifestyle. The Pecos Community functions primarily as a center of renewal and healing. Dove Publications, which publishes and sells Christian literature of all types, makes its home here.

Types of Retreats/Programs Offered: Directed/Group; Directed/Private; Conference; Charismatic; Special; Miscellaneous Programs including School for Charismatic Spiritual Directors
Open to: Everyone
Person to Contact: Reservations Office
Address: Pecos, NM 87552
Telephone: 505-757-6415
Office Hours: 10:00 A.M. to 12:00 noon, 1:00–3:00 P.M. weekdays
Notice Required: Variable

Sacred Heart Retreat Center
Diocesan, staffed by the Franciscan Sisters of the Immaculate Conception

The Sacred Heart Retreat Center is two miles from downtown Gallup, New Mexico. Facilities include 3 small cabins, called "hogans," with a total capacity of 18 beds, and one large hogan with 14 beds; all have modern conveniences. The center is at an altitude of 7,200 feet and sits on a hilltop with a 360-degree view of the surrounding desert. Among the practices taught are centering prayer and the Ignatian Exercises. Closed Thanksgiving, Christmas, and New Year's days.

Types of Retreats/Programs Offered: Directed/Group; Directed/Private; Conference; Hermitage/Solitary; Ecumenical; Charismatic; Prayer Days; Parent-Teen; Encounters; Cursillos; Special; Miscellaneous Programs
Open to: Everyone
Person to Contact: Father Daniel F. Resendes, Director
Address: P.O. Box 1989, Gallup, NM 87305
Telephone: 505-722-6755
Office Hours: Anytime
Notice Required: 6 months

New York

At Home Retreats International Center
Cenacle

At Home Retreats is not a center as such, but rather our retreats are conducted in home situations all over the United States and in several foreign countries. Groups of individuals meet once a week for 13 weeks, usually in their homes. Under the direction of a team of two people (most often one layperson and one religious), the group is led through an adaptation of the Ignatian Exercises. At Home Retreats was begun by Sister Mary Sullivan, a Religious of the Cenacle, and Mrs. Dot Horstmann, wife and mother. They have also designed a three-day program for developing a team to direct the At Home Retreats in their area. Closed summers.

Types of Retreats/Programs Offered: Special; give retreats at individual homes
Open to: Men, women, couples
Person to Contact: Lois Caputo, Secretary
Address: 310 Cenacle Road, Lake Ronkonkoma, NY 11779
Telephone: 516-585-1871
Office Hours: 9:00 A.M. to 4:00 P.M.

Bishop Molloy Passionist Retreat House
Passionist Community

The Bishop Molloy Retreat House is in the beautiful Jamaica Estates section of Queens, a borough of New York City. Facilities include private rooms, elevator service, monastery gardens for meditation and walks, a quiet chapel, and a library. Regular weekend retreats start on Friday at 6:30 P.M. and end on Sunday at 2:00 P.M. A retreatant is free to take part in the program or spend time at whatever is meaningful for him or her. The atmosphere is quiet and reflective, with the added dimension of the experience of Christian community. A retreat at Bishop Molloy is a rich experience in sights and sounds and silence. Closed in August.

Types of Retreats/Programs Offered: Directed/Group; Charismatic; Prayer Days; Parent-Teen; Special
Open to: Everyone except families
Person to Contact: Father Paul Wierichs, Director
Address: 86-45 Edgerton Boulevard, Jamaica Estates, NY 11432
Telephone: 718-739-1229
Office Hours: 9:00 A.M. to 5:00 P.M.
Notice Required: 2 weeks

Cenacle Retreat House
Congregation of Our Lady of the Cenacle

The Cenacle Retreat House is in picturesque and historic Bedford Village, 45 minutes northeast of major New York City bridges. Facilities include private rooms for 9 persons. The retreat house provides a space for prayer and spiritual growth in a quiet reflective atmosphere, homelike, and informal. Our orientation/ministry is on a one-to-one basis. We do not accept people seeking only "hospitality," but presume they desire to have some individual guidance. This would usually be during an hour or less each day, involving spiritual direction and/or counsel. Closed in September.

Types of Retreats/Programs Offered: Directed/Private; Prayer Days; Special; Miscellaneous Programs
Open to: Everyone except youths and families
Person to Contact: Sister Thelma Hall or Sister Kathleen O'Brien, Co-Directors
Address: P.O. Box 467, Bedford Village, NY 10506
Telephone: 914-234-3344
Office Hours: 9:30 A.M. to 9:30 P.M.
Notice Required: Variable

Center of Renewal
Sisters of St. Francis of Penance & Christian Charity

The Center of Renewal is on the banks of the Niagara River, near the village of Lewiston. The center is part of the Stella Niagara Education Park, on the 130-acre site where the Sisters of St. Francis established their Motherhouse in 1908. The campus also includes the Sisters' administrative offices, retirement residence, and health center, as well as a private school that makes available the use of an auditorium, gymnasium, and outdoor athletic fields. Facilities include single and double rooms, a large modern chapel with a newly designed prayer alcove, and the tower hermitage, a secluded prayer space overlooking the river. Elevators and ramps make the center handicapped accessible. Our holistic focus of programming—to touch the spirit, body, mind, and emotions—is encompassed in a year-round calendar including retreats, programs, and workshops.

Types of Retreats/Programs Offered: Directed/Group; Directed/Private; Conference; Hermitage/Solitary; Ecumenical; Prayer Days; Engaged Encounter; Special; Miscellaneous Programs
Open to: Everyone except youths and families
Person to Contact: Sister Catherine Gale, Administrative Secretary
Address: 4421 Lower River Road, Stella Niagara, NY 14144
Telephone: 716-754-7376
Office Hours: 8:30 A.M. to 4:30 P.M.
Notice Required: At least 1 week

Chrysalis House
Roman Catholic lay community

Chrysalis House is a Christian live-in community of women and men with a life-style that facilitates a personal journey into union with God. Chrysalis House is a part of National Contemplative Outreach, founded by Father Thomas Keating; it is also affiliated with the Archdiocese of New York. Father Keating continues to guide the community in living the contemplative dimension of the Gospel through a shared life of prayer, work, and solitude. Chrysalis House is a large contemporary-style home set on 50 acres of wooded hill country, in a semirural valley 50 miles northwest of New York City. Accommodations during retreats are in shared rooms. Home-cooked vegetarian meals are served. The community is committed to deepening their life in the Spirit by sharing their contemplative practice of centering prayer, meditation, worship, study, dialogue, and household work, including the arts of cooking and gardening.

Types of Retreats/Programs Offered: Various types of centering prayer retreats
Open to: Everyone
Person to Contact: Director
Address: 21 Ball Road, Warwick, NY 10990
Telephone: 914-986-8050
Notice Required: Variable

Dominican Retreat House
Dominican Sisters of St. Catherine di Ricci

Our retreat house accommodates 50 persons in private rooms that have running water, bed linens, and towels. The building is all one level and handicapped accessible. The weekend begins with registration Friday at 7:00 P.M. and concludes Sunday after Mass around 2:30 P.M.. All our retreat weekends include conferences, prayer services, quiet time for reflection, opportunity for private conferences with team members, Eucharistic celebration, group sessions, and opportunities to share if one chooses. A quiet atmosphere is recommended, and there is time for walks outside, contemplative prayer inside. We offer a wide variety of programs for weekends, days, evenings, or lectures. Closed week after Christmas, Holy Week, and a few weeks in the summer.

Types of Retreats/Programs Offered: Directed/Group; Conference; Charismatic; Prayer Days; Special; Miscellaneous Programs
Open to: Everyone except families
Person to Contact: Dominican Sisters
Address: 1945 Union Street, Schenectady, NY 12309
Telephone: 518-393-4169
Office Hours: 8:00 A.M. to 4:00 P.M.
Notice Required: 1 year

Island Retreat

The Island Retreat is not an institutional-type retreat house. There is a home-like atmosphere in which the individual needs of each retreatant (our maximum is 12) are respected. Island Retreat is a large former estate in the middle of Tupper Lake. In a wilderness setting on 50-acre Bluff Island, the buildings are perched on a high rock bluff overlooking the beautiful lake. The large living room-library features a huge fireplace. The Island Retreat has all modern conveniences, including electricity, water, and cable telephone to the mainland. Retreats begin with dinner every Sunday evening and extend until the following Saturday after breakfast. There is a daily Eucharistic celebration and an input session each day for those who wish but, otherwise, the program is unstructured. Private counseling is readily available. Twice a week, Mass is celebrated outdoors: once on a large pontoon boat on the lake, and once at sunset on a high ledge. There is also a 20-mile boat ride to Bog River Falls with a cookout on board. Centering prayer is taught. Closed October through May.

Types of Retreats/Programs Offered: Conference; Hermitage/Solitary; Ecumenical
Open to: Everyone except youths and families
Person to Contact: Father Tom Middendorf, Director
Address: After June 15: Moody Road, Bluff Island, Tupper Lake,

NY 12986. *Before June 15:* c/o The Hermitage, 6800 Rabbit Hash Road, Burlington, KY 41005
Telephone: 518-359-7027
Notice Required: 1 week, space available basis

Linwood Spiritual Center
Sisters of St. Ursula

Linwood sits on 55 acres high on a hill overlooking the Hudson River. A regional center for the Sisters of St. Ursula, Linwood is a center for spiritual renewal that welcomes women and men, lay people and members of religious communities. Linwood's programs are directed toward the goal of personal development, in which our spiritual and human dimensions are integrated so that we may be people fully alive for the glory of God. Facilities include all private rooms.

Types of Retreats/Programs Offered: Directed/Group; Directed/Private; Conference; Hermitage/Solitary; Prayer Days; Special; Miscellaneous Programs
Open to: Everyone
Person to Contact: Sister Elizabeth A. Geary, Director
Address: 139 South Mill Road, Rhinebeck, NY 12572
Telephone: 914-876-4178
Office Hours: 9 A.M. to 4 P.M. weekdays
Notice Required: At least 2 weeks

Our Lady of Hope Center
Oblates of Mary Immaculate

Our Lady of Hope Center is a unique house of prayer serving the Catholic Church through the charismatic renewal. Nestled in the heart of the Hudson Valley, the Center serves as a spiritual oasis to countless people who come to pray and be prayed for, to worship and to be led. The center has dorm-style living, a definite charismatic slant, and a strong outreach to the poor.

Types of Retreats/Programs Offered: Directed/Private; Conference; Hermitage/Solitary; Ecumenical; Charismatic; Prayer Days; Cursillos; Special; Miscellaneous Programs
Open to: Everyone except families
Person to Contact: Joe Brennan, Bursar
Address: 434 River Road, Newburgh, NY 12550
Telephone: 914-561-0685
Office Hours: 9:00 A.M. to 9:00 P.M.
Notice Required: 1 month

Passionist Spiritual Center of Riverdale
Passionist Fathers and Brothers
Description not available.

Types of Retreats/Programs Offered: Directed/Group; Directed/Private; Conference; Prayer Days; Special; Miscellaneous Programs
Open to: Everyone except families
Person to Contact: Father Eugene Bonacci, Director
Address: 5601 Palisade Avenue, Riverdale, NY 10471
Telephone: 212-549-6500
Office Hours: 9:00 A.M. to 5:00 P.M.
Notice Required: Variable

St. Andrew's House
Passionist

More like a large home than a formal retreat house, St. Andrew's House is on 14 acres of rural lawn and woodland with outdoor shrines and Stations of the Cross. Facilities include double rooms with semiprivate baths, conference rooms and lounges, library, special prayer room and a semicircular chapel. Additional features include a stone cottage for families or small religious groups and a newly created hermitage within the main house. St. Andrew's House does not schedule a yearly program of retreats. Rather, we offer hospitality to groups of various sizes (up to 60) to come with their own retreat director. Approved by diocesan authority and recognized as a place of spiritual nourishment in the *House of Prayer Directory,* we maintain a restful atmosphere where you can feel at home for a few days of refreshing prayer.

Types of Retreats/Programs Offered: Conference; Hermitage/Solitary; Ecumenical; Prayer Days; Marriage Encounter; Special
Open to: Everyone
Person to Contact: Father Andrew Ansbro, Director
Address: 89A St. Andrew's Road, Walden, NY 12586
Telephone: 914-778-3707
Office Hours: Anytime
Notice Required: 3 to 4 months

St. Joseph Spiritual Life Center
Holy Cross Brothers

Situated in the Hudson River Valley 18 miles south of Albany, St. Joseph Center is a nonprofit spiritual life center available for retreats and conferences. The center is on 400 acres with tennis courts and a spring-fed pond. The area is noted for its scenic beauty and historic background, and the hills and fields make cross-country skiing possible in winter. Facilities include main chapel, conference room and lounge, single and double rooms, small parlors, meeting rooms, and small chapel. The center is staffed by both religious and laypersons, and provides a peaceful atmosphere for relaxation and reflection. Individuals and groups of all faiths are welcome. Closed only on major holidays.

Types of Retreats/Programs Offered: Directed/Group; Directed/Private; Hermitage/Solitary; Prayer Days; Youth; Special; Miscellaneous Programs

Open to: Everyone
Person to Contact: Brother Aubert Harrigan, Administrator
Address: R.D. #5, Box 113, Valarie, NY 12184
Telephone: 518-784-9481
Office Hours: 9:00 A.M. to 5:00 P.M.
Notice Required: Variable

Wainwright House
Nonsectarian

Wainwright House is an educational and conference center with a spiritual focus on interdisciplinary programming. Wainwright House was founded in 1941 by a group of distinguished businessmen, who also worked for the establishment of the United Nations, for the purpose of bringing ethical and spiritual values into professional and personal lives. Four institutes provide seminars, conferences, and ongoing core programs in health, psychology, business leadership, global issues, spirituality, and the arts. Wainwright House is on Long Island Sound, overlooking Milton Harbor in Rye. The beautiful gardens and rolling lawns, gracious meeting rooms and library provide a congenial and relaxed atmosphere. Rooms are single, double, or dorm-style.

Open to: Everyone
Address: 260 Stuyvesant Avenue, Rye, NY 10580
Telephone: 914-967-6080

North Carolina

Aqueduct Conference Center
Interdenominational

The center can house 40 overnight guests. Each bedroom, with private bath, sleeps two people. Various guest speakers present

Directory of Retreat and Renewal Centers 191

a wide variety of conferences at the center. A description of the buildings and grounds was not available.
Types of Retreats/Programs Offered: Directed/Group; Conference; Ecumenical; Charismatic; Special; Miscellaneous Programs
Open to: Everyone
Person to Contact: Thomas E. Tyson, Executive Director
Address: Route 6, Box 508, Chapel Hill, NC 27514
Telephone: 919-933-5557
Office Hours: 8:30 A.M. to 5:00 P.M.

Avila Retreat Center
Diocesan

Sponsored by the Roman Catholic Diocese in Raleigh, Avila is nestled on 51 acres in northern Durham County. The country setting of fields, forest, streams, and hillsides affords peace and quiet to guests. Avila has accommodations for both single day and overnight guests sponsoring their own programs. In addition, guests may attend many special programs sponsored by Avila. Single and double rooms are located in 7 cottages, each with outdoor patio and located close to conference facilities. A hermitage in a wooded setting can provide visitors a very private and serene stay. Facilities also include a chapel, craft room, dining room with home-cooked meals, library, and store.

Types of Retreats/Programs Offered: Directed/Group; Directed/Private; Conference; Hermitage/Solitary; Ecumenical; Charismatic; Prayer Days; Encounters; Special; Miscellaneous Programs
Open to: Everyone except families
Person to Contact: Sister Damian Marie Jackson, Director
Address: 711 Mason Road, Durham, NC 27712
Telephone: 919-477-1285
Office Hours: 8:00 A.M. to 9:00 P.M.
Notice Required: 1 to 2 weeks

Avila Retreat Center, Durham, North Carolina

Jesuit Hikers' Hostel and House of Prayer
Society of Jesus (Jesuit)

We are located in the scenic mountains of the Pisgah National Forest, alongside the Appalachian Trail, in the small town of Hot Springs. The French Broad River and Spring Creek flow through our town. We're off the beaten track in a very beautiful part of the world. Because of our tiny staff and varied involvements, we are very much a self-help operation. We welcome hikers, retreatants, and folks who just want to get away. You supply the program, the purpose, the direction, sometimes even the food, for your stay here. We try to help in any way we can. Because of our tradition and experience and interests, we especially welcome those who are struggling to integrate their faith with a commitment to the poor and an involvement in justice and peace concerns. Our property includes a residence/house of prayer, hikers' hostel and cabin, and an A-frame chapel.

Types of Retreats/Programs Offered: Hermitage/Solitary; occasional workshops and directed or guided retreats
Open to: Everyone
Address: P.O. Box #7, Hot Springs, NC 28743
Telephone: 704-622-7366
Office Hours: 9:00 A.M. to 5:00 P.M.
Notice Required: Variable

The McAuley Center
Sisters of Mercy of North Carolina

The McAuley Center attempts to meet the religious needs of the people of the diocese of Charlotte by offering at minimal cost programs in adult religious education as well as retreat programs. The center is staffed by Sisters of Mercy who have studied theology, spirituality, the Bible, religious education, and liturgical music on the graduate level at leading Catholic universities. We have accommodations only for private overnight retreats and day group retreats. We do weekend retreats for parishes at their request in the place of their choice.

Types of Retreats/Programs Offered: Directed/Private; Conference; Miscellaneous Programs
Open to: Everyone
Person to Contact: Sister Mary Hugh Mauldin, Director
Address: Sacred Heart Convent, Belmont, NC 28012
Telephone: 704-825-5126
Notice Required: 2 to 3 weeks

Society of St. John the Evangelist: St. John's House
Anglican

The Society of St. John the Evangelist is a community of lay and ordained men who take life vows of poverty, celibacy, and obedience. Founded by Richard Meux Benson in Oxford, England in 1866, the society is the oldest Anglican religious order for men. All services of worship, celebrated from the Book of Common Prayer, are open to guests and to the public. St. John's House was opened in 1983 as a quiet spot in the city for individual retreats and spiritual direction. Renovations underway now will change the use of the rooms and expand guest facilities.

Types of Retreats/Programs Offered: Directed/Group; Directed/Private; Hermitage/Solitary; Special
Open to: Everyone except youths and families
Person to Contact: Guestmaster
Address: 702 West Cobb Street, Durham, NC 27707
Telephone: 919-688-4161
Notice Required: Variable

Ohio

Franciscan Renewal Center
Conventual Franciscans—Sisters of St. Francis

The Franciscan Renewal Center, comprising the Pilgrim House and the Retreat Center, is a place filled with the Spirit of God and alive with the spirit of St. Francis of Assisi. In this place, an individual can reside for a time to dwell with God in peace and let the mysteries of God unfold through prayer, reflection, study, community, conferences, dialogue, leisure. Simplicity and joy are the values expressed in a comfortable environment with few luxuries. In a rural small-town setting, the center provides conference rooms, lodging, meals,

Franciscan Renewal Center, The Pilgrim House, Carey, Ohio

prayer-chapel space, and the campus of the Shrine of Our Lady of Consolation.

Types of Retreats/Programs Offered: Directed/Group; Directed/Private; Conference; Hermitage/Solitary; Ecumenical; Charismatic; Prayer Days; Engaged Encounter; Cursillos; Special; Miscellaneous Programs such as planned family retreats
Open to: Everyone
Person to Contact: Father Donald Halpin or Sister Joan Froning, Retreat Directors
Address: 320 West Street, Carey, OH 43316
Telephone: 419-396-7635 or 396-7970
Office Hours: 8:30 A.M. to 4:30 P.M.
Notice Required: Variable

Friarhurst Retreat Center
Order of Friars Minor

The Friarhurst Retreat Center includes beautiful grounds with outdoor Stations of the Cross and a grotto for prayer and meditation. The main lodge contains a large conference room and dining room, and retreatant rooms are private. Weekend retreats begin on Friday night after dinner and end at 1:30 P.M. on Sunday. In addition to the regular program of retreats, the facilities may be rented by nonprofit groups. Usually closed in August.

Types of Retreats/Programs Offered: Conference; Special
Open to: Everyone except families and couples
Person to Contact: Marilyn Seibert, Secretary-Supervisor
Address: 8136 Wooster Pike, Cincinnati, OH 45227
Telephone: 513-561-2270
Office Hours: 8:00 A.M. to 4:00 P.M.
Notice Required: 2 weeks

Jesuit Renewal Center
Society of Jesus (Jesuit)

The Jesuit Renewal Center is 30 minutes from downtown Cincinnati, along the Little Miami River. In addition to retreat offerings, the center has established a rural retreat center on a wooded farm halfway between Cincinnati and Indianapolis. The farm offers 7-day personally directed retreats, 5-day prayer workshops, and hermitage retreats. The 2 hermitages are large, all-weather tents in which short or long solitary retreats may be scheduled. Massage therapy is also available.

Types of Retreats/Programs Offered: Directed/Group; Directed/Private; Engaged Encounter; Youth; Special; Miscellaneous Programs
Open to: Everyone except families
Person to Contact: Father Richard Bollman, Director
Address: 5361 S. Milford Road, Milford, OH 45150

Directory of Retreat and Renewal Centers 197

Telephone: 513-831-6010
Office Hours: 8:30 A.M. to 4:30 P.M. weekdays
Notice Required: 4 to 6 weeks

Jesuit Retreat House
Society of Jesus (Jesuit)

As America's first lay retreat center, all forms of ministry at Jesuit Retreat House are done in the spirit of the spiritual exercises of St. Ignatius. Retreatants and those receiving individual spiritual direction are guided through Christ-centered, Gospel experiences that call one to greater spiritual freedom. Jesuit Retreat House is on 57 acres of peaceful woods, fields, and pathways in an urban area. Facilities include private single rooms, prayer and music rooms, and air-conditioned chapels and dining room. Closed between Christmas and New Year's.

Types of Retreats/Programs Offered: Directed/Group; Directed/Private; Conference; Hermitage/Solitary; Ecumenical; Prayer Days; Marriage Encounter; Special; Miscellaneous Programs
Open to: Everyone except families
Person to Contact: Barbara Leggott, Office Manager
Address: 5629 State Road, Cleveland, OH 44134-2292
Telephone: 216-884-9300
Office Hours: 8:30 A.M. to 5 P.M. weekdays
Notice Required: 10 days

Maria Stein Center
Sisters of the Precious Blood

Situated on 200 acres of rural woodland in Mercer County, Maria Stein Center offers 60 bedrooms, each with private bathroom. The grounds and rural area are conducive for walking, jogging, and biking. Also on the grounds are the Shrine of the Holy Relics, the Adoration Chapel, the Maria Stein Heritage

Museum, the Pilgrim Gift Shop and several outdoor shrines and Stations of the Cross.

Types of Retreats/Programs Offered: Directed/Group; Directed/Private; Conference; Hermitage/Solitary; Ecumenical; Charismatic; Prayer Days; Engaged Encounter; Special; Miscellaneous Programs
Open to: Everyone except families
Person to Contact: Sister Anna Maria Sanders, Administrator
Address: 2365 St. Johns Road, Maria Stein, OH 45860
Telephone: 419-925-4538
Office Hours: 8:00 A.M. to 4:30 P.M. weekdays
Notice Required: 1 day

Milford Retreat Center
Society of Jesus (Jesuit)

The Milford Retreat Center is on 40 acres of beautiful, parklike surroundings just 20 miles east of Cincinnati. The quiet setting is conducive to prayer, reflection, and resting. Retreats are led by professional retreat masters (priests) and counseling is provided by a joint lay and religious staff. Facilities include private rooms with all necessities furnished. Special programs can be provided with staff from the Jesuit Renewal Center. No overnight accommodations for families.

Types of Retreats/Programs Offered: Directed/Group; Conference; Prayer Days; Parent-Teen; Special
Open to: Everyone except youths
Person to Contact: Father John J. Beckman, Director
Address: 5361 So. Milford Road, Milford, OH 45150
Telephone: 513-831-5151
Office Hours: 9:00 A.M. to 4:30 P.M.
Notice Required: 2 weeks

Mount St. Joseph Retreat House
Sisters of Charity of Cincinnati

Mount St. Joseph Retreat House is part of the mother house complex. It is 20 miles out of Cincinnati. All rooms are single, with running water (no air-conditioning). There is a kitchenette for snacks on each floor, 40 acres provide walking areas, and there is a swimming pool in summer. The large chapel has Exposition all day, plus there is a small prayer room with pillows. Plenty of good praying space, excellent library of books, tapes, records, and always someone available for spiritual companioning.

Types of Retreats/Programs Offered: Directed/Group; Directed/Private; Conference; Hermitage/Solitary; Prayer Days; Miscellaneous Programs
Open to: Women and female religious, priests
Person to Contact: Sister Annina Morgan, Retreat Coordinator
Address: Mount St. Joseph, OH 45051
Telephone: 513-244-4219
Office Hours: 9:00 A.M. to 5:00 P.M.
Notice Required: 2 weeks

Our Lady of the Pines Retreat and Renewal Center
Sisters of Mercy

Our Lady of the Pines is on 63 acres of woods and beautifully landscaped grounds conducive to reflection and solitude, but spacious enough for active sharing. The grounds include a grotto with an altar dedicated to Our Lady of Lourdes, and outdoor Stations of the Cross, as well as an outdoor swimming pool, bicycles, and trails for walking and jogging. The building is handicapped accessible and offers private, semiprivate, and dorm rooms. The library/meeting room and dining area are air-conditioned. There is a chapel with nonstationary seating, a Blessed Sacrament prayer room, and a listening room. Available are opportunities for

Our Lady of the Pines, Fremont, Ohio

individuals and groups to come together for prayer, personal growth, support, relaxation, and solitude. The center staff is trained and experienced in offering ongoing spiritual direction and counseling.

Types of Retreats/Programs Offered: Directed/Group; Directed/Private; Conference; Hermitage/Solitary; Ecumenical; Charismatic; Prayer Days; Encounters; Special; Miscellaneous Programs
Open to: Everyone except families
Person to Contact: Sister Marianne Longo, Director
Address: 1250 Tiffin Street, Fremont, OH 43420
Telephone: 419-332-6522
Office Hours: 9:00 A.M. to 4:00 P.M. weekdays
Notice Required: Variable

Sacred Heart Retreat and Renewal Center
Missionaries of the Sacred Heart

Sacred Heart Retreat House was originally a private home. Retreat rooms were added when the home was purchased. We can accommodate 55 retreatants in private rooms, all with semi-baths. We are in a quiet residential area on 27 acres of woods, paths, and lakes. There are two large conference rooms, several small ones, dining facilities for 80 people, a large chapel and a small one, and a private prayer house that will house 7 people with a small kitchen and prayer room.

Types of Retreats/Programs Offered: Directed/Group; Directed/Private; Conference; Ecumenical; Prayer Days; Special; Miscellaneous Programs
Open to: Everyone except families
Person to Contact: Barbara Witt, Office Manager
Address: 3128 Logan Way, P.O. Box 6074, Youngstown, OH 44501
Telephone: 216-759-9539
Office Hours: 9 A.M. to 5 P.M.
Notice Required: 6 months to 1 year

St. Joseph Renewal Center
Franciscan

Formerly a home for retired men, then a convent and later a motherhouse, the St. Joseph Renewal Center is a three-story brick building with private double rooms, 2 large meeting rooms, a large kitchen-dining area, a comfortable lounge, a chapel, and an elevator. Laity, priests, and religious come to spend time alone at the center. Directed retreats are available, and outside groups also use the center for their own retreats. Located in northeastern Ohio, the building has been modernized.

Types of Retreats/Programs Offered: Directed/Group; Directed/Private; Conference; Hermitage/Solitary; Ecumenical; Charismatic; Prayer Days; Encounters; Special; Miscellaneous Programs
Open to: Everyone except youths and families
Person to Contact: Sister Barbara Westrick, Director
Address: 200 St. Francis Avenue, Tiffin, OH 44883

Telephone: 419-447-0435
Office Hours: 8:00 A.M. to 5:00 P.M.
Notice Required: Variable

Oklahoma

Archdiocesan Pastoral Center
Archdiocesan

The Archdiocesan Pastoral Center is at the chancery offices. The chapel is on the main floor, but the bedroom area is separate and quiet. Most of the retreats offered at the center are only one day, due to lack of personnel and funds. However, the center is affiliated with the Sisters of Benedict at the Red Plains Priory in Oklahoma City and with the Villa Teresa of the Carmelite Sisters there. In this way, there is access to more traditional retreats.

Types of Retreats/Programs Offered: Directed/Group; Directed/Private; Conference; Hermitage/Solitary; Ecumenical; Charismatic; Prayer Days; Encounters; Cursillos; Miscellaneous Programs
Open to: Everyone except youths and families
Person to Contact: Sister Mary Kevin Rooney, Co-Director of Office of Worship and Spiritual Life
Address: 7501 N.W. Expressway, P.O. Box 32180, Oklahoma City, OK 73123-0380
Telephone: 405-721-5651
Office Hours: 9:00 A.M. to 4:30 P.M.
Notice Required: Variable

O + M (Osage + Monastery) Forest of Peace
Benedictine Sisters of Perpetual Adoration

This small monastic community seeks to blend Eastern ashram living and the monastic tradition of the West. It is composed of permanent and temporary members: Benedictine Sisters, laypersons and a Trappist monk. Located on a 40-acre tract of trees and canyons in eastern Oklahoma, Osage Monastery is open to people of all religions. The community strives to maintain an atmosphere of radical simplicity dedicated to contemplative prayer and work. There are 6 small hermitages within a short distance of the main building that contain simple sleeping facilities, bath and shower. They are available for overnight or extended retreats. Retreatants may share in community life and prayer, or complete solitude is possible. The community has two one-hour periods of contemplative sitting daily, which retreatants may attend. Closed two weeks before Holy Week.

Types of Retreats/Programs Offered: Directed/Private; Hermitage/Solitary
Open to: Men, women, male religious, female religious
Address: 18701 W. Monastery Road, Sand Springs, OK 74063
Telephone: 918-245-2734
Office Hours: 9:00 A.M.–12:00 noon; 1:00–4:30 P.M.; 6:30–8:30 P.M.
Notice Required: 2 months

Oregon

Alton L. Collins Retreat Center
United Methodist

Description not available.

Types of Retreats/Programs Offered: Directed/Group; Conference; Ecumenical; Parent-Teen; Encounters; Special; Miscellaneous Programs
Open to: Everyone except youths and families
Person to Contact: Bob Buescher, Director
Address: 32867 S.E. Highway 211, Eagle Creek, OR 97022
Telephone: 503-637-6411
Office Hours: 8:30 A.M. to 5:00 P.M.
Notice Required: Individuals, call for space available; groups, 2 years

Franciscan Renewal Center
Sisters of St. Francis

The Franciscan Renewal Center is on a 20-acre sylvan setting in the hills of southwest Portland, adjacent to Lewis and Clark College. Attractively landscaped grounds, orchards, and evergreens surround the worshiping, conferencing, living, and dining facilities. A former French chateau-style mansion dominates the entrance to the center, which has been known since 1943 as Our Lady of Angels Convent. Other buildings have been added to the complex and the center has been renovated. Accommodations include single and double rooms, and the center is handicapped accessible. Practices taught include centering prayer. Closed during Christmas holidays.

Types of Retreats/Programs Offered: Directed/Group; Directed/Private; Conference; Hermitage/Solitary; variety of Special; Miscellaneous Programs
Open to: Everyone except families
Person to Contact: Sister Carolyn Snegoski, Director
Address: 0858 SW Palatine Hill Road, Portland, OR 97219
Telephone: 503-636-1590
Office Hours: 8:30 A.M. to 4:30 P.M.
Notice Required: Several days to several weeks

The Grotto, National Sanctuary of Our Sorrowful Mother
Order of Servants of Mary (Servites)

Our facility is a shrine. The retreats we offer are one-day spiritual growth opportunities. We also offer some extended courses and spirituality conferences for those who seek such input. We try to appeal to an ecumenical audience. No overnight facilities, although we consider this a future goal.

Types of Retreats/Programs Offered: Directed/Group; Directed/Private; Ecumenical; Charismatic; Prayer Days; Miscellaneous Programs
Open to: Everyone

Person to Contact: Sister Ruth Arnott, or Sister Sylvia Swanke, Hospitality Coordinators
Address: Box 20008, corner Northeast 85th and Sandy Boulevard, Portland, OR 97220
Telephone: 503-254-7371
Office Hours: 8:30 A.M. to 4:30 P.M.
Notice Required: 2 weeks

Loyola Retreat House
Society of Jesus (Jesuit)

Loyola Retreat House is in a quiet neighborhood in southeast Portland. The beautiful, landscaped grounds screen out the noise of the city and provide a peaceful atmosphere. In addition to landscaped and forested grounds, facilities include private rooms, a chapel, spacious dining room, music room, and a library and fireplace area for quiet reflection. As an Ignatian center of spirituality and using the gift of the *Spiritual Exercises,* we choose, in solidarity with the poor, to help people with the process of integrating faith and justice with love.

Types of Retreats/Programs Offered: Directed/Group; Directed/Private; Conference; Hermitage/Solitary; Prayer Days; Special; Miscellaneous Programs, including 19th Annotation Retreats
Open to: Everyone except families
Person to Contact: Father Jack Kennedy, Director
Address: 3220 S.E. 43rd, Portland, OR 97206
Telephone: 503-777-2225
Office Hours: 8:30 A.M. to 4:30 P.M.
Notice Required: Variable

Mount Angel Abbey Retreat House
Benedictine Monastery

Mount Angel Abbey is a Benedictine monastery northeast of Salem on a mountain overlooking the Willamette Valley. In

Mount Angel Abbey, St. Benedict, Oregon

addition to the retreat house, the extensive abbey complex includes a world-renowned library, a Russian Center, the Abbey Museum, the Benedictine Press, and track and tennis courts. Retreat facilities include single and double rooms with private baths, meeting rooms, and a Blessed Sacrament prayer chapel; handicapped accessible. Men and women are welcome individually or in groups. No guests or retreatants on holiday weekends except for the Christmas and Easter celebrations.

Types of Retreats/Programs Offered: Directed/Group; Directed/Private; Conference; Hermitage/Solitary; Ecumenical; Parent-Teen; Marriage Encounter
Open to: Everyone
Person to Contact: Father Bernard Sander, Director
Address: St. Benedict, OR 97373
Telephone: 503-845-3025
Office Hours: 8:00 A.M. to 4:30 P.M.
Notice Required: Individual, anytime; groups, 6 months to a year

Our Lady of Peace, Franciscan Missionary Sisters, Beaverton, Oregon

Our Lady of Peace Retreat House
Franciscan Missionary Sisters of Our Lady of Sorrows

The retreat house property is a suburban tract of 20 acres in the beautiful Tualatin Valley, about 10 miles from the center of Portland. Facilities include private rooms. Central to the house is the chapel, where the Mass, Rosary and Benediction of the Blessed Sacrament are integral to the order of each day. All lectures and discussion sessions are held in 2 commodious lounges, adjoining one of which is the dining room. Surrounding the one-story house with its ranging wings are wide lawns, an orchard and a grove of native evergreens. This religious community was originally dedicated to the Chinese mission and still has schools in Hong Kong and Taiwan, but is also engaged in parochial and retreat work on the Pacific Coast.

Types of Retreats/Programs Offered: Directed/Group; Directed/Private; Hermitage/Solitary; Ecumenical; Charismatic; Prayer Days; Parent-Teen; Special; Miscellaneous Programs, including a Pontifical Catechetical Program
Open to: Everyone
Person to Contact: Sister Anne Marie, Retreat Director

Address: 3600 SW 170th Avenue, Beaverton, OR 97006
Telephone: 503-649-7127
Office Hours: 7:30 A.M. to 8:00 P.M.
Notice Required: Variable

Shalom Prayer Center
Benedictine Sisters

Shalom Prayer Center is in the quiet rural setting of Mount Angel, close to both ocean and mountains, run by the Benedictine Sisters of Queen of Angels Priory. All programs are open to men and women of all faiths.

Types of Retreats/Programs Offered: Directed/Group; Directed/Private; Conference; Hermitage/Solitary; Ecumenical; Prayer Days; Special; Spiritual Direction Programs
Open to: Everyone except youths and families
Person to Contact: Sister Antoinette Traeger, Director
Address: 840 S. Main, Mount Angel, OR 97362
Telephone: 503-845-6773
Office Hours: 9:00 A.M. to 5:00 P.M.
Notice Required: 3 months

Pennsylvania

Fatima Renewal Center
Diocesan

Ten miles southeast of Scranton, Our Lady of Fatima Center sits atop 300 acres in the northern Pocono Mountain region. As the Scranton Diocesan Center for Spiritual Renewal, we seek to refresh God's people by presenting experiential and educational programs geared to those who thirst to renew their Christian commitment. Numerous meeting rooms, 2 of which accommodate 200 people comfortably, chapels for both intimate reflection and large liturgical celebrations, a large dining area, and varied sleeping quarters comprise the main building.

Types of Retreats/Programs Offered: Directed/Group; Conference; Hermitage/Solitary; Ecumenical; Charismatic; Prayer Days; Parent-Teen; Encounters; Cursillos; Youth and Young Adult; Special; Miscellaneous Programs including family retreats
Open to: Everyone except priests, male religious, and female religious
Person to Contact: Father Michael M. Bryant, Director
Address: Box 163, Griffin Road, Elmhurst, PA 18416
Telephone: 717-842-8101
Office Hours: 8:30 A.M. to 4:30 P.M.; may call evenings
Notice Required: Usually 1 month

Jesuit Center for Spiritual Growth
Society of Jesus (Jesuit)

The center is at the Novitiate of St. Isaac Jogues, nine miles west of Reading, near the land of the Amish. The Ignatian exercises form the foundation of the retreats given, and the full 30-day Ignatian retreat is offered. Closed the last week of August and the first two weeks of September.

Types of Retreats/Programs Offered: Directed/Group; Directed/Private; Hermitage/Solitary; Ecumenical; Miscellaneous Programs, including Training in Retreat Direction
Open to: Everyone except youths, families, and couples
Person to Contact: Father C. Kevin Gillespie, Business Manager
Address: Church Road, Wernersville, PA 19565
Telephone: 215-678-8085
Office Hours: 9:00 A.M. to 4:30 P.M.
Notice Required: Usually 1 month

Kirkridge
Nondenominational

Kirkridge was founded in 1942 by John Oliver Nelson, a Presbyterian minister inspired by the Christian community on the

Scottish island of Iona. Kirkridge welcomes pilgrims seeking solitude and community, rest and discernment, toward personal and social transformation. Our purpose has often been expressed in the phrase: Picket and Pray. For us, those words signify the integration of personal growth and social change. We are committed to working out peace and justice imperatives in our own lives and in the structures of our society. Our intention is to address pressing human issues with the resources of biblical faith. Kirkridge is on 270 acres of mountainside in northeastern Pennsylvania. The Appalachian Trail runs through our property at the top of the mountain, where vistas are long. In the valley, gentle pastureland surrounds our 1815 farmhouse, one of several buildings available for programs. We also have several hermitage-style facilities available for individual private retreats.

Types of Retreats/Programs Offered: Various workshops and conferences; Hermitage/Solitary
Open to: Everyone
Person to Contact: Director
Address: Bangor, PA 18013
Telephone: 215-588-1793
Office Hours: 9 A.M. to 5 P.M. weekdays
Notice Required: Variable

Mount St. Macrina Retreat Center
Sisters of the Order of St. Basil the Great (Byzantine Rite)

Mount St. Macrina Retreat Center is on 210 acres of rolling hills in the Laurel Mountains of southwestern Pennsylvania. The retreat center itself, once the mansion of a coal baron, features spacious rooms and a dining area. Sponsored by a Byzantine religious order of Sisters, the liturgical services are celebrated in the tradition of the Byzantine Church. The center also houses a shrine to Our Lady of Perpetual Help. Sleeping accommodations are dormitory-style, with 4–7 in a room. Closed August and September 1–20.

Types of Retreats/Programs Offered: Directed/Group; Directed/Private; Conference; Hermitage/Solitary; Ecumenical; Prayer Days; Miscellaneous Programs including Iconography
Open to: Everyone except families
Person to Contact: Sister Margaret Ann Andrako, Director
Address: 510 W. Main Street, Box 878, Uniontown, PA 15401
Telephone: 412-438-7149
Office Hours: 9:00 A.M. to 4:30 P.M. weekdays
Notice Required: 1 to 2 months

Pendle Hill
Religious Society of Friends (Quakers)

Pendle Hill, grounded in the social and spiritual values of the Religious Society of Friends, is a 53-year-old venture in adult education that welcomes persons of all faiths who are committed to learning, open to exploring religious reality, and ready to take a responsible part in the common life of an adult community. Located 12 miles southwest of Philadelphia, Pendle Hill is in a suburban area with easy access to public transportation and 25 minutes from the Philadelphia airport. Pendle Hill offers a resident program of three terms of 10 weeks each, from October to June. It also presents 15 weekend conferences yearly, a New Year gathering, and several weeklong summer sessions. In addition, persons may sojourn at Pendle Hill for up to three weeks. Closed last 2 weeks in August and 1 week at Christmas.

Types of Retreats/Programs Offered: Conference
Open to: Adults of all ages and faiths
Address: 338 Plush Mill Road, Wallingford, PA 19086
Telephone: 215-566-4507
Office Hours: 9:00 A.M. to 5:00 P.M. weekdays

Pendle Hill, Wallingford, Pennsylvania (Photo: Ted Hetzel)

Precious Blood Spirituality Center
Adorers of the Blood of Christ

Located between Lancaster and York among rolling green fields of Pennsylvania Dutch country, the center provides a quiet, reflective atmosphere conducive to contemplation and quiet walks through tree-shaded areas. Clean, well-maintained, modern, air-conditioned dormitories (double occupancy, sinks in room), conference rooms, dining hall, and lounges are all located in one building. Elevator is available. Linens and towels provided. Ramp for handicapped.

Types of Retreats/Programs Offered: Directed/Group; Directed/Private; Conference; Hermitage/Solitary; Ecumenical; Charismatic; Prayer Days; Encounters; Special; Miscellaneous Programs
Open to: Everyone except families
Person to Contact: Sister Immaculata Markovich, Director
Address: St. Joseph Convent, Columbia, PA 17512
Telephone: 717-285-4536
Office Hours: 9:00 A.M. to 5:00 P.M. weekdays
Notice Required: Individuals, 2 weeks; groups, 1 year

Precious Blood Spirituality Center, Columbia, Pennsylvania

St. Francis Center for Renewal
School Sisters of St. Francis, Monocacy Manor

Description not available.

Types of Retreats/Programs Offered: Directed/Private; Conference; Hermitage/Solitary; Ecumenical; Charismatic; Prayer Days; Encounters; Special; Miscellaneous Programs
Open to: Everyone
Person to Contact: Sister M. Anita Kuchera, Retreat Administrator
Address: 395 Bridle Path Road, Bethlehem, PA 18017
Telephone: 215-867-8890 or 866-2597
Office Hours: 9:00 A.M. to 4:00 P.M.
Notice Required: 1 month

St. Paul's Retreat Center
Passionist Fathers and Brothers

We see ourselves as an oasis, a center where people pause in their life journey to look at the road map, examine where they've been and where they are going, and seek refreshment and strength to continue their journey. They also discover, or deepen their awareness, that God is with them as they make their way. Life is so busy for so many people today. Some people are wounded and hurting. Others are just worn out and frazzled. Still others are wandering and lost. St. Paul's Retreat House is a place where people can come and rest awhile. The married deacon, Sister and two Passionist priests on staff are experienced guides who provide the atmosphere where God works. Through conferences, prayer together, workshops with discussion, and quiet time, the retreatant experiences God's oasis.

Types of Retreats/Programs Offered: Conference; Prayer Days; Special; Miscellaneous Programs
Open to: Everyone except families
Person to Contact: Father Donald Ware, Retreat Director
Address: 148 Monastery Avenue, Pittsburgh, PA 15203
Telephone: 412-381-7676
Office Hours: 9:00 A.M. to 5:00 P.M. weekdays
Notice Required: 1 to 2 weeks

Villa Maria Community Center
Sisters of the Humility of Mary

Villa Maria Community Center is 1 mile east of the Ohio state line and 11 miles west of New Castle, Pennsylvania in a rural setting. The facilities include private rooms, Magnificat Chapel, Crucifix Prayer Room, Icon Room, Adoration Chapel, and a music listening room. There is also an art house with potter's wheel, an area for painting and a Zen room upstairs. In addition to a swimming pool and tennis courts, we have spacious grounds for walking and quiet contemplation. An herb garden in the back, a lake in the front, and a brook provide an atmosphere for prayer, as do shrines to Our Lady, the Sacred Heart, and St. Joseph. VMCC offers a full program of retreats year-round.

Types of Retreats/Programs Offered: Directed/Group; Directed/Private; Conference; Hermitage/Solitary; Prayer Days; Special; Miscellaneous Programs
Open to: Everyone except youths and families
Person to Contact: Sister Maria Ruegg, Programmer, or Patty Gessler, Registrar
Address: Villa Maria, PA 16155
Telephone: 412-964-8861
Office Hours: 8:30 A.M. to 4:30 P.M.
Notice Required: At least 1 month

Rhode Island

Carmel Retreat Center
Corpus Christi Carmelites

Carmel Retreat Center is on picturesque grounds overlooking Narragansett Bay. Facilities include private rooms as well as double accommodations for couples, beautiful shrines, and a Gothic chapel. Open to all groups and individuals, programs are custom-designed. Arrangements may be made for days of recollection, private retreats, summer sojourns, etc. July and August are open for private retreat guests only.

Types of Retreats/Programs Offered: Conference; Hermitage/Solitary; Ecumenical; Charismatic; Special
Open to: Everyone except families
Person to Contact: Sister Carmencita Correia, Retreat Director
Address: 21 Battery Street, Newport, RI 02840
Telephone: 401-847-6165 or 846-7839
Office Hours: 8:00 A.M. to 6:00 P.M.
Notice Required: 1 month

Father Marot CYO Center

Most of our retreats are for high school and college students. We also do many retreats for those preparing to receive confirmation. The retreat in which we specialize is called the Search For Maturity Retreat, which was founded at our center. To the search are attached other programs, such as weekly prayer meetings, Phase II and III, conclave as follow-through.

Types of Retreats/Programs Offered: Conference
Open to: Men, women, youths, and couples
Person to Contact: Ms. Fernande Dery, Executive Secretary
Address: 53 Federal Street, P.O. Box 518, Woonsocket, RI 02895
Telephone: 401-762-3252
Office Hours: 9:00 A.M. to 5:00 P.M.

Mount St. Joseph Spiritual Life Center
Sisters of St. Dorothy

Mount St. Joseph Spiritual Life Center is near the Mount Hope Bridge overlooking Mount Hope Bay, a natural oasis for anyone seeking spiritual refreshment. The center has 25 acres of peaceful scenery and a creative environment conducive to prayer, reflection, and relaxation. Rooms are double occupancy, with 1 dormitory that contains 4 beds.

Types of Retreats/Programs Offered: Conference; Hermitage/Solitary; Prayer Days; Teen
Open to: Everyone
Person to Contact: Sister Cecilia Ferro, Director
Address: 13 Monkey Wrench Lane, Bristol, RI 02809
Telephone: 401-253-5434
Office Hours: 9:00 A.M. to 5:00 P.M.
Notice Required: 2 weeks to preferably 1 month

Nazareth Center
Sisters of St. Chretienne

Description not available. Closed July 1 to August 31.

Types of Retreats/Programs Offered: Directed/Private; Hermitage/Solitary; Prayer Days; Special; Miscellaneous Programs
Open to: Everyone except youths and families
Person to Contact: Sister Rachel Gonthier, Director
Address: 12 Cliff Terrace, Newport, RI 02840
Telephone: 401-847-1654
Office Hours: 9:00 A.M. to 5:00 P.M.
Notice Required: 2 months

South Carolina

The Oratory—Center for Spirituality
Oratory

The Oratory is on 6 acres in a quiet residential area. The grounds of the center, the neighborhood, and 2 nearby parks offer opportunities for meditation, prayer, and relaxation. Housing facilities are varied, but all rooms are air-conditioned with linens furnished. The church and main residence which includes the dining room are handicapped accessible. The YMCA next door offers use of its pools (indoor and outdoor) for Oratory guests. The center desires to accommodate persons who are seeking to grow spiritually. We serve church groups of all denominations and seekers of quiet time and space; we also offer one-on-one guidance or direction, spiritual friendship, and prayer companioning.

Types of Retreats/Programs Offered: Directed/Group; Directed/Private; Conference; Hermitage/Solitary; Ecumenical; Prayer Days; Engaged Encounter; Special; Miscellaneous Programs
Open to: Everyone except families
Person to Contact: Sarah Morgan, Coordinator
Address: 434 Charlotte Avenue, Rock Hill, SC 29730
Mailing Address: P.O. Box 11586, Rock Hill, SC 29731
Telephone: 803-327-2097
Office Hours: 8:15 A.M.–12:00 noon daily
Notice Required: Individuals, variable; groups, 3 months

Spring Bank Retreat Center
Dominican

Spring Bank is an ecumenical center located in a quiet, rural setting on 58 wooded acres with magnificent live oak and magnolia trees, good biking and walking areas, and excellent beaches 1 hour away. Facilities include a large, air-conditioned conference and chapel area, an art studio, and mostly private air-conditioned rooms. The Spring Bank staff feel in harmony with a holistic approach to life, centered in the Word, conscious of the importance of spiritual, mental, and physical health, and the extraordinary power of creative energy. All retreats begin at 7:30 P.M. the first evening and end after the noon meal on the last day. Our daily prayer is centered on the Scripture readings of the Church, and all who come are welcome to join us. The Liturgy is usually celebrated on Tuesday and Thursday at 5:30 P.M. Thirty-day and 60-day sabbatical programs are available. Limited availability in August, September, and December.

Types of Retreats/Programs Offered: Directed/Private; Conference; Hermitage/Solitary; Ecumenical; Charismatic; Prayer Days; Special; Miscellaneous Programs
Open to: Everyone except youths and families
Person to Contact: Betty Condon or Ursula Ording, Coordinators
Address: Springbank Route #2, Box 180, Kingstree, SC 29556
Telephone: 803-382-3426
Office Hours: 9:00 A.M. to 5:00 P.M.
Notice Required: 1 month

South Dakota

Harmony Hill Center
Benedictine Sisters, Mother of God Monastery

Harmony Hill is a community adult education center that offers a full range of services. The retreat house provides time and place for personal reflection and meditation. In addition to the days of reflection, group retreats, and spiritual direction offered throughout the year, the retreat house may be reserved by an individual or a group as a host facility. Center facilities include library, lounge, chapel, exercise room, and outdoor auditorium. The center is a fully accredited branch campus of Mount Marty College and specializes in quality, affordable college education for nontraditional students. Practices taught include centering prayer.

Types of Retreats/Programs Offered: Directed/Group; Directed/Private; Conference; Ecumenical; Prayer Days; Encounters; Miscellaneous Programs, including Lay Ministry Program
Open to: Everyone except youths and families
Person to Contact: Sister Leona Gauer, Hospitality Manager
Address: Route 3, Box 254, Watertown, SD 57201
Telephone: 605-886-6777
Office Hours: 9:00 A.M. to 4:30 P.M.
Notice Required: 8 to 14 days

Tennessee

House of the Lord
Religious of the House of the Lord

Our retreat center is open and available to all people. Many non-Catholics come for quiet as well as for our programs. Our facility is an old monastery and exudes a sense of sacred space. Five Sisters live here, and we invite our guests and retreatants to share our lives with us. Our center is simple, comfortable, and has an intimate feeling. We welcome our guests because we are grateful they come and share Emmanuel; the House of the Lord is Our Father's House and therefore all are welcomed.

Types of Retreats/Programs Offered: Directed/Group; Directed/Private; Conference; Ecumenical; Prayer Days; Special
Open to: Everyone
Person to Contact: Sister Susan Erdman, House Director

Address: 1306 Dellwood Avenue, Memphis, TN 38127
Telephone: 901-357-7398
Office Hours: 9:00 A.M. to 9:00 P.M.
Notice Required: 2 weeks

Texas

Bishop DeFalco Retreat Center
Diocesan; staffed by Redemptorists

Bishop DeFalco Retreat Center is a diocesan renewal center with 50 private rooms with twin beds and bath/shower, dining room, chapel, and four conference rooms. The center is available to other denominations, nonprofit groups for retreats, seminars, conferences, etc. Redemptorists administer the center and specialize in teaching contemplative life-style amidst an active involvement with one's family, job, society. Contemplative path retreats are offered for weekends, 5 and 7 days. Residency programs of one month to a year, teaching the Christian contemplative tradition, including centering prayer and the Ignatian Exercises, or the Eastern Zen tradition. To ensure quiet atmosphere, one wing with 14 bedrooms, dining room/kitchen, and prayer room is reserved.

Types of Retreats/Programs Offered: Directed/Group; Directed/Private; Conference; Hermitage/Solitary; Ecumenical; Charismatic; Prayer Days; Encounters; Cursillos in Spanish and English; Miscellaneous Programs
Open to: Everyone except families
Person to Contact: Father Robert Curry, Director
Address: 2100 N. Spring, Amarillo, TX 79107
Telephone: 806-383-1811
Office Hours: 8:00 A.M. to 5:00 P.M. weekdays
Notice Required: 1 week

Cedarbrake Renewal Center

Cedarbrake is strictly a host facility that rents its accommodations to groups only, not individuals. Located in a grove of cedar trees, the Cedarbrake woods offer serenity and beauty for contemplation.

Types of Retreats/Programs Offered: Directed/Group; Ecumenical; Prayer Days; Engaged Encounter; Cursillos; Miscellaneous Programs
Open to: Everyone
Person to Contact: Sister Jean Burbo, Director
Address: P.O. Box 58, Belton, TX 76513-0058
Telephone: 817-780-2436
Office Hours: 9:00 A.M. to 5:00 P.M.
Notice Required: 6 months for groups

Christ the King Retreat Center
Diocesan

Christ the King Retreat Center, operated by the Diocese of San Angelo, is a multifaceted complex of modern buildings in a setting of tranquility and peaceful introspection. Stretching along the south bank of the Concho River, the center blends harmoniously with the stands of live oak and pecan and rolling grassy hillside. A winding path through the 19 acres offers solitude amid the statuary marking the 14 Stations of the Cross. At the heart of the complex is a peaceful courtyard leading to the chapel. Center facilities include single or double rooms, conference and counseling rooms, offices, dining room, kitchen, and a library. The variety of activities and programs mark the center as the focal point of the diocese. Family accommodations are being developed.

Types of Retreats/Programs Offered: Directed/Group; Directed/Private; Hermitage/Solitary; Charismatic; Prayer Days; Encounters; Cursillos; Miscellaneous Programs

Open to: Everyone
Person to Contact: Father Jim Chamont, Director, or Mary Ann Lewis, Administrator
Address: 802 Ford, San Angelo, TX 76903
Mailing *Address:* P.O. Box 3745, San Angelo, TX 76902
Telephone: 915-658-3900
Office Hours: 8:00 A.M. to 5:00 P.M.
Notice Required: 2 weeks to 1 month

Holy Family Retreat Center
Diocesan

Holy Family Retreat Center is in northwest Beaumont on 55 acres of pine woods. The quiet and solitary grounds include outdoor Stations of the Cross carved through a natural pathway in the woods. Center facilities include 3 guest houses, each with a large meeting room, a kitchenette, a large screened porch, and double rooms with private baths. There are also a large conference center, a small Blessed Sacrament chapel, and a library. The center sponsors programs such as traditional weekend retreats, lectures, and days of recollection. It also hosts programs sponsored by other groups. Closed Christmas through New Year's, Triduum and Easter weekend, and July 4 weekend.

Types of Retreats/Programs Offered: Conference; Charismatic; Prayer Days; Encounters; Special; Miscellaneous Programs
Open to: Everyone except families
Person to Contact: Father Michael A. Jamail, Director; Sister Lauren Beck or Sister Maria Geheb, Assistant Directors
Address: 9920 North Major Drive, Beaumont, TX 77713-9316
Telephone: 409-899-5617
Office Hours: 8:30 A.M. to 5:00 P.M. weekdays
Notice Required: Variable

Mount Carmel Center
Discalced Carmelite Fathers

Founded in 1974 by Father Anthony Morello, OCD, Mount Carmel Center is a monastery of Discalced Carmelite friars dedicated to a life of contemporary austerity and to the search for God through contemplation and the service of His Church. The extent of an individual retreatant's involvement with the community prayer schedule varies with each person's needs and wishes. Located on 30 hilltop acres overlooking Dallas, Mount Carmel Center is an informal institute of Christian spirituality. The House of Silence offers simple, rustic accommodations, and a small guest house is available. A small Byzantine oratory and a larger contemporary chapel are always available, and the wooded grounds are spacious and inviting.

Types of Retreats/Programs Offered: Directed/Private; Conference; Hermitage/Solitary; Ecumenical; Prayer Days; Miscellaneous Programs
Open to: Everyone except youths, families, and couples
Person to Contact: Father Mary Philip, Director
Address: 4600 W. Davis Street, Dallas, TX 75211-3498
Telephone: 214-331-6224
Office Hours: 8 A.M.–12:00 noon; 12:15–5 P.M.; 6:30–10 P.M.
Notice Required: Variable

Our Lady of the Pillar Marianist Retreat Center
Congregation of the Daughters of Mary Immaculate (Marianist Sisters)

Our Lady of the Pillar Marianist Retreat Center is dedicated to the proclamation of the Word of God to people of all backgrounds, denominations, and walks of life in order to vivify their personal and communitarian faith life and Christian commitment. The nonprofit center, staffed by Marianist Sisters and

Our Lady of the Pillar Marianist Retreat Center, San Antonio, Texas

laity, offers opportunities for all Christians to grow in their spiritual lives through retreats and various types of renewal programs in both Spanish and English. Groups of all denominations are welcomed who wish to conduct their own spiritual or educational program. The environment is uniquely designed for reflection in a peaceful atmosphere away from the bustle of daily living.

Types of Retreats/Programs Offered: Directed/Private; Conference; Charismatic; Prayer Days; Marriage Encounter; Special; Miscellaneous Programs
Open to: Everyone except youths and families
Person to Contact: Sister Marcy Loehrlein, Director
Address: 2507 N.W. 36th Street, San Antonio, TX 78228
Telephone: 512-433-1408
Office Hours: 8:30 A.M. to 5:30 P.M. weekdays
Notice Required: Variable

Directory of Retreat and Renewal Centers 225

Virginia

Dominican Retreat
Dominican Sisters of St. Catherine de Ricci

Dominican Retreat is a spacious, beautiful property 4 miles from Washington, D.C., enclosed in a wooded area that offers quiet, solitude, and solid spiritual nourishment to anyone seeking the Lord. The Sisters at Dominican Retreat offer not only a comfortable, at-home place, but a rich heritage of spiritual experience and walk with the Lord. Our programs are primarily geared to Catholic women, but all faiths are welcome and do enjoy our home. When you come, expect a restful, unpressured experience of kindness, hospitality, and respect for your spiritual journey. Expect us to give you the best fruit of our contemplation. Closed in August.

Types of Retreats/Programs Offered: Conference; Charismatic; Prayer Days; Special; Miscellaneous Programs
Open to: Everyone
Person to Contact: Sister Anne Lythgoe, Retreat Ministry Director
Address: 7103 Old Dominion Drive, McLean, VA 22101-2799
Telephone: 703-356-4243
Notice Required: 2 months

The Franciscan Center
Third Order Regular of St. Francis

Located at Sacred Heart Monastery on 150 acres of land 5 miles south of Winchester, the Franciscan Center facilities include private rooms, beautiful chapel, dining room, library, large and small meeting rooms, and large recreational lounge. We see hospitality as our ministry, and we provide a place, an atmosphere of quiet and reflection where people can get in touch with themselves and their God. Retreatants are welcome to join the friars for prayer and meals. Closed Christmas week, Holy

Week (Thursday–Sunday), Thanksgiving weekend, and early July to early August.

Types of Retreats/Programs Offered: Directed/Group; Directed/Private; Conference; Hermitage/Solitary; Prayer Days; Special; Miscellaneous Programs
Open to: Everyone except youths, families, and couples
Person to Contact: Brother Paul McMullen, Director
Address: P.O. Box 825, Route 642, Winchester, VA 22601
Telephone: 703-869-1599
Office Hours: 9:00 A.M. to 4:30 P.M.
Notice Required: Usually a few weeks

Missionhurst Mission Center
Missionhurst

Missionhurst is about 20 minutes by car from the Mall in Washington, D.C., and only two blocks from Marymount University. The center facilities include single or double rooms with semiprivate baths. There are also a chapel, a dining room, a conference room, a small meeting room, and beautiful grounds with tennis court. The director is available for spiritual direction and individually directed retreats. The center provides facilities for groups bringing their own program and director. Preference is given to missionary groups, those with interest in the Third World and in missionary spirituality.

Types of Retreats/Programs Offered: Directed/Group; Directed/Private; Hermitage/Solitary; Miscellaneous Programs
Open to: Everyone except families
Person to Contact: Father Bill Wyndaele, Director
Address: 4651 North 25th Street, Arlington, VA 22207
Telephone: 703-525-6557
Office Hours: 9:00 A.M.–12:00 noon
Notice Required: 2 weeks

The Well Retreat Center
Diocesan

The Well is nestled on 13 acres of pine woods near a spring-fed lake in Isle of Wight County. Since 1981 the center has grown from a small house of prayer into a complex containing a retreat center, conference rooms, chapel, and hermitage accommodations for retreatants. Four hermitages—each containing 4 bedrooms and 4 baths—are available for groups, as well as private rooms for individual retreatants. Accommodations are available for the handicapped. The Well has a special membership at the Suffolk YMCA, 12 miles away, where individuals making private or directed retreats may use the exercise room and pool for a nominal fee. Practices taught include centering prayer. Usually closed Christmas to New Year's.

Types of Retreats/Programs Offered: Directed/Group; Directed/Private; Conference; Hermitage/Solitary; Ecumenical; Prayer Days; Encounters; Cursillos; Special; Miscellaneous Programs
Open to: Everyone except families
Person to Contact: Sister Nancy Healy or Diane Weymouth, Co-Directors
Address: Route 1, Box 468, Smithfield, VA 23430
Telephone: 804-255-2366
Office Hours: 10:00 A.M. to 5:00 P.M. and 7:00–9:00 P.M. weekdays
Notice Required: Prefer 1 month

Washington

Kairos House of Prayer
Roman Catholic; privately incorporated

Kairos House of Prayer is located 11½ miles north of downtown Spokane on 27 acres of forested hills and beautiful meadows conducive to the prayer experience. Kairos has been established to provide a place for all who wish to avail themselves of a contemplative experience. Kairos offers a program to facilitate integrated prayer, that in which the whole person prays, including the following: Eucharist, Sacrament of Reconciliation, centering meditation, Jesus chant and prayer, deep relaxation and concentration, breathing methods, physical postures. We have 3 group meditations a day plus 2 hermit days each week (Wednesday and Sunday); a hermit chaplain is in residence. Hermitages are available upon request. Vegetarian diet. Closed Christmas through New Year's.

Types of Retreats/Programs Offered: Directed/Private; Hermitage/Solitary
Open to: Everyone except youths and families
Person to Contact: Sister Florence Leone, Coordinator
Address: Route 5, Box 490, Spokane, WA 99208
Telephone: 509-466-2187
Office Hours: 9:00 A.M. to 6:00 P.M.
Notice Required: At least 1 week to 1 month

The Priory Spirituality Center
Benedictine

The Priory Spirituality Center, a monastic setting in a wooded area, is an outgrowth of the St. Placid Community's commitment to Benedictine peace and hospitality. We welcome individuals and groups of all faiths who, seeking a closer relationship with God, desire time and space for inner renewal, spiritual studies, faith experiences, holistic psycho-spiritual integration, or recollection in an atmosphere of creative quiet. Guests are also invited to share in the richness of the Benedictine tradition by joining the Sisters in their daily prayer and worship. Centering prayer is among the practices taught.

Types of Retreats/Programs Offered: Directed/Group; Directed/Private; Conference; Hermitage/Solitary; Ecumenical; Prayer Days; Encounters; Special; Miscellaneous Programs
Open to: Everyone except families
Person to Contact: Sister Lucy Wynkoop, Director

Address: 320 College Street N.E., Lacey, WA 98506
Telephone: 206-438-1771
Office Hours: Anytime
Notice Required: Variable

The Redemptorist Palisades Retreat
Redemptorist

The Redemptorist Palisades Retreat is perched on a bluff 100 feet above Puget Sound. We offer everyone, young and old, men and women, religious and laity, rich and poor, the opportunity to experience heaven here on earth. God created our magnificent natural location with its beauties of water, sky, trees, and mountains for all to enjoy. The 35 acres include gardens and lawns for meditation and an outdoor Stations of the Cross. Facilities include private rooms and baths, a large chapel and lounge, and an Annex House.

Types of Retreats/Programs Offered: Directed/Group; Directed/Private; Conference; Hermitage/Solitary; Ecumenical; Charismatic; Prayer Days; Engaged Encounter; Special; Miscellaneous Programs
Open to: Everyone except families and small children
Person to Contact: Jacqueline Peterson, Secretary, or Brother William Roberts, Registrar
Address: 4700 SW Dash Point Road, Federal Way, WA 98023
Mailing Address: P.O. Box 3739, Federal Way, WA 98063
Telephone: 206-927-9621 (Tacoma) or 206-838-9583 (Seattle)
Office Hours: 9 A.M. to 3 P.M. weekdays
Notice Required: Variable

Still Point
Roman Catholic; incorporated

Still Point is a spacious old home on Seattle's Capitol Hill, with a lovely view of the beautiful Cascade Mountains and Lake

Washington. A nonprofit corporation, Still Point is staffed by religious women of various congregations and a laywoman. The house offers a chapel, library, private and double rooms, a large living and dining room area, and a second meeting room. Still Point is a homelike center for spiritual renewal near the heart of Seattle. Although our grounds are not large, we are in a very fine, quiet residential area near a park where retreatants enjoy walks. Still Point offers atmosphere, programs, and services to individuals and groups, laity, religious, and clerics of all faiths in their common hunger for God. Practices taught include centering prayer. No overnight facilities for families.

Types of Retreats/Programs Offered: Directed/Group; Directed/Private; Conference; Hermitage/Solitary; Prayer Days; Special; Miscellaneous Programs
Open to: Everyone
Person to Contact: Sister Eleanor Adams, Director
Address: 2333 13th Avenue East, Seattle, WA 98102
Telephone: 206-322-8006
Office Hours: 9:00 A.M. to 5:00 P.M.
Notice Required: Variable

West Virginia

John XXIII Pastoral Center

John XXIII Pastoral Center is a religious pastoral center. We do not have a retreat staff. Basically we offer our facility primarily for religious groups that plan and direct their own programs, which could be of a religious nature as well as workshops, seminars, or simply programs of an organizational or planning nature. Facilities include double rooms and two dormitories, a large dining area, conference rooms, a library, and a spacious and beautiful chapel. Handicapped accessible.

Open to: Everyone
Person to Contact: Group Coordinator

Directory of Retreat and Renewal Centers 231

Address: 100 Hodges Road, Charleston, WV 25314
Telephone: 304-342-0507
Office Hours: 9:00 A.M. to 5:00 P.M. weekdays

Wisconsin

Archdiocesan Retreat Center
Archdiocesan

Description not available.

Types of Retreats/Programs Offered: Ecumenical; Encounters; hosts Miscellaneous Programs
Open to: Everyone except youths
Person to Contact: Donna Rugolo, Director of Building Services
Address: 3501 S. Lake Drive, P.O. Box 07912, Milwaukee, WI 53207-0912
Telephone: 414-769-3491
Office Hours: 8:00 A.M. to 4:30 P.M.
Notice Required: As soon as possible

Dominican Education Center
Dominican

Located in the southwestern tip of Wisconsin on a geological mound, the Dominican Education Center is a large and varied complex centered on a mother house for Dominican Sisters. Facilities include private guest rooms, chapels, a large library, a book shop, dining rooms, lounges, and a beautiful archives and museum. Morning and evening prayer and daily Eucharist are available for all guests. As much as possible, the food is grown on the Sisters' large farm and gardens, cultivated with an awareness of natural and healthful methods. The premises also include a health center and a wellness center. In addition to hosting groups, we sponsor a weeklong centering retreat each summer and offer centering prayer evenings and days. We have also sponsored Zen retreats.

Types of Retreats/Programs Offered: Directed/Group; Directed/Private; Conference; Ecumenical; Prayer Days; Special; Miscellaneous Programs
Open to: Everyone
Person to Contact: Sister Joan Brichaecek, Director
Address: County Z, Sinsinawa, WI 53824
Telephone: 608-748-4411
Office Hours: 8:00 A.M. to 4:30 P.M. weekdays
Notice Required: Normally 3 weeks

Franciscan Spirituality Center
Franciscan Sisters of Perpetual Adoration

Description not available.

Types of Retreats/Programs Offered: Directed/Group; Directed/Private; Conference; Hermitage/Solitary; Ecumenical; Prayer Days; Marriage Encounter; Special
Open to: Everyone except youths and families
Person to Contact: Sister Mary Kathryn Fogarty, Director
Address: 920 Market Street, La Crosse, WI 54601
Telephone: 608-782-8899
Office Hours: 8:00 A.M. to 4:30 P.M. weekdays
Notice Required: 1 month

Ministry and Life Center
Norbertine Fathers

Located at St. Norbert's Abbey, the Ministry and Life Center facilities include private rooms. Meals are taken in the abbey dining room, and the Eucharist and Liturgy of the Hours are celebrated with the Norbertine Community. There are over 100 acres of fields to roam, with beautiful courtyard gardens, tennis courts, and an indoor pool. Practices taught include centering prayer.

Types of Retreats/Programs Offered: Directed/Group; Directed/Private; Conference; Hermitage/Solitary; Ecumenical; Encounters; Special; Miscellaneous Programs
Open to: Everyone except youths, families, and couples
Person to Contact: Anne Egan, Director, or Sister Ruth Burhart, Associate Director
Address: St. Norbert Abbey, De Pere, WI 54115-2697
Telephone: 414-336-2727
Office Hours: 9:00 A.M. to 3:00 P.M.
Notice Required: 3 to 5 days for individuals

Monte Alverno Retreat Center
Capuchin Franciscan

Ours is a silent retreat, more of a contemplative experience. We have four Capuchin Franciscans on our retreat team. We give conferences to the group and have material to guide them during the time between conferences. Our center is on the Fox River—a beautiful setting conducive to prayer and reflection. Most of our retreats are filled to capacity. Each retreatant has his own room, and there are lounge areas for common use. The chapel is furnished with comfortable chairs. Our center has a very good reputation for the meals that are served. All of this makes for a good retreat experience.

Types of Retreats/Programs Offered: Directed/Group; Directed/Private; Charismatic; Special
Open to: Men, women, priests, male religious, female religious, couples
Person to Contact: Father Kieran Hickey, Director
Address: 1000 N. Ballard Road, Appleton, WI 54911
Telephone: 414-733-8526
Office Hours: 9:00 A.M. to 5:00 P.M.

St. Benedict Center
Sisters of St. Benedict

St. Benedict Center is open to serious seekers of diverse backgrounds. You are welcome to join the praying community in our chapel three times daily. Our craft studio, monastic library, and bookstore will enhance your stay. Your private bedroom contains a comfortable chair, bed, desk, sink, and wardrobe. Heart-healthy meals are served in our central dining room. Our 135 acres include woods, glacial pond, rolling meadows, orchard, and garden. There are an outdoor pool and tennis courts. We are a nonsmoking, handicapped-accessible facility twenty minutes from downtown Madison, the University of Wisconsin, the airport and two interstate highways. Practices taught include centering prayer as well as Benedictine lectio and meditatio.

Types of Retreats/Programs Offered: Directed/Group; Directed/Private; Conference; Hermitage/Solitary; Ecumenical; Prayer Days; Cursillos; Miscellaneous Programs
Open to: Everyone. Have a limited number of family suites
Person to Contact: Christine Melland, Guest Coordinator
Address: 4200 County Highway M, Middleton, WI 53562
Telephone: 608-836-1631
Office Hours: 8:00 A.M. to 4:30 P.M. weekdays
Notice Required: Minimum 24 hours

St. Clare Center for Spirituality
Felician Sisters (Chicago)

We have a country atmosphere in spite of the fact that we are 10 miles from Stevens Point. Most of our retreats and programs are daylong, because our overnight facilities are very limited, available only to very small groups or individuals. Closed June through August.

Types of Retreats/Programs Offered: Directed/Private; Conference; Hermitage/Solitary; Ecumenical; Prayer Days; Parent-Teen; Miscellaneous Programs
Open to: Everyone
Person to Contact: Sister Mary Therese Lukas, Director
Address: 7381 Church Street—Polonia, Custer, WI 54423
Telephone: 315-592-4680
Office Hours: 9:00 A.M. to 5:00 P.M.
Notice Required: At least 2 weeks

St. Francis Friary and Retreat Center
Franciscan

St. Francis Friary is 3 miles north of Burlington on 160 acres of God's natural beauty. We are a Franciscan sponsored center for prayer and renewal with a team of Franciscan friars committed to sharing the spirit of St. Francis of Assisi with those who spend time here. In addition to traditional retreat facilities and programs, theologians and a canon lawyer are available for consultation. The center's housing includes individual bedrooms with common lavatories and showers. There are 8 lounges, ranging from a parlor-style room to a large meeting room. The weekend retreat schedule usually includes daily liturgy, conferences and discussions, time for communal and personal prayer, reflection, reading, and relaxation. Arrangements may be made by groups to use the facilities, and individuals may make arrangements for private directed or undirected retreats.

Types of Retreats/Programs Offered: Directed/Group; Directed/Private; Conference; Hermitage/Solitary; Charismatic; Prayer Days; Miscellaneous Programs
Open to: Everyone except families
Person to Contact: Father Edward Tlucek, Guardian/Director of Retreats
Address: 503 South Browns Lake Drive, Burlington, WI 53105

Telephone: 414-763-3600
Office Hours: 8:30 A.M. to 4:30 P.M.
Notice Required: At least 1 year

St. Francis Friary and Retreat Center, Burlington, Wisconsin

St. Joseph Retreat
Priests of the Sacred Heart

St. Joseph Retreat is on Kangaroo Lake in Door County, Wisconsin. We have a spacious area with a rustic, farm atmosphere. The property includes 400 acres to roam, a mile of lakeshore, totem trails, outdoor Stations of the Cross, and a Marian walk. In appropriate weather we also have a kiva-like chapel, bicycles, a hermitage, and cross-country ski trails. Accommodations include single and double occupancy rooms.

Types of Retreats/Programs Offered: Directed/Group; Directed/Private; Conference; Hermitage/Solitary; Prayer Days; Special
Open to: Everyone except youths and families
Person to Contact: Sister S. Lorraine Aspenleiter, Director
Address: 3035 O'Brien Road, Bailey's Harbor, WI 54202
Telephone: 414-839-2391
Office Hours: Anytime
Notice Required: Variable

Schoenstatt Retreat Center
Schoenstatt Sisters of Mary

Located on 200 acres of rolling hills and trees, the Schoenstatt Center includes not only the retreat center, but also the Shrine of Our Mother and Queen of Schoenstatt, the provincial house of the Schoenstatt Sisters of Mary, and the residence of the Schoenstatt Fathers. A group founded in the early 1900s by Father Joseph Kentenich in Germany, the Schoenstatt movement is a community dedicated to the world in Christ through Mary. Its main body is a lay apostolate working in conjunction with priests. Schoenstatt retreats emphasize a covenant of love with the Blessed Mother, everyday sanctity, and being an instrument in the hands of God. Facilities include single and double rooms and dormitories, conference halls and meeting rooms, large and small dining rooms, and a reading area.

Types of Retreats/Programs Offered: Directed/Group; Conference; Hermitage/Solitary; Ecumenical; Charismatic; Prayer Days; Encounters; Special; Miscellaneous Programs
Open to: Everyone except families
Person to Contact: Elisabeth M. Heisig, Coordinator
Address: W. 284 N. 698 Cherry Lane, Waukesha, WI 53188
Telephone: 414-547-7733
Office Hours: 8:30 A.M. to 3:30 P.M.
Notice Required: Individuals, 4 weeks; groups, 1 to 2 years

Siena Center Retreats
Sisters of St. Dominic (Racine)

Siena Center Retreat Wing is wonderfully located on Lake Michigan in Racine, Wisconsin. The beauty of the environment and the prayerful mood of the center bring people back again and again. There is plenty of space for walking, as the center is outside the city but close enough for convenience. Great care is taken that only the best is offered. Hospitality, too, is one of our happy virtues. Community retreats only in June and July; closed in August.

Types of Retreats/Programs Offered: Directed/Private; Conference; Hermitage/Solitary; Ecumenical; Charismatic; Prayer Days; Special; Miscellaneous Programs
Open to: Everyone except youths and families
Person to Contact: Sister Mary Michna, Director of Retreats and Activities
Address: 5635 Erie Street, Racine, WI 53402
Telephone: 414-639-4100
Office Hours: 9:00 A.M. to 5:00 P.M.
Notice Required: Variable

The TYME OUT Youth Ministry Center, Inc.
School Sisters of Notre Dame

The TYME OUT Center is an independent not-for-profit organization that serves the moral and faith development of youths in southeastern Wisconsin. The objectives of the center are to provide retreats and other value-related experiences for youths, and to provide a comfortable space where other accredited agencies can present programs for youths. TYME OUT is housed in St. John Center, which is owned and operated by the Archdiocese of Milwaukee. The space allotted to TYME OUT includes 3 separate retreat centers with dormitory-style accommodations, and shared use of the cafeteria, gym, and grounds.

Types of Retreats/Programs Offered: Directed/Private (rare); Conference; Prayer Days; Special Youth Retreats; Miscellaneous Youth Programs
Open to: Youths
Person to Contact: Sister Kieran Sawyer, Director
Address: 3680 S. Kinnickinnic Avenue, Milwaukee, WI 53207
Telephone: 414-769-2680
Office Hours: 9:00 A.M. to 3:00 P.M. weekdays
Notice Required: 1 week

Canada

Bethany Center
Congregation of Sisters of St. Martha

Bethany Center is a renovated wing of the congregation's headquarters on the outskirts of the small town of Antigonish in rural Nova Scotia. The spacious grounds surrounding the center provide opportunity for peaceful nature walks. In July and August, beaches suitable for swimming are within 20–30 minutes driving time. The center provides a quiet comfortable atmosphere conducive to prayer and reflection. Ten 8-day retreats are scheduled yearly, and private retreats or days of prayer may be arranged. Bookings for weekend programs must be made a year in advance. We are two hours' driving time from the nearest airport, so retreatants need connecting ground transportation. The Ignatian Exercises are taught.

Types of Retreats/Programs Offered: Directed/Group; Directed/Private; Conference; Prayer Days; Special (hosted); Miscellaneous Programs
Open to: Everyone except families
Person to Contact: Director
Address: Antigonish, Nova Scotia B2G 2G6, Canada
Telephone: 902-863-4726
Office Hours: 9:00 A.M. to 4:15 P.M.
Notice Required: Variable

Canterbury Hills
Anglican Diocese of Niagara

Year-round conference, retreat, and camping center operated by the Anglican Diocese of Niagara. Houses up to 160 people (2-4 per room) in the main lodge and 10 log cabins. Located on 72 rolling acres of Carolinian forest at the headwaters of Hermitage Creek at the foot of the Niagara Escarpment. Reserved for church use on weekends and in July and August; available for educational, social service, and nonprofit groups on weekdays. Individual retreatants welcome on weekdays. Director is available to consult with individuals or to direct groups.

Types of Retreats/Programs Offered: Conference; Hermitage/Solitary; Vocations Conference
Open to: Everyone
Person to Contact: The Reverend William C. (Bill) Thomas, Director
Address: 509-575 Lions Club Road, P.O. Box 7068, Ancaster, Ontario L9G 3L3, Canada
Telephone: 416-648-2712
Office Hours: 9:00 A.M. to 5:00 P.M. weekdays
Notice Required: 1 month

Crieff Hills Community
Presbyterian Church in Canada

Crieff Hills Community, formerly a private country estate, is in the heart of Ontario's picturesque farming country. Two hundred fifty acres of rolling countryside provide a natural setting for hiking and cross-country skiing. Easily accessible from airport and major metropolitan centers, Crieff Hills feels far removed from the pressures of the city. Our two modern electrically heated lodges have a lounge area with fireplace. Each of the twin bedded rooms is equipped with a private bath. Our dining-room serves excellent meals. We also have self-contained retreat facilities available for small groups of 6–24 or a hermitage for one. Practices taught include Celtic meditation— focusing on the common daily activities and finding Christ there.

Types of Retreats/Programs Offered: Directed/Group; Directed/Private; Conference; Hermitage/Solitary; Ecumenical; Encounters; Miscellaneous Programs
Open to: Everyone
Person to Contact: The Reverend Robert Spencer, Director
Address: R.R. #2, Puslinch, Ontario N0B 2J0, Canada
Telephone: 519-829-7898
Office Hours: 9 A.M. to 5 P.M.
Notice Required: Individuals, 2 weeks; groups, 6 months

Holy Cross Centre
Passionist Community of Canada

Holy Cross Centre, just 2 hours from Toronto on Lake Erie, was established by the Passionist Community and is dedicated to developing a spirituality for the new ecological age. A resident core community, supported by a group of associates committed to a Christian articulation of new age values, maintains the retreat, including a chapel, library, and extensive grounds, where the Stations of the Cosmos celebrate the evolution of the earth and serve as a focus for meditation. The center sponsors activities that explore the relation of humans to the other natural life systems, with special reference to the Canadian region, and considers the spiritual and religious resources available to people as they seek to enhance and preserve life throughout the planet earth.

Types of Retreats/Programs Offered: Directed/Group; Directed/Private; Conference; Hermitage/Solitary; Ecumenical; Prayer Days; Special; Miscellaneous Programs
Open to: Everyone
Person to Contact: Lynda Nevins, Office Manager
Address: R.R. #1, Port Burwell, Ontario N0J 1T0, Canada
Telephone: 519-874-4502
Office Hours: 9:30 A.M. to 4:30 P.M. weekdays
Notice Required: 24 hours

Loyola House—Guelph Centre of Spirituality
Society of Jesus (Jesuit)

Loyola House is one kilometer north of Guelph, Ontario, on the beautiful farmland of Ignatius College. The college is a residence and novitiate of the Upper Canada Province of the Society of Jesus; it also contains facilities for individual directed retreats in an atmosphere of silence. Since 1969, Loyola House has been a center for the personally directed retreat; and the directed retreat experience continues to be at the heart and foundation of most of our programs. The purpose of our programs is the personal growth in prayer and awareness of the individual participant. More specialized programs intend to assist participants in their capacity to guide others spiritually. Our methodology is one that always moves from experience through reflection toward judgment and action. It is a dynamic of discernment following the principles of the spiritual exercises of St. Ignatius. We hope to expose and encourage many to contemplation and to decision-making through discernment.

Types of Retreats/Programs Offered: Directed/Private; Conference; Ecumenical; Charismatic; Miscellaneous Programs including training for spiritual direction
Open to: Everyone except youths and families
Person to Contact: Father Paul Dungan, Director, or Jane Crawford, Secretary
Address: Box 245, Guelph, Ontario N1H 6J9, Canada
Telephone: 519-824-1250
Office Hours: 9:30 A.M. to 4:30 P.M.
Notice Required: Variable

Marywood
Congregation de Notre Dame

Marywood is a diocesan retreat center staffed by the Sisters of the Congregation de Notre Dame. Marywood provides retreatants with an atmosphere of silence and peace, a small chapel, an opportunity for walking and hiking through the woods and mountains, a beautiful view of the Rockies, a comfortable fireside room for prayer and study, private rooms and bath, simple meals, and a personal approach. Families welcome for day programs only.

Types of Retreats/Programs Offered: Directed/Group; Directed/Private; Conference; Hermitage/Solitary; Ecumenical; Charismatic; Prayer Days; Special; Miscellaneous Programs
Open to: Everyone
Person to Contact: Nancy Hurren, Coordinator
Address: R.R. 2, Site 13-68, Cranbrook, B.C. V1C 4H3, Canada
Telephone: 604-426-8117
Notice Required: Variable

M.O. Renewal Centre
Missionary Oblate Sisters of S.H. and of M.I.

Located at the mother house of the Missionary Oblate Sisters on the east side of the Red River in Winnipeg, the M.O. Renewal Centre is in a bilingual environment. The center provides a space for spiritual renewal for individuals and groups of various religious denominations. There is an annual calendar of programs sponsored by various groups or organizations as well as by the Spiritual Exercises Apostolate, based on the Ignatian Exercises, under the sponsorship of the Missionary Oblate Sisters. Facilities include single and double rooms, 2 chapels, a cafeteria, 2 large and 2 small conference rooms, and an auditorium. Closed July, August, and Christmas season.

Types of Retreats/Programs Offered: Directed/Group; Directed/Private; Conference; Ecumenical; Prayer Days; Engaged Encounter; Special; Miscellaneous Programs
Open to: Everyone except families
Person to Contact: Sister Therese Brule, Program Director, or Sister Albertine Peloquin, Coordinator
Address: 601 Aulneau Street, Winnipeg, Manitoba R2H 2V5, Canada
Telephone: 204-233-7287
Office Hours: 8:00 A.M. to 5:00 P.M. weekdays
Notice Required: Variable

Mount Carmel Spiritual Centre
Carmelite Order, Province of the Most Pure Heart of Mary

Situated at the edge of the promontory overlooking Canadian Horseshoe Falls, Mount Carmel has 20 acres of beautiful, spacious grounds in a quiet and peaceful setting. Mount Carmel Centre consists of 2 facilities: the monastery building has single and double rooms, dorms, meeting rooms, dining rooms, and several chapels; Avila Hall has single rooms, kitchen, chapel, and meeting room. In the same place will be found the historic Shrine of Our Lady of Peace and Our Lady of Mount Carmel Chapel, a religious gift shop and bookstore. Closed between Christmas and New Year's.

Types of Retreats/Programs Offered: Directed/Group; Directed/Private; Conference; Hermitage/Solitary; Ecumenical; Charismatic; Prayer Days
Open to: Everyone except youths and families
Person to Contact: Father Gregory L. Klein, Director, or Mrs. Jean Yazaroglu, Reservations Director
Address: 7035 Portage Road, Niagara Falls, Ontario L2G 7B7, Canada
Telephone: 416-356-4113
Office Hours: 8:30 A.M. to 4:30 P.M.
Notice Required: Individuals, 2 months; groups, 10 months

Mount St. Francis Retreat Centre
Franciscans O.F.M.

Located on spacious grounds in the Rocky Mountain foothills, Mount St. Francis consists of a turn-of-the-century sandstone mansion that has been expanded and renovated into the present retreat center. The work at Mount St. Francis is inspired by the life of St. Francis of Assisi. Francis' concerns for the environment, unity among people and issues of justice were based on the Gospel values of Christ. As a Franciscan center we strive to live and to help others live out these values in our contemporary world. To do this we provide an atmosphere of welcome, quiet, and peace, a place of prayerful listening where people can grow spiritually as they deepen their awareness of God, of themselves, of others, and of the world in which they live. Closed in July.

Types of Retreats/Programs Offered: Directed/Group (August); Directed/Private; Conference; Hermitage/Solitary; Ecumenical;

Charismatic; Prayer Days; Special
Open to: Everyone except families
Person to Contact: Retreat Director
Address: Box 430, Cochrane, Alberta T0L 0W0, Canada
Telephone: 403-932-2012
Office Hours: 9:00 A.M. to 5:00 P.M.; closed Mondays
Notice Required: 1 month

Nova Nada, Spiritual Life Institute
S.L.I. Community

Nova Nada is in a woodland of tall white pines overlooking 3 connecting lakes in Kemptville, Nova Scotia, 1 hour outside Yarmouth. We are a small monastic community of hermits founded for men and women in 1960 by Father William McNamara with a mandate from the visionary Pope John XXIII. We live like the early Carmelites who followed the example of the prophet Elijah and lived on Mt. Carmel under a common monastic rule characterized by simplicity and minimal structure to enable them to offer God a pure and undivided heart. We live in separate hermitages, and our monastic life is a rhythm of work and play, solitude and togetherness, fast and feast, discipline and wildness, sacrifice and celebration, contemplation and action. Retreatants participate in our monastic rhythms or choose solitude in their own hermitages. Each hermitage is self-contained with a small kitchen. Mondays and Tuesdays are days of complete solitude, Wednesday through Saturday are days with some community activity and some solitude, and Sundays are holy days of leisure "wasted" in praying and playing.

Types of Retreats/Programs Offered: Hermitage/Solitary
Open to: Everyone except youths and families
Person to Contact: Mark letters "Retreat Request"
Address: Kemptville, Nova Scotia B0W 1Y0, Canada
Notice Required: 6–8 months summer, 2–3 months winter

Our Lady of the Prairies, House of Prayer
Lay Associates of the Congregation of Our Lady of the Missions

We are a house of prayer where religious and lay Catholics live in community, follow the Liturgy of the Hours in community prayer, and are open to "hearing the cry of the poor" (spiritually, emotionally, as well as physically). We apply a holistic approach to our ministry, and there is also a charismatic dimension to our prayer that has been found helpful in healing prayer. We have a home rather than an institute atmosphere, and our guests are encouraged to participate in community life and prayer as much as possible. On extended stays of a week to a month, people are requested to participate in the prayer and work of the house and grounds. The community library, tapes, and videos are available for use, and there is access to nature walks, canoeing, and cross-country skiing. Rooms are either double or dormitory-style.

Types of Retreats/Programs Offered: Directed/Group; Directed/Private; Conference; Hermitage/Solitary; Ecumenical; Charismatic; Prayer Days; Special; Miscellaneous Programs
Open to: Everyone
Person to Contact: John Duma, Bursar
Address: Box 37, Elie, Manitoba R0H 0H0, Canada
Telephone: 204-353-2440
Office Hours: 9 A.M. to 5 P.M.
Notice Required: 2 weeks

Providence Renewal Centre
Sisters of Providence

Providence Renewal Centre is a facility with accommodations and staff resources for groups and individuals in a hospitable environment. Its location offers both peace and rest and proximity to city services and transportation. A qualified staff provides resources for retreats, workshops, conferences, and spiritual direction. Retreats and programs offered by us address a variety of needs for human and religious development in the Church. The staff is committed to a spirituality that is essentially linked to interaction with others in service. Ultimately, our mission is to foster authentic Christian spirituality for a changing world, a spirituality centered in Christ in whom is recognized the need for justice in reordering the world for the coming of the kingdom of God.

Types of Retreats/Programs Offered: Directed/Group; Directed/Private; Ecumenical; Charismatic; Prayer Days; Encounters; Special; Miscellaneous Programs
Open to: Everyone
Person to Contact: Sister Betty Kaczmarczyk, Director
Address: 3005-119 Street, Edmonton, Alberta T6J 5R5, Canada
Telephone: 403-436-7250
Office Hours: 8:00 A.M. to 5:00 P.M. weekdays
Notice Required: Usually 1 month, but variable

Queen of Apostles Renewal Centre
Oblate Fathers of Assumption Province

Queen of Apostles is an ecumenical Christian center for people who want to meet for a few hours, or in residence for a day or more. Situated on 12 landscaped acres overlooking the Credit River Valley in the heart of Mississauga, the center has private bedrooms, an outdoor swimming pool, lounges, and a dining room. It features a well-appointed, large broadloomed conference room, the scenic "blue" room for smaller meetings, and private space for individuals who are on retreat. All facilities, including the uniquely designed chapel, are wheelchair accessible. Queen of Apostles Renewal Centre is the space where people of all ages and physical conditions can come together to grow intellectually, emotionally, and spiritually.

Types of Retreats/Programs Offered: Directed/Private; Conference; Encounters; Miscellaneous Programs
Open to: Everyone except youths and families

Person to Contact: Director or Secretary
Address: 1617 Blythe Road, Mississauga, Ontario L5H 2C3, Canada
Telephone: 416-278-5229
Office Hours: 9:00 A.M. to 5:30 P.M.
Notice Required: 3 to 4 months

Queen's House Retreat and Renewal Centre
Oblates of Mary Immaculate

Queen's House seeks to be a community of hospitality, a place of renewal for persons and institutions, and a sign of hope for the larger church as it renews itself through many changes. The facilities and riverside grounds are simple, spacious, and restful. Women and men of all ages, denominations, and backgrounds come to be refreshed, challenged, and changed through the creative blending of leisure, solitude, community, inner stretching ,

Queen's House, Retreat and Renewal Center, Saskatoon, Saskatchewan, Canada

widened horizons, and creation-centered quietness. The Spirit is at work and at play through pervasive prayerfulness, exciting the awe-filled sense of God in all. Practices taught include Christian Meditation (John Main) and Christian Zen.

Types of Retreats/Programs Offered: Directed/Group; Directed/Private; Conference; Hermitage/Solitary; Ecumenical; Prayer Days; Encounters; Special; Miscellaneous Programs
Open to: Everyone
Person to Contact: Glenn M. Zimmer, OMI, Director
Address: 601 Taylor St. West, Saskatoon, Saskatchewan S7M 0C9, Canada
Telephone: 306-242-1916
Office Hours: 9:00 A.M. to 4:30 P.M.
Notice Required: 1 week to 1 month

St. Benedict's Educational Centre
Benedictine

St. Benedict's is on 72 acres of beautiful scenic grounds on the Red River. Facilities include modern air-conditioned double occupancy bedrooms. There are a Peace Room/Chapel, a large conference room, smaller meeting rooms, and lounges. Recreational facilities include a lounge with TV and a game room with billiards, table tennis, and shuffleboard; baseball and badminton equipment is available. The grounds are ideal for cross-country skiing, and a walking path winds through the wooded area to the garden.

Types of Retreats/Programs Offered: Directed/Group; Directed/Private; Conference; Hermitage/Solitary; Ecumenical; Prayer Days; Engaged Encounter; Special; Miscellaneous Programs
Open to: Everyone except families
Person to Contact: Sister Virginia Evard, Director
Address: 225 Masters Ave., R.R. 1B, Winnipeg, Manitoba R3C 4A3, Canada

Telephone: 204-339-1705
Office Hours: 8:30 A.M. to 4:30 P.M.
Notice Required: Variable

St. Michael's Retreat
Franciscan Friars
Description not available.

Types of Retreats/Programs Offered: Directed/Group; Directed/Private; Hermitage/Solitary; Ecumenical; Charismatic; Teen; Engaged Encounter; Special; Miscellaneous Programs
Open to: Everyone except families
Person to Contact: Donna Fischer, Retreat Director
Address: Box 220, Lumsden, Saskatchewan S0G 3C0, Canada
Telephone: 306-731-3316
Office Hours: 8:30 A.M. to 4:00 P.M.
Notice Required: 1 week

Star of the North Retreat House
Oblates of Mary Immaculate
Star of the North Retreat House is on a hill overlooking historic St. Albert. It is a quiet setting with room to walk, to think, and to reflect. Facilities include single and/or double rooms, a chapel and prayer room, and a large lounge and conference room. Closed in July.

Types of Retreats/Programs Offered: Directed/Group; Directed/Private; Conference; Hermitage/Solitary; Ecumenical; Charismatic; Prayer Days; Parent-Teen; Encounters; Cursillos; Special
Open to: Everyone except families
Person to Contact: Father Al Roy, Director
Address: 3 St. Vital Avenue, St. Albert, Alberta T8N 1K1, Canada
Telephone: 403-459-5511
Office Hours: 9 A.M. to 4:30 P.M.
Notice Required: At least 6 months

Stillpoint House of Prayer
Ursulines of Jesus

In the heart of Edmonton, Stillpoint House of Prayer is nevertheless an oasis of peace and spiritual silence. The property includes a garden courtyard where visitors may sit in the sun. A main goal at Stillpoint is to teach people how to pray. Retreats vary from short sessions of a few hours to daylong, weekend, and extended programs, from scheduled group retreats to tailor-made sessions where individual attention is given. An attempt is being made to use Stillpoint as a vehicle for education in the area of social justice. No overnight facilities for families.

Types of Retreats/Programs Offered: Directed/Group; Directed/Private; Hermitage/Solitary; Ecumenical; Prayer Days; Marriage Encounter; Special; Miscellaneous Programs including Social Justice
Open to: Everyone
Person to Contact: Sister Mary Clare Stack, Director, or Sister Elizabeth Beaton, Receptionist
Address: 10647-81 Avenue, Edmonton, Alberta T6E 1Y1, Canada
Telephone: 403-433-1342
Office Hours: 9:30 A.M. to 5 P.M.
Notice Required: 1 week

Villa Maria Retreat House
Oblates of Mary Immaculate

Villa Maria is a nonprofit retreat and learning center that sponsors programs of its own and also offers its facilities to other groups for religious, educational, and charitable programs. Religious communities of various denominations and different lay organizations have found Villa Maria ideal for residential weekday and weekend programs. We offer our own programs of spiritual enrichment. Located in a lovely country setting, Villa

Maria is an extensive complex of buildings and grounds conducive to peace and prayer.

Types of Retreats/Programs Offered: Directed/Group; Directed/Private; Conference; Hermitage/Solitary; Ecumenical; Charismatic; Prayer Days; Encounters; Miscellaneous Programs
Open to: Everyone
Person to Contact: Father Joseph Alarie, Director
Address: 100 Villa Maria Place, St. Norbert, Manitoba R3V 1A9, Canada
Telephone: 204-269-2114
Office Hours: 8:30 A.M. to 5 P.M.
Notice Required: Variable

Appendix

Roman Catholic Beliefs in Brief

This information is intended as an aid for those who are not familiar with Roman Catholic beliefs. If you are considering making a retreat in one of the Roman Catholic facilities listed in this book, it would be helpful for you to have some rudimentary knowledge of the basic assumptions of faith you will encounter there. There are many popular misconceptions about Roman Catholicism, and people who take time to read a brief synopsis of its doctrines often express surprise at having those misconceptions dispelled.

The following information is a very spare presentation of only the most important points of faith. For a more in-depth treatment, refer to Resources for a list of recommended reading.

Dogma

"Dogma" is the term preferred in Roman Catholicism to refer to those doctrines that are considered essential items of faith in the Church. Another term often encountered, "deposit of faith," concerns all of the teachings of the Church—revelation, tradition, etc.—taken collectively. The primary source for revelation in the Roman Catholic Church is the Scriptures, both the Old Testament and the New Testament. Some formal declarations made by the Church in explication or elaboration of what is found in the Scriptures are considered to be protected from error by God. Finally, there is the term "canon law," which is a body of rules formulated over the centuries by the Church to describe the proper way in which a Roman Catholic lives his or her life in accordance with Church doctrine; it also includes more technical rules governing specific members and functions within the Church.

Dogma is a much more important factor in Roman Catholicism than in most Protestant denominations. "Magisterium" is the name given to the formal teaching authority of the Church, which includes the responsibility for identifying and explaining correct doctrine. According to the 1988 edition of the *Catholic Almanac,* "This authority is personalized in the pope, the successor of St. Peter as head of the Church, and in the bishops together and in union with the pope, as it was originally committed to Peter and to the whole college of apostles under his leadership. They are the official teachers of the Church." Thus, there exists a standard in the Roman Catholic Church against which any individual member is able to measure his or her own understanding of, for example, personal reading of the Scriptures, in order to avoid the potential pitfalls of self-validation.

The most important way in which the Roman Catholic Church identifies and develops its teaching is through ecumenical councils. An ecumenical council is a gathering of the Church hierarchy (cardinals, archbishops, bishops, abbots, etc.) together with and under the pope. Although an ecumenical council has supreme authority in the Church in matters of faith and morals, decrees from such a council have a binding effect on Church members only when declared by the pope. The Roman Catholic Church recognizes 21 ecumenical councils in its history, the most recent being the Second Vatican Council, which took place over the course of four sessions held between October 11, 1962, and December 8, 1965. This council spurred into action much of the renewal and reform that has taken place in the Church in the past 25 years.

Creed

A "creed" is a formal statement of belief. The word comes from the Latin verb "credo," which literally means "I believe." The two most fundamental creeds in Christianity are the Nicene Creed and the Apostles' Creed. The latter has come to be the creed used most frequently in the Roman Catholic Church. The Apostles' Creed is a very succinct statement of the most basic beliefs in Roman Catholicism; its text reads as follows:

Appendix

I believe in God, the Father almighty, Creator of heaven and earth.

And in Jesus Christ, his only Son, our Lord; who was conceived by the Holy Spirit, born of the Virgin Mary, suffered under Pontius Pilate, was crucified, died, and was buried. He descended into hell; the third day he arose again from the dead; he ascended into heaven, sits at the right hand of God, the Father almighty; from thence he shall come to judge the living and the dead.

I believe in the Holy Spirit, the holy Catholic Church, the communion of saints, the forgiveness of sins, the resurrection of the body, and life everlasting. Amen.

Basic Beliefs

Trinity: The Trinity refers to the triune nature of God. This dogma holds that there are three persons (Father, Son, and Holy Spirit) in one God. The Trinity is considered one of the mysteries of the faith, which means that it does not contradict reason but it is not fully accessible by means of reason alone. Much of the early formulation of doctrine in the ecumenical councils was concerned with defining the Trinity and defending it from specific misinterpretations. The doctrine of the Trinity is considered central to the Roman Catholic faith.

Jesus Christ: In Roman Catholicism, Jesus Christ is a historical figure, the subject of the New Testament, who was the actual Son of God incarnated (i.e., born as a human being) in this world. He is considered the Messiah referred to in the Old Testament, whose mission was the redemption and salvation of humankind. Jesus Christ is both true God and true man in Church teaching. Because human beings had separated themselves from God, God-become-man was required to show us the way back to unity with God; this is the redemption and salvation which is effected and offered by Jesus Christ.

Mary: As the Mother of God, Mary is held in high esteem in the Roman Catholic Church and doctrines about her essentially pure, albeit human, nature and her virginity have been formulated. Note that the Apostles' Creed states that Jesus was "conceived by the Holy Spirit, born of the Virgin Mary." The Incarnation and virgin birth of Jesus Christ fall into the category of mysteries of the faith.

The Church: The Roman Catholic Church holds that it is the original church founded by Jesus Christ, because it traces itself back to the individual person of the apostle Peter. The *Dogmatic Constitution on the Church,* one of the primary documents issued by the Second Vatican Council, affirms the basic belief that "the Church . . . is necessary for salvation." But it also goes on to state:

"The Church recognizes that in many ways she is linked with those who, being baptized, are honored with the name of Christian, though they do not profess the faith in its entirety or do not preserve unity of communion with the successor of Peter.

"We can say that in some real way they are joined with us in the Holy Spirit, for to them also he gives his gifts and graces, and is thereby operative among them with his sanctifying power."

Papal Primacy: The Roman Catholic Church holds that the pope (the bishop of Rome) has primacy not only in honor, but also in actual power. This power covers all aspects of the Church, not only faith and morals, but also discipline and Church government. Although the Church bases its belief in the primacy of the pope on its interpretation of Scripture, the history of this belief is strewn with problems exacerbated by secular matters—notably the ninth century forgeries known as the *False Decretals* and the *Donation of Constantine.* The actual dogma was not formally proclaimed until 1870, in the fourth session of the First Vatican Council, when it was felt necessary to reaffirm the position of the pope in the face of the loss of the Papal States.

Sacraments: There are seven Sacraments in the Roman Catholic Church: Baptism, Confirmation, Eucharist, Penance, Holy Orders, Marriage, Anointing of the Sick.

The Code of Canon Law states: "The sacraments of the New Testament . . . stand out as the signs and means by which the faith is expressed and strengthened, worship is rendered to God and the sanctification of humankind is effected, and they thus contribute in the highest degree to the establishment, strengthening and manifestation of ecclesial communion . . ."

In other words, Sacraments are formal actions or ceremonies within the life of the Church in which the outward signs employed (e.g., the bread and wine of the Eucharist) signify and become a means of salvation.

Liturgy: The liturgy is the public worship of the Church, and it culminates in the celebration of the Eucharist, most commonly referred to as "Mass."

Appendix

The Roman Catholic Church has a very rich liturgy, consisting of a system of public prayer (called the Divine Office), sacred music and art, numerous rites and celebrations, and a liturgical calendar of feasts. However, the Mass is the most common form of the liturgy encountered by lay people, and anyone considering making a retreat at a Roman Catholic center needs to be aware of one essential point concerning the celebration of the Eucharist: in Roman Catholicism (as well as in Orthodoxy), the Eucharist is believed to be the actual Body and Blood of Christ. This distinguishes it from many Protestant denominations. By means of a process usually called "transubstantiation," the outward signs of bread and wine actually become the real Body and Blood of Christ in the Eucharistic celebration, and one who takes communion thus becomes united with Christ in a very real sense. Although intercommunion normally continues to be forbidden, the Roman Catholic Church now acknowledges conditions under which it would be justified. If there is any doubt whether one will be allowed to take communion at a retreat in a Roman Catholic center, the subject should be raised beforehand and the director queried on that center's practice.

Conclusion

Although the basic tenets of Roman Catholicism have remained fixed throughout the history of the Church, and it has always been the position of the Roman Catholic Church that the deposit of faith must be safeguarded, it is obvious that there is a constant and ongoing evolution in how doctrine is understood and applied in the life of the Church.

Resources

The books listed in this Appendix have proven helpful in the preparation of this book. A good source of material is usually your own retreat center. Many centers maintain a small bookstore with books and tapes pertaining to making retreats, as well as spiritual material used for meditation purposes.

Books

Chitty, Derwas J. *The Desert A City* (Crestwood, N.Y.: St. Vladimir's Seminary Press, 1966)
Climacus, John. Trans. Colm Luibheid and Norman Russell. *The Ladder of Divine Ascent* (Ramsey, N.J.: Paulist Press, 1982)
Foy, Felician A., O.F.M., ed. *1988 Catholic Almanac* (Huntington, Ind.: Our Sunday Visitor Publishing Division, 1987)
Hopko, Thomas. *Spirituality*—Volume IV of *The Orthodox Faith* (New York: The Orthodox Church in America, 1976)
Ignatius of Loyola. Trans. Louis J. Puhl, S.J. *The Spiritual Exercises* (Chicago, Ill.: Loyola University Press, 1951)
———. Trans. Anthony Mottola. *The Spiritual Exercises* (Garden City, N.Y.: Image Books, 1964)
Jager, Willigis. Trans. Matthew J. O'Connell. *The Way to Contemplation* (Mahwah, N.J.: Paulist Press, 1987)
Keating, Thomas, O.C.S.O. *Crisis of Faith* (Petersham, Mass.: St. Bede's Publications, 1979)
——— et al. *Finding Grace at the Center* (Petersham, Mass.: St. Bede's Publications, 1978)
———. *The Mystery of Christ* (Amity, N.Y.: Amity House, 1987)
———. *Open Mind, Open Heart* (Amity, N.Y.: Amity House, 1986)
Maloney, George A., S.J. *Alone with the Alone* (Notre Dame: Ave Maria Press, 1982)
———. *Prayer of the Heart* (Notre Dame: Ave Maria Press, 1981)
McNamara, William, O.C.D. *Christian Mysticism* (Amity, N.Y.: Amity House, 1981)
———. *The Human Adventure* (Amity, NY: Amity House, 1981)
Merton, Thomas. *Contemplation in a World of Action* (London, Eng.: Unwin Paperbacks, 1980)
———. *Contemplative Prayer* (Garden City, N.Y.: Image Books, 1971)

———. *The Last of the Fathers* (San Diego, Calif.: Harcourt, Brace Jovanovich, 1982)
———. *Mystics and Zen Masters* (New York, N.Y.: Farrar, Straus and Giroux, 1967)
———. *Thoughts in Solitude* (New York, N.Y.: Farrar, Straus and Giroux, 1987)
———. *What Is Contemplation?* (Springfield, Ill.: Templegate Publishers, 1981)
———. *The Wisdom of the Desert* (New York, N.Y.: New Directions Books, 1970)
Palmer, G. E. H., Philip Sherrard and Kallistos Ware, trans. *The Philokalia.* 3 vol. (London, Eng.: Faber and Faber, 1979)
Ratzinger, Joseph. *Journey Towards Easter* (New York, N.Y.: The Crossroad Publishing Co., 1987)
Russell, Norman, trans. *The Lives of the Desert Fathers* (London, Eng.: Mowbray, 1980)
Steindl-Rast, David. *Gratefulness, The Heart of Prayer* (Ramsey, N.J: Paulist Press, 1984)
———. *A Listening Heart* (New York, N.Y.: The Crossroad Publishing Co., 1983)
Ward, Benedicta, trans. *The Sayings of the Desert Fathers* (Kalamazoo, Mich.: Cistercian Publications, 1984)
Ware, Kallistos. *The Orthodox Way* (Crestwood, N.Y.: St. Vladimir's Seminary Press, 1986)
Wolters, Clifton. *The Cloud of Unknowing* (Middlesex, Eng.: Penguin Books, 1978)

Tapes, Periodicals, Miscellaneous

1. To obtain tapes of Mother Tessa, Brother David, Father Robert Arida, and Dr. Jim Finley from the conference on meditation practices where I met them, contact: Sounds True, 1825 Pearl St., Boulder, CO 80302, 303-449-6229. Request their order form for the tapes from the 1988 conference at the Naropa Institute on "Theism and Nontheism."

2. Taped talks by Father William McNamara and Mother Tessa Bielecki are available from The Spiritual Life Institute, Nada Hermitage, Box 119, Crestone, CO 81131. They also publish a periodical entitled *Desert Call* and a newsletter, *Nada Network.*

3. Audio- and videotapes by Father Thomas Keating on the subject of centering prayer are available from Contemporary Communications, Walt Lawson, 7 Mesa Lane, Colorado Springs, CO 80906, 719-632-7320.

Appendix 265

4. Books and audio- and videotapes by Father Basil Pennington on the subject of centering prayer are offered for sale by: Food for the Poor, Inc., 1301 W. Copans Road, Pompano, FL 33064, 305-975-0000.

5. The Pecos Community has its own publishing house, which offers both books and tapes: Dove Publications, Pecos, NM 87552, 505-757-6597.

6. To find out if there is a centering prayer group in your own area, write to Father Thomas Keating, St. Benedict's Monastery, 1012 Monastery Road, Snowmass, CO 81654.

Again, a good place to check for materials is your local retreat center.

Other Books from John Muir Publications

22 Days Series
These pocket-size itineraries are a refreshing departure from ordinary guidebooks. Each author has an in-depth knowledge of the region covered and offers 22 tested daily itineraries through their favorite destinations. Included are not only "must see" attractions but also little-known villages and hidden "jewels" as well as valuable general information.

22 Days Around the World by R. Rapoport and B. Willes (65-31-9)
22 Days in Alaska by Pamela Lanier (28-68-0)
22 Days in the American Southwest by R. Harris (28-88-5)
22 Days in Asia by R. Rapoport and B. Willes (65-17-3)
22 Days in Australia by John Gottberg (65-40-8)
22 Days in California by Roger Rapoport (28-93-1)
22 Days in China by Gaylon Duke and Zenia Victor (28-72-9)
22 Days in Dixie by Richard Polese (65-18-1)
22 Days in Europe by Rick Steves (65-05-X)
22 Days in Florida by Richard Harris (65-27-0)
22 Days in France by Rick Steves (65-07-6)
22 Days in Germany, Austria & Switzerland by R. Steves (65-39-4)
22 Days in Great Britain by Rick Steves (65-38-6)
22 Days in Hawaii by Arnold Schuchter (28-92-3)
22 Days in India by Anurag Mathur (28-87-7)
22 Days in Japan by David Old (28-73-7)
22 Days in Mexico by S. Rogers and T. Rosa (65-41-6)
22 Days in New England by Anne Wright (28-96-6)
22 Days in New Zealand by Arnold Schuchter (28-86-9)
22 Days in Norway, Denmark & Sweden by R. Steves (28-83-4)
22 Days in the Pacific Northwest by R. Harris (28-97-4)
22 Days in Spain & Portugal by Rick Steves (65-06-8)
22 Days in the West Indies by C. & S. Morreale (28-74-5)
All 22 Days titles are 128 to 152 pp. and $7.95 each, except 22 Days Around the World, which is 192 pp. and $9.95.

"Kidding Around" Travel Guides for Children
Written for kids eight years of age and older. Generously illustrated in two colors with imaginative characters and images. An adventure to read and a treasure to keep.
Kidding Around Atlanta, Anne Pedersen (65-35-1) 64 pp. $9.95
Kidding Around London, Sarah Lovett (65-24-6) 64 pp. $9.95
Kidding Around Los Angeles, Judy Cash (65-34-3) 64 pp. $9.95
Kidding Around New York City, Sarah Lovett (65-33-5) 64 pp. $9.95
Kidding Around San Francisco, Rosemary Zibart (65-23-8) 64 pp. $9.95
Kidding Around Washington, D.C., Anne Pedersen (65-25-4) 64 pp. $9.95

Asia Through the Back Door, Rick Steves and John Gottberg (28-76-1) 336 pp. $13.95

Buddhist America: Centers, Retreats, Practices, Don Morreale (28-94-X) 400 pp. $12.95

Bus Touring: Charter Vacations, U.S.A., Stuart Warren (28-95-8) 168 pp. $9.95

Catholic America: Self-Renewal Centers and Retreats, Patricia Christian-Meyer (65-20-3) 325 pp. $13.95

Choices & Changes: Preparing for Pregnancy and Parenthood, Brenda E. Aikey-Keller (65-44-0) 256 pp. $13.95

Complete Guide to Bed & Breakfasts, Inns & Guesthouses, 1989-90 Edition, Pamela Lanier (65-09-2) 520 pp. $14.95

Elderhostels: The Students' Choice, Mildred Hyman (65-28-9) 224 pp. $12.95

Europe 101: History & Art for the Traveler, Rick Steves and Gene Openshaw (28-78-8) 372 pp. $12.95

Europe Through the Back Door, Rick Steves (28-84-2) 404 pp. $12.95

Floating Vacations: River, Lake, and Ocean Adventures, Michael White (65-32-7) 256 pp. $17.95

Gypsying After 40: A Guide to Adventure and Self-Discovery, Bob Harris (28-71-0) 264 pp. $12.95

The Heart of Jerusalem, Arlynn Nellhaus (28-79-6) 312 pp. $12.95

Indian America: A Traveler's Companion, Eagle/Walking Turtle (65-29-7) 336 pp. $14.95

Mona Winks: Self-Guided Tours of Europe's Top Museums, Rick Steves (28-85-0) 450 pp. $14.95

The On and Off the Road Cookbook, Carl Franz (28-27-3) 272 pp. $8.50

The People's Guide to Mexico, Carl Franz (28-99-0) 608 pp. $15.95

The People's Guide to RV Camping in Mexico, Carl Franz with Steve Rogers (28-91-5) 256 pp. $13.95

Ranch Vacations: The Complete Guide to Guest, Fly-Fishing, and Cross-Country Skiing Ranches, Eugene Kilgore (65-30-0) 256 pp. $17.95

The Shopper's Guide to Mexico, Steve Rogers and Tina Rosa (28-90-7) 224 pp. $9.95

Ski Tech's Guide to Equipment, Skiwear, and Accessories, edited by Bill Tanler (65-45-9) 200 pp. $14.95

Ski Tech's Guide to Maintenance and Repair, edited by Bill Tanler (65-46-7) 200 pp. $14.95

Traveler's Guide to Asian Culture, Kevin Chambers (65-14-9) 356 pp. $13.95

Traveler's Guide to Healing Centers and Retreats in North America, Martine Rudee and Jonathan Blease (65-15-7) 240 pp. $11.95

Undiscovered Islands of the Caribbean, Burl Willes (28-80-X) 216 pp. $12.95

Automotive Repair Manuals

Each JMP automotive manual gives clear step-by-step instructions together with illustrations that show exactly how each system in the vehicle comes apart and goes back together. They tell everything a novice or experienced mechanic needs to know to perform periodic maintenance, tuneups, troubleshooting, and repair of the brake, fuel and emission control, electrical, cooling, clutch, transmission, driveline, steering, and suspension systems and even rebuild the engine.

How to Keep Your VW Alive (65-12-2) 424 pp. $17.95
How to Keep Your Golf/Jetta/Rabbit/Scirocco Alive (65-21-1) 420 pp. $17.95
How to Keep Your Honda Car Alive (28-55-9) 272 pp. $17.95
How to Keep Your Subaru Alive (65-11-4) 480 pp. $17.95
How to Keep Your Toyota Pickup Alive (28-81-3) 392 pp. $17.95
How to Keep Your Datsun/Nissan Alive (28-65-6) 544 pp. $17.95

Other Automotive Books

The Greaseless Guide to Car Care Confidence: Take the Terror Out of Talking to Your Mechanic, Mary Jackson (65-19-X) 224 pp. $14.95

Off-Road Emergency Repair & Survival, James Ristow (65-26-2) 160 pp. $9.95

Road & Track's Used Car Classics, edited by Peter Bohr (28-69-9) 272 pp. $12.95

Ordering Information

If you cannot find our books in your local bookstore, you can order directly from us. Your books will be sent to you via UPS (for U.S. destinations), and you will receive them approximately 10 days from the time that we receive your order. Include $2.75 for the first item ordered and $.50 for each additional item to cover shipping and handling costs. UPS shipments to post office boxes take longer to arrive; if possible, please give us a street address. For airmail within the U.S., enclose $4.00 per book for shipping and handling. All foreign orders will be shipped surface rate. Please enclose $3.00 for the first item and $1.00 for each additional item. Please inquire for airmail rates.

Method of Payment

Your order may be paid by check, money order, or credit card. We cannot be responsible for cash sent through the mail. All payments must be made in U.S. dollars drawn on a U.S. bank. Canadian postal money orders in U.S. dollars are also acceptable. For VISA, MasterCard, or American Express orders, include your card number, expiration date, and your signature, or call (505)982-4078. Books ordered on American Express cards can be shipped only to the billing address of the cardholder. Sorry, no C.O.D.'s. Residents of sunny New Mexico, add 5.625% tax to the total.

Address all orders and inquiries to:
John Muir Publications
P.O. Box 613
Santa Fe, NM 87504
(505)982-4078